DATE DUE

	PRINTED IN U.S.A.

ALSO BY J. FREDERICK ARMENT

The Elements of Peace: How Nonviolence Works
(McFarland, 2012)

The Economics of Peace

*Freedom, the Golden Rule and
the Broadening of Prosperity*

J. FREDERICK ARMENT

McFarland & Company, Inc., Publishers
Jefferson, North Carolina

LIBRARY OF CONGRESS CATALOGUING-IN-PUBLICATION DATA

Arment, J. Frederick, 1953–
    The economics of peace : freedom, the golden rule and
the broadening of prosperity / J. Frederick Arment.
        p.   cm.
    Includes bibliographical references and index.

    ISBN 978-0-7864-9638-9 (softcover : acid free paper) ∞
    ISBN 978-1-4766-1890-6 (ebook)

    1. International economic relations.   2. Federal government.
    3. Peace—Economic aspects.   4. Social change.   I. Title.
    HF1365.A76 2015
    174'.4—dc23   2014042328

BRITISH LIBRARY CATALOGUING DATA ARE AVAILABLE

On the cover: Rotary Peace Fellows from a class at International Christian
University (Rotary International); Presidential Medal of Freedom recipient the
Rev. Martin Luther King, Jr., with the Rev. Theodore M. Hesburgh at an Illinois
rally for civil rights, 1964 (National Portrait Gallery, Smithsonian Institution;
gift of the University of Notre Dame in honor of the Rev. Theodore M.
Hesburgh, C.S.C); background image © 2015 iStock/Thinkstock

Printed in the United States of America

McFarland & Company, Inc., Publishers
  Box 611, Jefferson, North Carolina 28640
    www.mcfarlandpub.com

Table of Contents

"*Thus we are impelled to rise from the economic processes to the mutuality, the give and take between man and man, and furthermore to that which will arise from this, namely the objective community-spirit working in the Associations.*"[1]

—Rudolf Steiner, *World Economy:*
The Formation of a Science of World-Economics;
1922 lectures on the threefold associative
economy for the rising global age

Introduction

Global Consciousness as Manifestation of the Golden Rule

First, a confession. It isn't often that a book begins with an admission by the author that he has, indeed, forgotten something. Yet such is the exact moment when I realized I was intimately connected to all other human beings: to a victim of rape in Congo, to a displaced refugee in Turkey, to the mother of a fallen soldier in Pakistan, to every person on earth who suffers violence or want of a simple meal.

This awareness is certainly not unique to me. For the first time in history, people are experiencing this realization as unified humanity. Due in large part to increasing connectivity through technology, the human race is suddenly and completely aware of itself, of our diversity and similarities, of our greatest innovations and deepest challenges. This intense globalization of consciousness has profound implications for how we, as humanity, make our living and how we govern. It is transforming how we live our individual and collective lives.

Much has been written about global commerce and global media, even global war. The globalization of culture certainly sends shivers down the spines of those who fear the homogenization of their heritage, yet there are advantages. Creative and effective global business practices such as monopolies, takeovers, leveraged buy-outs, consolidations, multinational corporations, state supported industries, and mergers have led to unprecedented individual accumulation of capital. They have also led to uncertainty in the marketplace and great inequities in standards of living. The last decades of exuberant bubbles and falls of global stock markets have further divided the "haves" from the "have-nots."

1

⌒

"We have seen the economic life of the entire Earth gradually merging into world-economy. And at this point the possibility of reaping further advantages by merger is at an end."[1]—Rudolf Steiner

There have been many harbingers of our modern global challenges, including Austrian social reformer Rudolf Steiner, as early as 1922. Today, we are at a point where prophecy has given way to reality. Our technologies and explorations have given us physical, intellectual, and spiritual access to the entire planet, to the great expanse of ideas, to the most intimate dreams of our seven billion companions.

How will a change in global consciousness make a difference in our lives? When the human race reaches a critical mass for a common understanding that we are intimately connected, will it change our world for the better? Can we ever be fully aware that the welfare of our family and friends depends, ultimately, on the welfare of everyone else on the planet?

Indeed, what happens in Singapore or Dubai affects the lives of Londoners and New Yorkers. Rumor of war in the Middle East quickly elevates the price of energy and sends quavers through stock markets from Shanghai to Sao Paulo. Even something as regional as the weather in Russia can greatly affect not only the price of bread in Europe but also the availability of biofuels in Los Angeles.

Thousands, even millions of people, who have lately been categorized as the one percent, are extremely adept at benefiting from the fluctuation of capital. Billions of people, those in the so-called ninety-nine percent, are not quite as lucky. Humanity is aware as never before that we are intimately associated economically, politically and socially—both haves and have-nots, forevermore.

⌒

"The association between inequality and violence is strong and consistent. The evolutionary importance of shame and humiliation provides a plausible explanation of why more unequal societies suffer more violence."[2]—Kate Pickett and Richard Wilkinson, *The Spirit Level*

Deep in our collective hearts we know something is wrong about systems that have created such inequity. When someone is favored by law and custom or disfavored by circumstance and prejudice, injustice is lightning-quick in its expression. Yet global consciousness is not just about how fat or empty are our pocketbooks. It entails a deeper understanding that the threats to our mutual survival are now global in nature: natural disasters, conflicts over resources, pandemic disease, sectarian violence, and endless wars. Our current systems are little prepared for the global challenges sure to come. With technological innovations in biological and genetic engineering comes the responsibility to predict the outcomes of our decisions.

Our ethics, our moral philosophies, our methods of understanding what is right and wrong, are straining under the dire challenges of a future where uncertainty is the rule of the day, where democracies are polarized, where mass destruction is in the hands of individuals. Our government and economic systems are, surely, reflections of our moral foundations.

Perhaps it is time to understand the technological reasons as well as to reflect on the ethical basis beneath our precipitous rise in global consciousness. What peace we have on earth—our safety, prosperity, and quality of life—has come in large part from accelerated innovations in food production, medicine, and communications. As governmental systems become more conflicted and polarized, these three factors have created the highest potential for longevity and standard of living in our history.

Though great progress is acknowledged by most people, we have a long way to go for the promise of peace. Millions still suffer from malnutrition and disease. Millions die from war and abuse. As long as there is gross inequality of wealth, there will be terrorism. As long as there is injustice, there will be victims who lash out with violence. And most frightening, the proliferation of the global arms trade—from small arms, land mines, and drones to chemical, nuclear, and biological weapons of mass destruction—has extended the reach of horrifying violence into the sanctified safety of our homes.

What basis do we have to be optimistic that global consciousness will be a boon to humanity? We know factually and intuitively that if we continue to be diverted by wars and economic downturns from doing what is necessary for peace—such as educating our children and extending the healthcare and nutritional needs for billions—the consequence will be violence as our constant companion. Our globalized world is certainly a long way from a culture of peace. Yet there is great hope. More powerful than fear, our tendency toward commensuration and empathy is evident in the surge of nonviolent actions. Witness the astounding humanitarian relief efforts after tsunamis and earthquakes. The news is rife with massive movements toward democracy. Trends toward expanded rule of law around the world point to a trajectory of global freedom.

More than the dreams of a few idealists, the proliferation of faith-based giving, nongovernmental organizations (NGOs), and the widow's mite of average citizens show that a just and equitable society is possible. As social philosophers as diverse in approach as Aristotle and Ayn Rand have written, it is the reciprocal call to imagination that allows for the evolution of humankind. One good deed may not lead in a straight path to another, but collectively we reap verifiable benefits. All actions are interconnected and interwoven. Our global consciousness calls us back to the ancient moral foundation that has allowed our species to thrive in times of the best and worst.

~

"I desire health and healthy conditions of life, therefore I must do all in my power to make them possible for others.... In general, I wish to be happy."[3]—English Philosopher Arthur T. Cadoux

The wisdom of practicing the Golden Rule is more than a primeval clarion call to "do the right thing." It is the two-way street upon which our humanity travels. Reciprocity, or mutual exchange, is the clear and profound operative of the Golden Rule. Its fundamental ethic is our call to peaceful interaction. An ancient moral principle passed down from generation to generation from earliest humans to the modern world, the Golden Rule underlies our common values and has allowed humanity to survive and flourish.

As the ethical prime of human conduct, the Golden Rule provides an ancient, genetically encoded or memetically transferred moral foundation to meet our challenges in the future. It is the dynamic energy, a conscious decision-making mechanism that, when applied to our economic, political, and social systems, results in fairness and sustainability. With depthless, yet understandable dimensions of mind, body, and spirit, the Golden Rule is the principle that guides us from self-centered and bordered consciousness toward the expansive love that lifts the wings of our evolution.

Golden Rule Values

All of us have experienced points along our journeys when we became aware of the wisdom of the Golden Rule. Sometimes people are down on their luck or experience personal rejection. They worry for their families, have moments of fear and times when they need to reach out to others, to family and friends. On the other hand, many of us are blessed in our circumstances and wish such blessings upon others. We clamor for justice and equity for all. We do our best to create a semblance of peace in the world through the expansive virtues of fairness and forgiveness. From the first light of birth, most of us receive the love of family. We absorb the moral teachings of our faith, learn through decades of schooling, often receive a journeyman's entry into the workplace. To build a life and succeed as part of the whole, we take threads from the rich tapestry of our communities.

Yet the gateway to fully embracing our common humanity is highly individual in nature. Our personal character traits, learning experiences, influential mentors, spiritual practices, and many other factors help make us unique as well as connect us with others. As long as each of us is free to pursue our dreams, there are seven billion prescriptions to find our way to peace. However, to fulfill our dreams does not depend entirely on us. The way we order our lives, the economy in which we make our living, and the government that provides guidelines for our interactions can each hinder or help in that search.

~

"We seek peace, knowing that peace is the climate of freedom."[4]
—Dwight D. Eisenhower

Individually and collectively, we move forward through time toward an unknown future that is both exciting and forbidding. Like a ship sailing uncharted waters, we make decisions based on the winds of our courage, moral convictions, and moral fiber. Through the millennia of history, we have set up institutions, religions, philosophies, and constitutions to help us preserve our freedom. Some of these institutions survive; others are abandoned. Beneath the tremulous history, we have held a deep-seated morality basic to us all.

It is this subtle and unheralded heritage that is, perhaps, humanity's greatest feat of intellect. Even in our darkest hours, when we lapse into crime and racism, genocide and religious wars, in our hearts we know there is a better way. Soldiers honor the fallen and curse the war. Mothers teach love and mourn children lost to violence. The skepticism we all feel toward achieving a peaceful world is, indeed, understandable. Recalling the horrors of the Holocaust, the killing of millions in Cambodia, the genocides in Rwanda, we ask: *Is inhumanity an essential part of our humanity?*

~

"Someone awakened to the universal humanity of reciprocity does not stop obeying laws or cultivating virtue, but the motivating ideal becomes the interpersonal communion of love."[5]—Benedictine monk Olivier Du Roy

The Golden Rule is the universal moral compass that has stood alone among all our philosophies, religions, and moral homilies. It has survived essentially undiminished throughout history. Its eternal wisdom pervades all cultures and national boundaries. Its simplicity makes it available to all regardless of age or creed. *Do to others as you would have them do to you.*

Powerful. Pervasive. Simple. The values inherent in these few words, written in so many different ways in a host of languages and styles, give the

Golden Rule a deep relevance unlike any other maxim in our languages. All of the virtues of humanity reside within its sublime moral artistry. Each one of us finds within its angelic truth our particular values and virtue that lift our actions into purpose.

Now with the rise of global consciousness, the necessity of a global morality to transcend cultural and regional differences has become more apparent. The Golden Rule is our common heritage. It is a tried-and-true maxim for behavior, yet the Golden Rule is not static. It is active. It has reasoning. Most importantly, it has an inherent power available by its use.

Global consciousness arises out of the Golden Rule's manifestation, but it is ours to use individually as well as the collective hope of humanity. It is a stimulus, a catalyst, and a force for good. Economically, politically, and socially, the moral compass handed down from our ancestors now shows us the way.

A Personal Note on Honesty

One of the reasons the Golden Rule has remained steadfast as our moral code throughout our history is that it holds the entire pantheon of our best characteristics. Humanity's greatest virtues, such as integrity, forgiveness, friendship, empathy, generosity, and discretion, are embodied by its wisdom. Each of us finds the truth in the Golden Rule through what we personally value, or the virtues we express through our actions. Our values come from our families, our communities, our faiths, and our cultures. We may resonate with the virtues of logic or compassion, or those of creativity or courage. We may excel in several at once. What we value gives us insight into what we need from others and what we give to them.

Each of us has a relationship with the Golden Rule and its expression through the personal values we hold. The contributing value that brought the Golden Rule to life for this author, as an example, was an overwhelming and simple need, or least the desire, to be honest, to stay true to myself. Honesty is the value for which I hold myself accountable as a standard of behavior and truth. At times I falter, as we all do. Yet at times I succeed, and when I do, life becomes much richer for the experience.

Indeed, a recent experience helped me understand why the virtue of honesty became so important as my personal gateway to the Golden Rule. The awakening of my global consciousness arose from watching my father: the way he reacted to situations, his life experiences, his take on *these times* in the wider perspective of history, his words and transactions all provided me with a window into the Golden Rule.

One of sixteen million Americans serving in the military during World War II, U.S. Army Corporal John Clinton Arment with his new bride, Monna Ruth Harrison, before he was deployed to fight in the Pacific. By recent estimates, 60 million or more people, or more than 2.5 percent of the global population, were killed in the war.

John Clinton Arment, with all his strengths and weaknesses, became my teacher, my touchstone for reciprocity. He was one of a generation of Americans who experienced the pre-war depression of the 1930s. He fought on the winning side in the hell of war, then reaped the benefits of his country's rise as a powerhouse of prosperity. His place in twentieth-century events had a profound impact on his life. As with so many of his compatriots, the searing effects of the Great Depression and Word War II were never far away. He was a solid member of society, yet he had an unsettled nature, an understanding, or fear perhaps, that economic collapse and fascism could rise again.

As an adherent of the 1960s U.S. president Lyndon Johnson's Great Society, my father exhibited an awareness and understanding that he was not alone on this earth. As a son who found in his father a companionable spirit, I saw that he sensed the fragile nature of society. With clear eyes, he was aware of the inequity in the world and the avarice of politicians and plutocracy. He was skeptical of public liars and angry at the ambition and success of those who would take advantage of their status or inequitable laws.

My father passed from this life two decades ago, but I recently came upon a letter that had been written by him during the war that gave me insight into his character. Eight years before my birth, John C. Arment was a corporal in the United States Army. According to his honorable discharge papers, he was a field radio operator deployed on the front lines of the Japanese-occupied islands of New Guinea and the Philippines. "My Dearest Wife," he wrote to my mother from the battlefield. "Yesterday was a day that I will remember for the rest of my life. We had a big battle with some Jap Tanks. I went on watch at 3:00 a.m. and a little later the battle began."[6]

Corporal Arment's unit was part of the army's 37th Division, which had already been embroiled in battle from the day it had been deployed from San Francisco in 1943. He and his fellow soldiers had been commanded to take a town that was occupied by a fierce and committed contingent of Japanese troops.

"I was in a hole with the radio and we had a tent up over it," he penned to my mother. "They fired at the tent three times and hit a small bank along the cross road. They hit about thirty feet from me and dirt sure did shower down on me. The tent was full of holes."

As a radioman, my father was the front-line connection between the soldiers at risk behind enemy lines and the rest of the Allied world. Part of his job was being as close as possible to the line of fire. "The burning tanks were exploding and I think some of the Japs who managed to get off the trucks and the tanks were firing mortars and machine guns at us. It sure was a fierce battle for a few hours. I was in that foxhole," he wrote in all honesty, "and I mean I was scared."

The firefight stopped for the night, Japanese and Americans holing up in preparation for another surge. That morning, a Japanese tank came fast out of the village and opened up with a barrage of fire. "There was a battle scene like you read about and see pictures of," he wrote. "The trees were all burned and buildings blown away."

What occurs to a soldier who goes through such hell? In a moment of introspection beyond searing fear, my father scripted words that emerged from that letter almost sixty years later as a revelation that would stay with him throughout his life. Few words, yet a battlefield honesty came through to me sixty-five years later with a clarity that rivaled the images of combat.

"I have seen all the war I want to," he wrote simply to my mother in a common prayer. It was a moment of quiet revulsion. One considered sentence separated by a metaphysical space from the other details of the letter. It was my father's conscious reaction, a thought formed then and there, an epiphany that every soldier, from general to grunt, must find as he contemplates the dead and dying. "It was a real battle ground," he wrote. "I sure hope we don't go through anything like that again."

When the Japanese tanks had gone silent and the battle was won, my father's unit began securing the area. They had combed the forests and fields, shooting anything that moved "like they were hunting rabbits." Many of his fellow soldiers and untold Japanese defenders were dead. My father was one of the lucky ones. At the end of the war, he received a Bronze Star medal for exhibiting valor during that battle behind enemy lines. "Don't worry," he concluded with a telling nod to his new bride, "because I am digging deeper all the time."

I knew from watching my father's preoccupied silences that digging deeper was exactly what he had done. He was a victim as well as a participant of war. Like soldiers on all sides of a conflict, John Clinton Arment had done his duty, served with distinction in the Second World War in a century that saw the destruction of millions of lives, including those in the Holocaust and at Hiroshima.

When he returned to his home in Xenia, Ohio, he joined millions of other veterans to enjoy the spoils of victory. The largest peacetime expansion in history reaped the doughboys good jobs, decent wages, union benefits, houses, and land. He had four children and a career that paid a retirement pension for nearly twenty years until his death at seventy-three.

My father and our family were the beneficiaries of a political and economic legacy that reached its astounding peak in the 1960s. There were prosperity and freedom, technological and scientific discoveries, a historic reduction in poverty and hunger. The American century and its capitalistic drive had lifted many out of poverty. Democracy was acknowledged as the form of government that rang true with freedom.

I am greatly appreciative of my father's valor. His Bronze Star and honorable discharge papers hold a hallowed place in my home. Yet the honesty that came through in his battleground letter, the honesty with which he lived his life, had the greatest influence on me. When honesty is your touchstone, the world of avarice and ambition hold no lies that can harm the essential truth—as you would have them do unto you, so do unto others.

It is not ironic that as a nonviolent peace advocate, I am soundly indebted to a warrior. I acknowledge that fact of history and do not consider it a paradox. The complexity of human history prevents us from making definitive conclusions on the choices of other times and other people. From our isolation, we become inadequately aware of their actions, fears, and motivations. As humans, we are capable of empathy but also of condemnation when we see wrongs done. We try to do what is right. We reap the reciprocal benefits of the Golden Rule, and whether we are warriors in wartime or peace, the Golden Rule is at our call.

Like most veterans, my father kept his war memories to himself. He never boasted about his medal or told battle stories. He worked each day and paid his debts. He was the kind of man who wouldn't sell a used car if there was something mechanically wrong with it. He was truthful and candid.

All in all, he seemed relatively unscathed by the racism and prejudices of his time. When he called his enemy "Japs" in that letter and later around the table, I detected no hate in his soul, only the bitterness of war, a grappling with the senselessness of war when time moves on. Our enemies become our allies; our allies become new enemies. Such temporary racism is a psychological necessity of discerning *them from us* in order to justify the killing. Among the fear and bravado of my father's battlefield letter was the introspection of an honest man thrown into a situation that demanded survival. There was courage in his admission of fear. When he said he had seen enough of war, there was honor in the statement.

My father, indeed, was a hero in my eyes, but not because of his war record. It was his peace record that made me respect and love him all the more. How could a man survive such hell and exhibit a global consciousness where all people were born equal and deserving? He supported President Johnson's Great Society at a time when prejudice and political power were conspiring to oppress and maintain the caste system of poverty and oppression. He reluctantly supported liberal presidential candidate McGovern when he knew his party needed someone to defeat "Tricky Dick," as he called the soon-to-be indicted Nixon. He was part of America's silent majority that, in a continuous fight against the ravages of economic injustice and threat of fascism, kept progressivism in power for decades.

I admire men who have seen war and survive without anger. Through hell they were fired with a sense of justice. I believe that in that jungle foxhole, my father took an honest look at his life. He had seen the belly of the beast, contemplated death, measured duty and patriotism with their antithesis of cowardice and greed.

When all is said and done, my father's honesty was the simple virtue that I believe led me closer to a global consciousness. It submitted my ego to a humble understanding that beyond victors and victims, we're all in this together. Survival may require us to defend ourselves, but there is recognition that even our enemies are caught in the same web of violence. Honesty, in ways deeper than victory, made my father part of the Greatest Generation that put their lives forward in an exhibition of the Golden Rule as applied to war and peace.

A New Call for Heroism

Today, we find ourselves in another great battle. This time it has become even more apparent that, as *Pogo* cartoonist Walt Kelly said, "We have found the enemy, and he is us."[7] Racism, colonialism, and wars for resources are entering a new and more critical phase. Yet things move so quickly these days that we are barely able to construct a plan before everything changes. Even war with our enemies has become more difficult, for even before the smoke has lifted they become trading partners or allies among shifting alliances.

The call for heroism in this time is clear. The world is reeling from hyper-change caused by technology. Running up against forces far greater than before are the status quo of wealth inequity and the oppressive political power of the few. Our common aspiration to be done with poverty and war has never been stronger or more practical in its expression.

My father's generation would have scowled at the inequity and injustice created by the current emanations of cowardice and greed. For their sons and daughters, we have reaped the benefits of an information boom and access to education. We can no longer plead ignorance, though our history books are still limited to the lives of kings and politicians. Our collective stories focus on the rise and fall of nations, on the *realpolitik* that built treaties like houses of cards in preparation for war. We know our challenges, the manipulation of power, the wars, and accumulation of money and power. We also know of the momentous victories, the eradication of disease, the agricultural revolution, the strides in science, the ideas and actions of justice, the stories of common men and women toiling with honesty and integrity.

Intuitively, we know there is a better way than violence and war. The spearhead for change has evolved from a dependence on iron weapons and explosives toward the compassion of expanded medical care and the enlightened ideas of justice and prosperity.

Now comes the most perplexing question. How do we organize to meet the challenges and potential of the next century? How can we ensure that our economic and governing systems will enable us to reap the benefits of a new globalization of consciousness?

To find a practical and honest answer to that question is what drove me to hypothesize, research, interview, and experiment with a future history. This book investigates forces already present and how they will play out in the next expression of human life. With highly powerful and potentially harmful technologies being developed, with the expansion of population and misuse of planetary resources, the means of our destruction have reached critical mass. As humankind, we need to take an honest look at our world and learn to capitalize on the best we have to offer so the future is ours to determine. Safety, prosperity, and quality of life are the consensus values of the global consciousness. For the first time in history, with all the valor and honesty we can muster, the possibility for an economy of riches and a governance system based on justice are finally within our grasp.

Thank goodness for the principle that is manifesting in our rising global consciousness. The Golden Rule is our heritage, a moral map we can fully comprehend and utilize to maintain our prophetic bearing in this age of change, in this time of capricious fair weather and impending storm. It is not just that the Golden Rule will come in handy to meet our future challenges. Its evolutionary wisdom necessitates fundamental change in our economic and governmental systems.

The Golden Rule is humanity's greatest power. Teach our children well.

The Relational Ethic of Freedom

"Classic economic theory, based as it is on an inadequate theory of human motivation, could be revolutionized by accepting the reality of higher human needs, including the impulse to self actualization and the love for the highest values."[1] —American psychologist Abraham Maslow

Chapter 1

The Motive of Freedom
in a Culture of Peace

From our antiquarian roots and survivalist evolution and on through the flow of history, human beings have struggled for two types of freedom: *freedom from* and *freedom to.*

First conceived by Eric Fromm in 1941, these distinctions represent complementary forms of our individual and collective search. *Freedom from* is to release us from negative and sometimes oppressive challenges in order for us to taste the fruits of freedom. On the other hand, *freedom to* is an unleashing of the positive creativity necessary to allow us to fulfill our basic needs, expansive desires, and individual purpose.

Some put emphasis on freedom from governments and institutions of oppression. Others put greater importance on our freedom to rise to greater levels of intellectual, material, and spiritual attainment. Most fundamentally, *freedom from* and *freedom to* represent humanity's strategy to escape Maslow's hierarchy of human survival, such as food, water, and shelter, as well as to achieve the safety required to maintain life. We organize not only to exist but also to flourish. We create governments and economic systems that need constant attention to release maximum ingenuity and prevent descending into a state of oppression or the bonds of slavery.

"Freedom from fear could be said to sum up the whole philosophy of human rights,"[1] said United Nations secretary-general Dag Hammarskjold. To be without such fears is a blessing to those who either live in a time and place with little violence, or who have the innate courage to flourish despite the challenges.

On the other hand, freedom to be, to act, and to prosper is the process of leveraging the power of our humanity to transcend the daily grind toward higher levels of attainment. Freedom to work and make a living, to just sit and think, or to paint or write and contemplate the great questions of existence is to experience the epiphanies to which poets aspire. Freedom to love a child, a life partner, a place to call home allows us to find a measure of solace and peace in our lives.

In Maslow's hierarchy, *freedom to* seeks even higher levels of existence: to find self-esteem and self-actualization, to tap into universal love. German philosopher Hegel said, "The history of the world is none other than the progress of the consciousness of freedom."[2]

"Let freedom ring!" concludes the anthem "America the Beautiful." "Keep on pushing" was guitarist Jimi Hendrix's call to action in his song "Freedom." Musician Alice Cooper spoke for the oppressed in his album "Raise Your Fist and Yell." In some ways the most universal of freedom's brave calls comes down through the decades from the Rev. Dr. Martin Luther King, Jr.'s 1963 speech "I Have a Dream": "Free at last! Free at last! Thank God Almighty, we are free at last!"[3]

Such music and oratory is the timbre of our drive to be free. It is an expression of what makes us get up each day and strive for freedom from and freedom to. At once overt and emotional, and also subtle and persistent, the call for life, liberty, and the pursuit of happiness is expressed succinctly in the threadbare cloaks of freedom's rising: Delecroix's *La Liberté* in a torn dress leading her people to revolution; the German artist Leutz's flag-draped *Washington Crossing the Delaware;* the images of fearful yet hopeful immigrant mothers and children at Ellis Island: "Give me your tired, your poor, your huddled masses yearning to breathe free ..."[4]

From the beginning of human existence, our physical nature began to evolve. Our jointed fingers enabled flexibility, our legs extended our reach, and our brains became far more complex than all other creatures as we struggled to achieve our species' greatest goal: to break free from the survival motive of existence. Through this evolution of physical characteristics, our human ancestors were coming up with new and better ways to organize in order to escape our biological and societal bonds. Our economic and governmental models evolved with us as our bodies adapted to our drive to go beyond our basic needs to have lives of quality, individuality, and society.

Freedom! Such an evolutionary concept. The travels and travails of human DNA are set within the framework of our struggle to be free. History is the story of the march toward freedom. The cuneiform cylinder of the Persian king Cyrus the Great, after he had conquered the "impious" Babylonian king Nabonidus, is considered to be the first document of toleration. He repatriated the population, allowed them to worship as they pleased.

The historical documents of freedom are cherished proof of progress in our history. The Magna Carta of 1215 tempered the power of the king. The Mayflower Compact of 1620 attested to the Pilgrims' freedom of worship. The eighteenth century saw Enlightenment language at the core of the two great revolutions of recent centuries. John Locke's *Two Treatises of Government* laid out the personal freedoms of contracts and private property. In *The Spirit of Freedom,* Montesquieu wrote of separation of power so that one governmental body could not dominate law.

The American and French revolutions and the establishment of the new age of democratic and efficient governments were documented in the Declaration of Independence, the French Declaration of the Rights of Man and Citizen, and the Constitution. The Bill of Rights was a later addition to the U.S. Constitution, but it has laid the foundation of liberty for many governments around the globe.

From Washington's farewell address to Lincoln's Gettysburg Address, the rhetoric of American freedom has provided the inspiration of Lincoln's "better angels of our nature." When Teddy Roosevelt railed against the financial aristocracy, he became a populist politician who tapped into the common drive toward freedom. Franklin D. Roosevelt in his 1941 State of the Union address outlined his famous four freedoms: freedom of speech and expression; freedom of worship; freedom from want; and freedom from fear. Herbert Hoover, president before Franklin, forwarded a fifth: economic freedom, which he contended underlay all the others.

"Freedom is an indivisible word," said U.S. president Lyndon Johnson. "If we want to enjoy it, and fight for it, we must be prepared to extend it to everyone, whether they are rich or poor, whether they agree with us or not, no matter what their race or the color of their skin."[5]

The quest for freedom is, indeed, central to the history of humankind. Everyone feels its draw. "Every tyrant who has lived," said Elbert Hubbard, "has believed in freedom for himself."[6] The attainment of freedom is not only at the core of self-realization but also at the center of peacemaking, as well as our economic prosperity and governance. In the end, freedom is a necessity if we are to have maximum latitude and capacity to find our individual purposes.

The Economy of Our Lives

How best to expand our freedom is the great debate entailed by our rising global consciousness. Do we, like parents who fear to spare the rod, seek the efficiency of authoritarianism? Akin to caged animals suddenly finding an open field, do we unleash all humans from the overbearing nature of societal laws? How much *freedom to* should we nurture to balance the *freedom from* that keeps slavemasters at bay?

For many of us, the vast majority of our lives is spent in relative calm. Depending on the day, we sleep, rise to the sun, eat breakfast, and go to work. After the day's labor we spend time with our families, eat dinner, watch television, surf the Internet, and make love if blessed. The next day, we get up and do it all again.

These are the basics of *the economy of our lives.* And for the most part, we enjoy our days. Trouble is, we are not alone in the safety of our family and friends. The world is far from perfect. The reality of domestic abuse, neighborhood crime, war, and violence create fear and isolation. Swindlers conspire to bilk us out of our retirement savings. Dishonest politicians manipulate the public interest. And if all that were not enough, there are terrorists, strong-arm dictators, and paid armies to plunder our global village.

To those of us sheltered from the worst by rule of law, such deplorable acts of violence often seem remote. We put safety measures in every aspect of our lives, from airport security to the neighborhood watch. Regions that suffer from the ravages of child conscription and sexual slavery are slowly being brought into the light of day. The horrors of war affect our daily existence mostly through the headlines of the day.

The challenges of violence that come from the need to be free from oppression as well as the need to survive have become our collective burden. "Freedom is never voluntarily given by the oppressor," said Martin Luther King, Jr., "it must be demanded by the oppressed."[7] If there is to be any peace, we must grapple with global hunger, poverty, crime, and war, wherever it occurs, in what has become our small, interconnected world. Violence is, indeed, *the diseconomy of our lives.*

A little-used word, diseconomy is defined as something that adds cost as opposed to something that contributes to economy or efficiency. Yet diseconomy is rampant in the world of violence. Crime, abuse, and war have great costs, not only in our standard of living and quality of life, but also in the lives and health of our children.

Many of us, especially in post-industrial countries, are living examples of the material peak of human existence. We are blessed with long lives, excellent opportunities for education, and freedom to worship. We have access to great works of art and recreation. Many of us experience the calm of knowing that we have safety nets for health care and a societal commitment to a safe retirement with little worry compared to times past.

However, the world is a disparate set of circumstances. The vast majority

Presidential Medal of Freedom recipient the Rev. Martin Luther King, Jr., with the Rev. Theodore M. Hesburgh at an Illinois rally for civil rights, 1964 (National Portrait Gallery, Smithsonian Institution; gift of the University of Notre Dame in honor of the Rev. Theodore M. Hesburgh, C.S.C).

of our seven billion fellow humans still suffer from disease and poverty. A woman in Uganda must fear rape and murder. A girl in Afghanistan must fear being stoned to death for seeking an education. Many live with horrible facial disfigurations after experiencing one of the brutal tactics of war. Child soldiers suffer fear of death or threats against their families if they don't do the bidding of their masters.

As a society, we have endeavored to prevent the worst abuses. We do what we can to empower people to live in safety, have a chance at prosperity, and enjoy high quality of life. When we consider our future economic models and systems of government, the *freedom from* and *freedom to* of seven billion must be the main goals of our global strategic plan. "Man is truly free only among equally free men"; said Mikhail Bakunin, "the slavery of even one human being violates humanity and negates the freedom of all."[8]

To move from a culture that in some ways accepts violence as a natural part of life, humanity has a long history of documents and thousands of organizations dedicated to shepherding the world toward a culture of peace. Before the turn of this new century, United Nations Resolution A/RES/52/13 defined a culture of peace as "a set of values, attitudes, modes of behavior and ways of life that reject violence and prevent conflicts by tackling their root causes to solve problems through dialogue and negotiation among individuals, groups, and nations."[9]

For peace to prevail, UNESCO's Culture of Peace initiative prescribes eight essential endeavors of evolutionary progress:

- Foster a culture of peace through education
- Promote sustainable economic and social development
- Promote respect for all human rights
- Ensure equality between women and men
- Foster democratic participation
- Advance understanding, tolerance, and solidarity
- Support participatory communication and the free flow of information and knowledge
- Promote international peace and security

Through the centuries, many societies have made advances in democracy, human rights, and equality. Yet the diseconomies of life are many, especially in the plight of women to achieve equal status, as well as sustainable development and overall peace and security. In many parts of the world, fear often reigns. The world can seem on the edge of chaos.

So as humankind, we organize our governments to prevent the worst from happening, to keep a culture of peace in our sights. We construct forts and fences. We define borders and cultural divides. We establish governments, prisons, laws, and armies. Our great story is plotted with the heartbreak of continuous wars.

As humankind, we also endeavor to organize an economy that will not only give us prosperity but also contribute to safety and quality of life. We conceive of trade and industry organizations, tariffs and embargos, incentives and taxes. We create our economies in the best way within the constraints of ignorance, avarice, and greed. It took millenniums to move from a hunter and gatherer economy to agriculture. The stabilizing force of seasonal crops led to the development of common fields and private property, then villages and cities. As we flourished and covered the planet, our cultures diversified, and the way we adapted to different environments accounted for the creation of new ways to make a living. Trade between stable societies birthed the commercial enterprises of merchants and those involved in the transport of goods.

As our economies become more complex, societies moved from tribal elders and chiefs to councils, Pharaohs and Caesars. Democratic institutions arose from the genius of the Greeks, though the universal spread of democracy is still a goal. Within the body politic, there was always wiggle room for avarice and ambition. The rise of dictators and petty kings paved the way for slaves and serfs of a feudal system to tie people to the land.

All along the way, change was ever present. Each way that we organized had an inherent conflict that led to its demise. Slavery was an abomination, and the call for freedom from servitude became a clamor. The use of armies to subjugate the world led to a succession of Caesars who killed one another until Romulus Augustus, the last one standing, was sent on his way by the German conquerors. Even *Pax Romana* couldn't survive the power of time.

Change is part of life, and each fixed organization lasted only a short time relative to human history. These temporary institutions included political systems as well as economic systems. The march of history is a reasoned dialogue between the good in a system and its inherent challenges, or contradictions.

The concept of the historical dialectic attributed to the German philosopher Wilhelm Hegel has long roots that go back to Socrates. A thesis, or idea, is considered the synthesis of a previous thesis, or previous idea. As all ideas are subject to the changes of time, the thesis also includes inherent contradictions. Each thesis develops a negation, or antithesis. The dynamic between the old thesis and the new antithesis is a conflict mediation and synthesis that results in a new thesis.

Such change is one way to see the movement of history. When a political or economic system is fresh, the contradictions caused by change are few. As time goes on, the contradictions grow and a new system is required. The way we make our living at present is subject to the same movement of history. Human society is now undergoing unprecedented change. Moore's Law predicted that the computing power of transistors would double every two years. That trend foretold a lightning-fast technological advance that would spread throughout our world. Industry after industry has gone through major transitions.

At first, people resisted the reality that change is a primary factor in the economy, but now most embrace change with a relish that can only be described as a new sense of discovery and freedom. Entrepreneurs and inventors are among our greatest heroes. Whereas politicians and managers have suffered under constant scrutiny, the innovators have been lauded and admired. From Thomas Edison to Bill Gates, the pioneers of industry and technology have entered the hallowed halls that were before reserved for kings and popes.

Today, Steve Jobs has become almost Jungian in the archetypical dreams of success. With attention to the mind and desires of the consumer, Jobs was able to grasp the products that were needed to match the imagination of users of computer technology. To be at the advent of change was his greatest attribute, and his company, Apple, was able to become for a time the highest-valued company in the world. Yet even Apple would fall to the currents of time, its products having inherent contradictions caused by the inevitable static quality of product conception. Time moves on, as do technologies, as do systems.

As our greatest modern philosophers note, change is about to become even more evident and pervasive. New rules of commerce are forming. The seeds of our future economy and accompanying political system are already present. If only we could see them clearly—if only we could have some understanding of the kind of society we are about to enter, then we could interject the requirement of peace.

To discern the future clearly, like the claim of fortune tellers, is not a requirement to create new models for government and economy. It requires an understanding of history, practical experience, imagination, and innovation. To make decisions on the next evolution of our systems based on what we want the future to be is a reasoned action. The alternative to not trying to see the future is to live with what comes. In effect, if we don't visualize the future, the future will visualize us.

"True individual freedom cannot exist without economic security and independence," said Franklin Delano Roosevelt. "'Necessitious men are not free men.' People who are hungry and out of a job are the stuff of which dictatorships are made."[10]

What may come in the future has the potential to be devastating. There are weapons of mass destruction and invasions of privacy. Financial disasters have wiped away trillions of dollars of personal wealth. And there are new threats from biological weapons and technologies that can affect our seed populations and change our genetic structure. Indeed, there is a foreshadowing of new kinds of slavery.

Yet the plodding history of humanity has always led to progress. "The

Golden Rule is the original of every political castigation, written and unwritten, and all of our reforms are but pains with which we strive to improve copy."[11] The rule of justice transforms the rule of reciprocity, or mutual exchange, into the rule of equality. We can only evaluate our claim to rights as objective if we recognize others' comparable rights.

Today, the potential for feeding the world, for lifting the world from poverty, for letting every human on earth reach his or her purpose is within our grasp. Yet we must keep a determined eye on change and steer the vessel of our history through troubled waters to a calmer sea. Freedom born of prosperity and justice already won from the imagination of our forefathers and foremothers can now imagine the economic and governing systems of tomorrow.

Fully understanding any model considered, of course, will not be the last word on the subject. Two hundred years from now, an entirely new set of conditions will evolve and the children of our children's children will respond in kind. Yet this book is dedicated to today, to a reasoned strategy to achieve new levels of freedom, to the next thesis of our lives, and to a new world expressed by the Golden Rule.

Chapter 2

The Imperative for an
Alternative Gold Standard

To imagine what our world will look like, how we will function one hundred years in the future, is a daunting task. Yet in this era of accelerated change and deep challenges, to contemplate the trajectory of our lives is essential. The welfare of our children, the billions upon billions yet to be born, hangs in balance. Will there be scarcity or plenty? Dictatorship or freedom? Continuous war or conscious peace?

Each generation plays out the actions of its forebears, and the next century will be born from our time of intense innovation. The precedent we leave will be the next generation's only stabilizing influence. What we teach our children, the institutions we preserve or create, the legacy we leave will not only cause their challenges but also be their tether in a spinning world.

Throughout our evolution, our ancestors' story is one of adaptation and success against the struggles of their time. Even a cursory reading of our history books, filled with war, slavery, pandemics, and natural disasters, instills a measure of shock and awe as well as pride in the tenacity of our species. Today the world remains rife with conflict, and our cities are overcrowded and dangerous. Climate change, pandemics, and the proliferation of destructive weapons make for a future clouded with fear.

Indeed, humanity finds itself in a time of dire consequence created by our successes—the very innovations that inspire such pride and optimism. We are uncomfortable global neighbors, connected within microseconds by technology and hours by faster travel. It is no longer the people in our communities who have immediate access to our lives. We are available 24/7/365, an open book to the world with details readily accessible about our unique avocations, faiths and businesses. Our lives are virtual fishbowls of revelation for anyone who takes an interest, for better or worse. Crime is no longer simply a neighborhood challenge. A corrupt person on the other side of the planet could just as easily affect our lives as the criminal down the street. The person on the other side of the world can no longer be ignored. No nation can be distanced or marginalized. No culture can be disrespected or overpowered.

Wary we are, and should be, by necessity. This astounding connectivity makes it imperative that we find better ways to get along. We need to understand and create better systems of government and economy. The responsibility to be the keeper of our brothers and sisters urges us to monitor and engage in a society that is no longer so distant and unaffected. The idea that we are all in this together has repercussions in every aspect of our lives. Each of us has a profound effect on the large world. To every action, there is an equal and opposite reaction. The economy of our lives is intimately connected to the economy of others, which has huge benefits and possibilities.

Fortunately, the abundance of connectivity and information can also create great advantages in fostering a culture of peace. We know a great deal about the *others* on our planet, their successes and sufferings, their customs and plights. This connectivity offers unprecedented opportunity for a reciprocal understanding, a deeper relationship with our companions around the world. With over seven billion people, when one person has an idea, there is a good chance that there are others also thinking the same. When we attempt an individual endeavor, there are those who have already put together a coalition to accomplish the same goal. Patents, trademarks, and copyrights have gone from national scope to international. The synergy within organizations has gone from division of labor to collaborative expansion.

Technology has enabled the human race to enter a new era of cooperation. We now associate with each other beyond the necessity of trade. We've gone beyond competing neighborhood businesses to where we must work together in order to compete in a larger world where it is easy to get left behind. Cooperation and collaboration have become standard practices of businesses and organizations, which will be detailed in later chapters. We associate with each other to bring synergies to our search for prosperity. We form associations to bring strength to our convictions and justice to society. Cooperation and collaboration are increasingly essential in both the way we work and the way we govern.

Beyond any forewarnings of doom are the simple and profound stories of work-a-day lives where we enjoy the support of family and friends. We find inspiration in amazing feats of strength, intelligence, and reciprocating love. As humans, we exhibit a genetic drive toward survival that has far exceeded our fellow creatures on this earth.

The Individual and the Collective

Freedom of association is a basic individual human right. The right to freely come together as friends or a group with common interests is as fundamental to our lives as it is natural. Like birds that flock together in species, human beings are drawn to seek communion with others. It is not only to find solace among the many, but it is also to learn and grow with innovative ideas and new ways of living.

Yet the freedom to commune, assemble, and organize has been abridged by governments throughout time. History is littered with laws that prevent freedom of worship and thought. Workers' rights to organize have been restricted. Legislation and intimidation by authorities have kept people from expressing certain viewpoints and organizing to defend common pursuits.

To prevent such abridgement of the essential right to congregate and work together for common goals, documents and laws have been written to ensure the right to assemble. The American Constitution's Bill of Rights prevents government interference with the right to peaceably assemble or prohibit groups from petitioning to redress grievances. The European Convention on Human Rights protects the right to freedom of assembly and association, including the right to form trade unions. The Universal Declaration of Human Rights is very specific on the rights of individuals to freely associate, or not associate. "Everyone has the right to freedom of peaceful assembly and association." To ensure no coercion, the Declaration's Article 20 affirms, "No one may be compelled to belong to an association."[1]

The rights of individuals and workers to associate is firmly established. From such diverse agreements as the Canadian Charter of Rights to the International Labor Organization Conventions, those rights include collective bargaining, forming political parties, and creating standards for child labor and the equality of women. It makes sense that the right to cooperate is a basic right. How could democracy possibly function without freedom of association? We come together for recreation and sports, culture and commerce, education and faith, arts and science, as well as to take care of our brothers and sisters in the great cause of humanitarianism. The right to associate is the right to society. And in many parts of the world we have done well in protecting that right.

In modern times, the changes caused by our technological advances can also be used to abridge the right to associate. As noted, privacy is a major concern not only of social networking but also of government and commercial surveillance. The right to assemble without the prying eyes of entities that would use information for purposes that abridge other freedoms is a constant concern. There is a struggle between the power of the individual and the power of the collective.

Historically, the power inherent in collaboration has caused the word to have duplicity of character. The positive form of collaboration is to form an association that can have beneficial outcomes in terms of new creativity and progress. Yet during historical conflicts and wars, to collaborate was to give aid and encouragement to the forces of opposition. In France during World War II, for instance, a collaborator was a traitor who worked with the Nazis.

These two sides of the collaborative coin can be easily differentiated. The essence of the struggle between the two types of collaboration is in our freedom. As individuals, we associate with those who have a positive influence on our lives. When there is coercion, the association no longer serves the individual or, in the broadest sense, humanity. As Nelson Mandela said, "Only free men can negotiate; prisoners cannot enter into contracts. Your freedom and mine cannot be separated."[2]

Negative, coerced associations serve the power of a group over the individual. Collaboration enforced by power from outside simply becomes corruption. As nineteenth-century British politician Lord Acton's saying goes, "Power tends to corrupt and absolute power corrupts absolutely."[3]

Collaboration and association are core to the amazing increase in freedom for the twenty-first-century world. Many of the reasons for this contemporary progress are detailed in Jeremy Rifkin's book, *The Third Industrial Revolution*. That well-researched and ideated book focuses on the convergence of communications and energy technologies and how, as a result, our economic realities will drastically change.

> If the industrial era emphasized the values of discipline and hard work, the top-down flow of authority, the importance of financial capital, the workings of the marketplace, and private property relations, the collaborative era is more about creative play, peer-to-peer interactivity, social capital, participation in open commons, and access to global networks.[4]

Rifkin's mid-century vision of an associated society provides many of the fundamental concepts that underlie how a twenty-second-century economy will adapt and organize. Many of the changes that will take place after the "Third Industrial Revolution," as he terms the new era, have already occurred.

What Rifkin and other futurists are alluding to is far different from the models of society imagined in the past. Most economists and political theorists have approached economic theory as the "mechanics" of prosperity. Capitalism, socialism, and other economic models are *amoral*, neither moral nor immoral. They are simply structures that measure right and wrong by the benefits and risks of participating. The mechanism of the *invisible hand* in supply-and-demand economics provides the amoral code of capitalism. The right and wrong in socialist systems is provided by projected benefits of public ownership of the means of production.

In the past, the wealth of the world was measured by a physical *gold standard* by which a government guaranteed the exchange rate of currencies. The success of a country's economy was measured by their rate of exchange. Today the use of gold is obsolete, but physical measures still provide the imperative for success. Continuous rises in the gross domestic product and the gross world product are necessary, or we risk a global slowdown, recession, or worse.

Instead of a material imperative, the new model of an economy of peace must have a moral imperative that comes from within our global consciousness. The collaborative era necessitated by constantly changing circumstances is shifting our measure of success from a purely physical basis to one of relationships. Success will be dependent on our ability to freely associate. Rather than founded upon fixed laws or decreed structures, any economy of the future must be able to adapt to shifting associations stabilized by a moral understanding. Whether a person is a plumber or a geneticist, the principle of right conduct must be held in consensus and understood by individuals. A sense of morality must underlie our next economic system, or, with the undeniable risks entailed by our innovations, all hell will break loose.

Reciprocity as an Economic Principle

Throughout history, the idea that we even have a morality has been seriously questioned. Englishman John Locke believed there were no innate ideas on which a sense of morality could be based. Austrian Gottfried Wilhelm Leibniz said morality was not self-evident and therefore suspect as part of the human condition.

The Age of Reason brought analytical skills to the question. Philosopher Immanuel Kant tucked the idea of reciprocity, or the morality of mutual exchange or cooperation, soundly into the categorical imperative. Rather than focusing on the religious foundations of the Good Samaritan, he determined a universal law was at play, a human element, a moral agent. Doing good was not based simply on the desire to do good but by a judgment based on reason.

Of course, Kant was not the first to apply reason to the Golden Rule.

The Roman Grotius said, "That we do unto others such things as reason dictates we should not unjustly desire from others."[5] Centuries later, Englishman John Stewart Mill said, "To do as one would be done by, and to love one's neighbor as oneself, constitutes the ideal perfection of utilitarian morality."[6]

In the twentieth century, the psychologist Jean Piaget presented a process of moral development in his observations of children. When they played games, there was always an exchange. There was give-and-take. Sometimes there was simply take. When "give" was achieved in play, mutual exchange came forward as a learned behavior.

> In our view, it is precisely this concern with reciprocity which leads one beyond the rather short-sighted justice of those children who give back the mathematical equivalent of the blows they have received.[7]

Reciprocity, according to Piaget, has two aspects, as a fact and an idea, or something that ought to be. A child begins by simply practicing mutual exchange. Then, once accustomed to finding a beneficial source of equilibrium in the action, the child's behavior is altered from within.

> What is regarded as just is no longer merely reciprocal action, but primarily behavior that admits of indefinitely sustained reciprocity. The motto 'Do as you would be done by' thus becomes to replace the conception of crude equality. The child sets forgiveness above revenge, not out of weakness, but because "there is no end" to revenge (a boy of 10).[8]

According to Piaget, a sense of morality begins in early childhood. Reciprocity as retaliation results in conflict and destroys a game. Reciprocal action in equitable proportion leads to a sense of justice and makes the game sustainable.

In his 1948 book, *Die Goldene Regel,* Hans Reiner put the Golden Rule and reciprocity on the level as a moral principle. He cautioned against the limitations placed on the Golden Rule by Locke, Leibnitz, and Kant and wrote about the transcendence of human nature. Reiner cautioned against "the mistake of taking the ... self-evident character of the golden rule as a sign of something final,"[9] incapable of further explanation or interpretation. He proposed three distinct forms for application of the Golden Rule:

- The Rule of Empathy, in which we move from self-centered actions to considerate ethical actions.
- The Rule of Autonomy, where our conduct is considered based on observation of others and the praise or blame we place on others. Equipped with this reflective and judgmental standard, we take right actions as autonomous moral beings.
- The Rule of Reciprocity, a mode of behavior that results from the

relationship of actions, or those actions that affect others. With the rule of reciprocity, we can exist peacefully in society and do right by ourselves and by others. Reciprocity functions as our social moral foundation.

The Golden Rule gives us the basis not only for a morality but also for natural law, or a sense of right action derived from nature. As humans, we try to understand the roots of ethical reasoning for our most basic actions. We develop norms of behavior for the treatment of ourselves and thereby for the treatment of others. Golden Rule reciprocity provides the fundamental reasoning for human rights and the language of our democratic constitutions. Equity, fairness, and goodness fall out of mutual exchange and the Golden Rule's subjective/objective analysis. The Golden Rule is a physical, emotional and spiritual force that helps us find right action. We move from egotism through sympathy to compassion. We transcend from a simple self-interested response to taking action based on a moral foundation.

Also inherent in the Golden Rule is the ability for course correction. We live and learn. We observe and incorporate right action into our behavior. The English philosopher Arthur T. Codoux said, "Unless, therefore, the Golden Rule, when we are willing to act upon it, modifies our own desires and therefore the standard by which we act, it affords no guidance. And since its guidance lies in this modification, it is ere that the good sought by the Rule will be manifest."[10]

The Golden Rule is the evolving moral foundation of freedom. It gives us the ability to learn and innovate. The Golden Rule does not exist as "a single meaning but as a symbol of a process of growth on emotional, intellectual and spiritual levels."[11] It gives us a moral basis for the personal associations and collaborations that are necessary to adapt to changing conditions.

As we endeavor toward personal freedom, we have always modified the way we live and govern. It is a necessity, an imperative proven by history. We evolve the way we make our living and the way we govern not only because it is a requirement of time but also because we see increasing potential for the greater freedom to which we aspire.

"The balanced practice of the golden rule, then," wrote author Jeffery Wattle, "evolves from conscientious striving, monitored by self-examination, to a level where the metaphysical-spiritual foundation so infuses the mind as to eclipse distracting and material urges."[12]

Chapter 3

The Archetype of
the Golden Rule

More than a poet's phrase, a mother's love for her children knows no bounds. It is proof that deep emotions exist, yet how far does love extend beyond the reciprocating womb? Is such kindred connectivity what ensures humanity's survival? Or is love a fundamental way of life that enables us to live in wider society, to engage in peacemaking efforts such as fair trade and just governance? In essence, does love abound?

It would certainly be wonderful for love to rule our lives, yet short of that utopian vision we make do with a more practical mechanism for creating peace. That most of our lives are spent in relative calm gives us some assurance that more than kinship is at play. Without a deep awareness of others, life would be a constant battle of the fittest. Without an extension of reasonableness, empathy, forgiveness, and generosity to others, we would have long since succumbed to zero-sum fighting among nations, cultures, and tribes.

Somewhere between survival and altruism, keeping in check the dire natures of greed and ambition, is a practical motive for sustaining our race. There is a tool, an idea, a moral foundation, a universal philosophy, an ancient standard by which we measure the actions of others as well as one's self and find our path to right behavior. That measure is, literally, the way in which we would like to be treated. Whether our actions are caused by self-interest or the greater good, that standard of measure provides the core of the Golden Rule and, hence, the reason for our survival.

The history of the Golden Rule undoubtedly goes back to the beginning of time, when the first humans became aware that the needs of others were, by clear reasoning, their own needs. That thought became the basis of human law as derived from a deeper understanding of the survival instinct inherent in natural law. The standard for our conduct toward others is, essentially, the compassionate treatment of one's self.

However, the first mention of the Golden Rule traditionally dates to the Chinese philosopher Confucius (551–479 B.C.E.). In *The Analytics,* written by his disciples, Confucius is said to have equated Golden Rule thought and action to the idea of consideration. "Do not impose on others what you do not desire others to impose on you."[1]

To Confucius, the highly valued *gentleman* has a sense of duty to others and to himself. His life is spent in the acquisition of moral virtues that allow for correctness of behavior. The result applied to economy and governance is a just society that benefits all. For thousands of years, we have known the simple wisdom that what goes around comes around.

What has made simple Golden Rule wisdom survive when concepts more complex and sophisticated come and go?

- The Golden Rule is intuitive. It is immediately understandable, almost obvious and self-evident.
- The Golden Rule is self-sufficient and does not depend on other axioms to be wholly useful.
- The Golden Rule is all-inclusive. A person can determine correct action in each and every case.

Yet there is subtlety in its wisdom. As noted, there is not a single meaning but a process of growth. According to Plato, there are four basic reasons for right action.[2]

- The Repayment Principle, where we do something with the intent of getting something in return.
- The Cosmic Justice Principle, where doing good has consequences.
- The Moral Prudence Principle, where we do good because it has long-range self-interest.
- The Principle of Humanity, the highest level beyond the first three that points to the "good," a perfect, eternal, unitary principle that we find by inquiry into the ultimate source of our humanity.

As the sustaining principle of humanity, the Golden Rule is the moral archetype of transcendent behavior and relationships. We have an objective understanding that our moral obligation is to our fellow humans. From time immemorial, we have inherited this moral sentiment by way of the primeval stream of our human evolutionary consciousness. Just as genetics, or the science of heredity, gives us insight into the transfer of physical characteristics, the study of culture provides a way to understand the evolution of ideas.

Indeed, the human capacity for new ideas far exceeds that of other species. The human brain, relative to body size, is approximately three times larger than that of other primates. Millions of years ago, our brains began to reorganize to ensure survival. High-level capacities and concepts such as fast decision making, good memory, and societal culture were key to our survival. The reciprocal altruism of the Golden Rule became essential in forming alliances and separation of good ideas from bad.

As human consciousness developed, the high-level concept we call culture came by way of the human capacity to selectively copy ideas, symbols, and behaviors. These items of cultural information, or *memes,* spread from person to person over space and time. Coined in the 1970s by biologist Richard Dawkins,[3] memes are *imitated things* that act like genes, from which he derived the name, to self-replicate, mutate, transfer, and change culture through interaction with the environment. This co-capacity for natural selection of the best ideas through genetic and memetic transfer has, according to this theory, allowed the Golden Rule to survive the ages and evolved our global consciousness.

Whether by genetic, memetic, or co-evolutionary transfer, the Golden Rule spirit comes to modern humanity as a straightforward survival mechanism, without supernatural or relativistic baggage. It is the one principle that has been embraced by our entire species regardless of race, creed, color, situation, or circumstance. This deep-set moral naturalism of the Golden Rule is also evident in other species.

Apes and dolphins, dogs and cats, monkeys and whales all show attachment and bonding, sharing and altruism. Animals cooperate as a species in packs and herds. In addition, there are many examples of cooperation between species. There is direct reciprocity between humans and dogs. Goats herd horses; pilotfishes eat crumbs left by sharks. Symbiotic relationships abound. There are complex social rules among the animals just as there is a survival instinct that turns living things into food in the respectful and natural cycles of life.

As a human moral imperative, the Golden Rule compels us, urges us and directs us toward action. It is an imperative that is so strong in a person's mind that going against the reasoning is seen to be self-defeating. For the individual to be in touch with the universal is a fundamental mode of survival—the tribal consciousness linked directly to a sustainable global consciousness. As Kant put it, "Act only according to that maxim whereby you can, at the same time, will that it should become a universal law."[4]

The Golden Rule is a consensus value proposition that has come down through the ages, the one idea that transcends all religious division and philosophical postulates. As such, the Golden Rule is a most ancient ethical code. It is the common maxim of every religion, stated in a host of different ways. The positive form of the Golden Rule is that you should treat others as you would like to be treated yourself. The negative version has essentially the same message: Do not treat others as you would not like to be treated yourself.

As all religious texts tell us, the Golden Rule is the ethical path that gives reason for beneficent actions. Be kind to others. Do the right thing. Perform random acts of kindness, and those actions will be repaid in this life or a life beyond. All Golden Rule actions, whether altruistic or reciprocal in payment, contribute to world peace. All religions contain this fundamental truth explicitly:

> *Blessed is he who preferreth his brother before himself.*—Baha'i: Tablets of Baha'ullah, 71
>
> *Hurt not others in ways that you yourself would find hurtful.*—Buddhism: Udana-Varga, 5:18
>
> *You shall love your neighbor as yourself.*—Christianity: Jesus, Mark 12:31
>
> *This is the sum of duty: Do naught unto others which would cause you pain if done to you.*—Hinduism: Mahabharata 5:1517
>
> *No one of you is a believer until he desires for his brother that which he desires for himself.*—Islam: Sunnah
>
> *In happiness and suffering, in joy and grief, we should regard all creatures as we regard our own self.* —Jainism: Lord Mahavira, 24th Tirthankara
>
> *What is hateful to you, do not to your fellowman. That is the law: All the rest is commentary.* —Judaism: Talmud, Shabbat 31a
>
> *Respect for all life is the foundation.*—Native-American: The Great Law of Peace
>
> *Don't create enmity with anyone as God is within everyone.*—Sikhism: Guru Arjan Devji 259, Guru Granth Sahib
>
> *That nature only is good when it shall not do unto another whatever is not good for its own self.*—Zoroastrianism: Dadistan-i-Dinik, 94:5

Though the sustainability of the Golden Rule through time may be due to the near perfection in its logic, many have forwarded counter-examples to question its eternal wisdom. Some have gone to extremes and contended, for instance, that the Golden Rule can easily be used for justification by a sadomasochist. If they want harm done to themselves, what prevents them from doing harm to others? Yet the need for a deeper understanding of what is good for self as well as others is implied in the Golden Rule. Self-correction is inherent in Golden Rule thought.

Others have said that our ancestors' tribal nature might conflict with the universal value of unity. Yet the purpose of tribal custom is to find safety and prosperity. History has taught us that true safety is less difficult when realized without the conflicts inherent in boundaries and isolation.

Still others have said that it sets the bar too low for justice. Yet the Golden Rule seeks a higher perspective in fairness rather than the leniency of low expectation.

Finally, there are those who believe that only God's love can help us transcend our evil nature. Indeed, the Golden Rule culminates in the transcendent practice of love. "Someone awakened to the universal humanity of reciprocity does not stop obeying laws or cultivating virtue, but the motivating ideal becomes the interpersonal communion of love."[5]

The Four Processes of Golden Rule Ethics

Though at first glance simple and direct, the Golden Rule contains profound wisdom that can only be mastered over a lifetime. It requires thought and training to be of greatest value, and there are steps toward fully utilizing its power. To become a master of the Golden Rule ethic and achieve its transcendent quality, four processes become apparent, as follows:

1. **Empathy:** We become aware of the *other*. Awareness comes from intellectual observation of the other's circumstances. From that remote identification, we use experience and intuition to form a greater understanding and enter into the other's thoughts and feelings. We feel sympathy, or empathy, as the other becomes like a mirror to one's self.

2. **Compassion:** We move from empathy to a stronger identification with the other's feelings and circumstances as if they were our own. We can feel happiness and seek to encourage, or we can feel distress or pity in the case of the other's misfortune. With a deeper feeling of compassion, we have a strong desire to help and encourage or to mitigate and alleviate the other's circumstance.

3. **Engagement:** From a compassionate desire to help the other we move to the reciprocal engagement of right action. Engagement comes through immersion of self in the other's experience as we begin to form strategies for action. We are bound to the other by concern and duty just as we are bound to our self. We are obliged, liable, and pledged to engage in actions that we would wish the other to engage in toward us.

4. **Unity:** From compassionate engagement, we begin to lose the separation we originally felt from the other. Through engagement we transcend our division and fully embrace the oneness and interconnectedness of the world. We experience a sense of concord and har-

mony not only with the other but also for all of humanity. This transcendent morality, as expressed in the Golden Rule ethic, has potential to achieve that state of transcendent love of which poets and theologians write.

A student of Plato and teacher of Alexander the Great, Aristotle contended that "virtue means doing the right thing, in relation to the right person, at the right time, to the right extent, in the right manner, and for the right purpose. Thus, to give money away is quite a simple task, but for the act to be virtuous, the donor must give to the right person, for the right purpose, in the right amount, in the right manner, and at the right time."[6]

The virtue of reciprocity starts with feeling empathy for the other person. In the framework of oneness that is at the base of religious and humanistic philosophy, psychology and sociology, the *other* is inclusive of the *I* or *self*. In essence, the other is one's self. "There, but for the grace of God, go I" is a recognition that another's misfortune could be ours. This individual awareness is just as profound when used by groups. Differences in culture, faith, race, creed, or any other identifier become less important than our commonality in being a part of the human race.

The virtuous practice that underlies the Golden Rule is the action taken with regard to reciprocity. The two-way relationship inherent in the maxim defines equal responsibility. The ethics of reciprocity speak to positive actions that come from other positive actions.

The Golden Rule is a reciprocal force because of the response generated. When reciprocity is the underlying intention, there is the expectation that the action will be returned in kind. Altruistic actions, on the other hand, may result in a positive reaction, but there is no necessity for a response. A social gift, as another example, is not given with the expectation of a like response.

The reciprocal in mathematics is called the multiplicative inverse. The ratio of reciprocity is the number that when multiplied by the inverse of itself, results in one or unity, as it is termed in mathematics. As physics tells us, the consequences of our actions have repercussions. What goes up comes down. A body in motion stays in motion until acted upon by an equal or stronger force. For every action there is an equal and opposite reaction.

The "thoughtful practitioner"[7] will grow in the wisdom and practicality of the Golden Rule. We begin to see others in relational form, as brothers and sisters, fathers and sons, mothers and daughters. Strangers become friends; customers become colleagues. With a greater understanding of the consequences of reciprocity, we lose our fear and find compassion.

The Golden Rule is a transcendent moral process. The axiom clarifies and sharpens our values. It builds upon our moral inclinations so that we discern our duty as more than isolated self-interest, but a self-interest that includes the needs and desires of others and humanity in general.

Intuition is the ability to have insight into the *other* and know how to do the right thing according to reason. Over our lives, we build on specific insights to gain general wisdom. With wisdom we fine-tune our characters and the values we hold dear. When our motivations are purely reciprocal within Golden Rule reasoning, our values are applied with love and we achieve an inspirational, transcendent morality. "Inspiration will finally organize the economic justice," said Christian social activist George Herron, "which law has no power to utter; which custom is impotent to procure."[8]

The Golden Rule, from empathy through compassion and engagement and on to transcendent unity and love, is the start and finish of ethics. According to Rabbi Hillel, "What is hateful to you, do not do to your neighbor; that is the whole Torah, while the rest is commentary thereon."[9] Rabbi Akiba posed the challenge "Teach me the whole law all at once!" which prompted a succinct answer, "That which you hate, respect yourself, do not do to your neighbor."[10]

Many religions ascribe the Golden Rule to their own traditions. In Christian texts, Matthew 7:12 says, "Therefore, all things whatsoever ye would that men should do to you, do ye even so to them: for this is the law and the prophets." In Luke 3:11, Jesus is written to have said, "And as ye would that men should do to you, do ye also to them likewise." In the story of the Good Samaritan, Jesus defines a good neighbor as anyone in need and asks us to reverse the situation and act kindly.

Today, there are many variations on the theme. Though not considered religion, many modern philosophies and spiritual practices have updated the Golden Rule. The power of positive thinking undoubtedly goes back to the beginning of time, yet the work of Norman Vincent Peale in the 1950s and contemporary books such as *The Secret* promote the idea that if one puts positive thoughts *out there*, then one can expect prosperous returns.

Quantum physics also has a Golden Rule tradition. The *enfolded order* of British-American physicist David Bohm saw a universe that was beyond space and time, where there is a deeper order of the *undivided whole*. We live in an implicit reality, attested by recent theories of quantum physics, that is a flowing stream in constant flux. Events in one part of the universe affect another part without regard to the speed of light. In this universal view, all of us are entangled and interconnected. What one does literally affects us all.

The implications of reciprocity as the consensus value of humanity are not only relevant to personal morality but also integral to the evolution of our economy and models of governance. There is a sense of duty inherent in the Golden Rule, beyond the simple expectation of future return for kindness done. In Japanese culture, the idea of *sumimasen* invokes the idea that *this will not end,* thereby addressing the need for future action. One good deed deserves another.

It is obvious that there can be a negative reciprocity as well as a positive reciprocity. "Violent means will give violent *swaraj* [independence],"[11] said Mahatma Gandhi. An eye-for-an-eye retaliation can be the response to a negative act. Cooperative reciprocity is a positive response. Gift giving, smiles, and honesty are all positive responses that have been witnessed by everyone.

Throughout the centuries, the Golden Rule has been called forth to make a better world. The idea of *the kingdom of God on earth* was promoted by a group of social reformers in the late nineteenth century. New York pastor Walter Rauschenbusch established the Brotherhood of the Knights of the Golden Rule with other *millionaire socialists.* These reformers pledged their bank accounts and believed that with the right systems, wealth used for the good of humanity will create wealth for all. "Only with the institutionalization of new forms, thus eliminating the old apparatus," said the nineteenth-century American progressive, "could the political economy of the golden rule be made operative."[12]

Today in our rapid drive to modify our economic and governing systems in order to adapt to new realities, the Golden Rule stands as a moral force for innovation and justice. It is our common heritage, the original model from which all philosophies, constitutions and religions are derived. As the Jungian archetype of consideration, the Golden Rule is universally present in our psyches and can be tapped at any time to offer clear direction. Association and collaboration, the life-giving prescription for a prosperous and just society, are inherent in the Rule's overarching principle. The Golden Rule is an imperative of our history, necessary for our survival. The Golden Rule is a catalyst for the next generation's evolution of society, their economy, and their form of governance.

It is clear that this generation's overarching responsibility is to establish an evolutionary precedent, to infuse the Golden Rule into the economic and governing systems we leave for generations to come.

Chapter 4

Vision of a Peace Economy

How do we maximize the benefit of this endowed gift of our ancient moral code, the Golden Rule? Can the virtue of reciprocal exchange provide the moral driver for an economy of peace? How do we create an economic and governance system that flows with changing technology and avoids the blocks of power that bring inequities?

According to the wisest of our philosophers throughout time, the Golden Rule can, indeed, free us from self-indulgence, greed, intolerance, and racism. In theory it is easy; in practice more difficult. We simply put ourselves in the other's shoes. Reciprocity as a personal choice frees us to learn what modern customer-focused businesses have lately taught us—that thinking of the *other* provides reciprocal giving and receiving that is measurable in benefits. For business, it might be more about profit, but individual measures come in all three of our consensus values of a peaceful life: in our safety, prosperity, and quality of life.

In order to realize the Enlightenment vision of our collective right to "life, liberty, and the pursuit of happiness," economic and governing systems must ensure freedom for the other as well as one's self. Relationships between people must be equal in opportunity and free of the powerful influences that corrupt those relations. Reciprocity in our economic activity as well as how we govern has identifiable dynamics toward freedom:

- Reciprocity in economic activity INCREASES freedom.
- Reciprocity as just governance PRESERVES freedom.

Historically, prosperity, power, and even justice, unfortunately, have been the gifts of the privileged few. While humanity evolved in consciousness, our economic and governance models were built, necessarily, on systems that have focused on keeping society from descending into the chaos of unsustainable tribalism and personal greed. Ensuring safety and stability in the face of the epic challenges of nature tilted our systems toward survival of the fittest. The boon of power was peace for *some*.

- Political power has been distributed vertically by reason of status and wealth.
- Competition was the main driver of economic activity, which necessitated winners and losers.
- Nation-states formed as competing entities with trade barriers and national armies to settle disputes.
- Allocation of resources has been based on proximity and availability rather than sustainable use.
- Money exchanges in trillions of dollars per day have become indicative of a speculative, chaotic economy.
- Individuals and small groups have few ways, some of which entail crime or violence, to address grievances.

The debate continues on whether these and other major trends of history have led to greater progress. Yet today, there are harbingers of change that offer profound insight into how society is moving toward safety, prosperity, and quality of life for a much larger percentage of humanity. In the twenty-first century, the following indicators show that we are evolving away from economic models built on self-interest as well as governing models that support centralized power. These undercurrents point to a more adaptable and equitable wealth-producing economic system and a governance system that is increasingly dependent on judicial rather than executive actions or legislative law.

- Technology is democratic in that it distributes power horizontally (laterally) rather than vertically.
- Innovation as a transformative action is replacing zero-sum competition as the driver for economic expansion.
- Global communication and international trade are rendering trade barriers and nation-states obsolete.
- Free flow of information through technology is enabling the valuation of goods and services based on fair, location-specific reciprocal exchanges.
- Sustainable allocation of resources has become critical to global economic stability.
- Transparency has made obvious the accumulation of power and wealth in the hands of a few.
- Individuals and small groups now have great destructive power to address grievances.

Greater technological advancement, innovation, globalization, networking, sustainability, transparency, and empowerment are demanding the evolution of our economic and governance systems. These telling trends arise from the necessity of meeting new challenges. They require higher levels of consciousness based on the reasonable application of reciprocity. They entail innovations in the means of production as derived from the motive of human reasoning. Though not without exception, they can be seen as timely and natural expressions of our evolving moral code.

A Relational Economy Preserves Freedom

Economic expressions of the Golden Rule have one action in common: association. They entail a relation or connection—an exchange of ideas, feelings, or sensations. The highest form of association is collaboration, when people work together in a more efficient manner than working alone. Technological advancements depend on putting individual ideas and capabilities together as an association to achieve the innovation necessary to go beyond what has been. Networking and globalization are the opposite of isolation.

Collaboration requires unity. The sustainability of an association depends on people cooperating. Otherwise one person's wasted resources, including potential creativity, become someone else's challenge, whether now or for future generations. Transparency opens up to others the information that was, historically, an asset of the wealthy. When the greater community is empowered, actions support the greater good.

As the active ingredient in associative relations, collaboration expands the relationships that give the opportunity for all to be successful. Relationships between human beings create a sustainable associative society that can supply our needs as well as give us freedom to achieve our individual purposes.

Over the last few decades, attention to customer needs and desires has become the mantra of the growing relational economy. One key reason for the unprecedented prosperity of the last few decades is simply expressed in Golden Rule value: delight your customers as you would have them delight you.

Yet an economy based on relationships is about more than pleasing customers. Relationships can be one-to-one, one-to-many, or many-to-many. Stakeholders in a person's economic activity can be family and friends, neighborhoods and communities, and the natural world as well as one's self. Fair and equitable relationships are the new standard for success, and the Golden

Rule is the method of exchange. A reciprocating economy allows people the freedom to innovate. A reciprocating economy also demands a governance system that is free from the power blocks that cause restrictions and unfair practices.

In economic systems of the past, dominance was the most efficient path to wealth. On the macro scale, armies provided stability and new markets. Colonialism provided resources. In democracies, legislative lobbying and money were the keys to political power, as in good measure they are now. The governing system reflected the zero-sum competitive economies of our evolutionary history. At the microeconomic level, companies depended on competitive strategies such as advertising to increase market share or offering product line extensions and incremental changes in legacy products to find new customers.

Today's successful companies largely depend on collaborative innovations. Partnerships combine technologies and distribution channels. Continuous improvements and new technologies create new markets and expand sales to entirely new customer bases.

Reflecting the change from competitive strategies to innovative relationships is an evolving model of government and process of making laws in order to accommodate new ways of doing business. The judiciary is being used to pave the way for progress. Inefficient lobbying activities are being replaced by legal briefs that outline complex conditions and factual testimony from *amicus curiae,* or friends of the court. Laws written to support unfair economic practices are being struck down in courts. The judicial process of discovery and increased transparency are limiting the accumulation of power that has notoriously corrupted human systems.

The relational economy is a citizens' economy not ruled by an invisible hand or commanded by government but rather by the interaction between the partners in a transaction with the goal of a culture of peace. At first glance, this may sound like many economic models proposed in the past. Indeed, the history of economics is peppered with both practical and idealistic endeavors to devise the next economic model. Some economic theorists put the focus on decisions by the individual; others put emphasis on the collective.

Social liberalism, for instance, emphasizes cooperation by the collective as the way individuals can benefit. The belief that government should support the good of the community in working issues such as unemployment, education, and health is seen as good for everyone. Keynsian economics is when the state intervenes in the economics of society by ingesting tax money to enliven the economy.

Neoliberalism, a reaction to social liberalism, deemphasized the reliance on the collective to embrace monetarist policy whereby manipulation of the money supply is used to encourage economic activity. The government is seen as highly inefficient in making economic decisions. Supply and demand are a better balance than a command economy, where bureaucrats make decisions rather than individuals. Deregulation rather than regulation and free market rather than controls are indicators of a free-market economy, according to Neoliberalism.

Adam Smith is considered the forefather of the free-market system. His 1776 tome, *An Inquiry into the Nature and Causes of the Wealth of Nations,* laid out the details of how self-interest can be relied upon to provide maximum benefit to society.

> As every individual, therefore, endeavours as much as he can both to employ his capital in the support of domestic industry, and so to direct that industry that its produce may be of the greatest value; every individual necessarily labours to render the annual revenue of the society as great as he can. He generally, indeed, neither intends to promote the public interest, nor knows how much he is promoting it. By preferring the support of domestic to that of foreign industry, he intends only his own security; and by directing that industry in such a manner as its produce may be of the greatest value, he intends only his own gain, and he is in this, as in many other cases, led by an invisible hand to promote an end which was no part of his intention. Nor is it always the worse for the society that it was no part of it. By pursuing his own interest he frequently promotes that of the society more effectually than when he really intends to promote it.[1]

This *invisible hand* of capitalism has, arguably, delivered great prosperity over the last several hundred years. It is essentially an amoral economic concept given credence by many theorists. Ayn Rand was a Russian-American economic and social philosopher whose books, screenplays, and writings hailed the virtues of *laissez-faire,* or free-enterprise capitalism. Rejecting religion and altruism, she wrote of Objectivism, where the reason of individuals was what would result in the best of all possible worlds.

With her novels *The Fountainhead* and *Atlas Shrugged,* Rand condemned statism and all forms of a controlled economy. All forms of centralized policy were antithetical to individual human rights. The Libertarian Party in the United States was an outgrowth of Rand and her followers, with repercussions in today's political debates.

Objectivism touts the virtue of selfishness. When an individual does what is truly best for the self, it inevitably will be what is best for society. In *The Virtue of Selfishness: A New Concept of Egoism,* Rand and Nathaniel Branden outlined a new code of ethics, which they contended is rational, based on self-identity and validation.

The Moral Basis for Economic Activity

In addition to icons of capitalism such as Smith and Rand, other economic models and theories have been proposed, debated, reviled, and abandoned. Joseph Schumpeter of the Austrian School and Milton Friedman of the Chicago School of economic thought, as well as others with diverse economic theories, are put into an uncomfortable bundle of capitalistic advocacy: private ownership, free market, free enterprise, *laissez faire* economics, creative destruction, private enterprise, and perfect competition.

What most of these economic models and theories lack is a moral imperative. In fact, many reject morality as bourgeois sensibility that is based on self-interest. Yet morality, as embodied in the Golden Rule, is fast becoming the new standard of our society. Reciprocal exchange is the most efficient mechanism of the economy. Reciprocal justice is the most efficient mechanism of a governance model.

The economic and political models of the future will determine whether the vision of a culture of peace becomes a historical dream or reality. The difference between failure and success lies in lifting from subconscious to conscious the moral code of humanity. One thing we know, according to history and science, is that things will inevitably change. Throughout the centuries, we have labored, suffered, and survived, even flourished, through the rise and fall of Pharaohs and Caesars, tribalism and slavery. There were lords and feudal estates, kings and kingdoms. Change is the one dependable aspect in the never-ending evolution of our economic and governmental systems.

Since the Middle Ages, we have developed grand systems, primarily based on capitalism and socialism, to organize our lives. Remnants of the old guilds and joint-stock companies are still with us. Yet as our technologies and thinking evolve at an ever-increasing rate, a new economic system will necessarily emerge and rise like sizzling fireworks from the old.

Our Current Amoral Economy

A working definition of *economy* is simply the relationships among people and nature for the purpose of producing, distributing, and consuming what we need to survive. Of course, we not only want to survive but also to thrive. Our current system, primarily capitalism mixed with socialism and some aspects of feudalism, is under constant stress due to advances in technology and repetitive legislative attempts to promote economic activity.

In addition, it has become obvious that some among us accumulate more power than others and are able to manipulate the system to excessive gain. If we fully comprehend that the future for our children's children depends on the decisions we make in the present—and if we act reasonably and with foresight—we will ensure that succeeding generations will reap the full benefit of human progress.

To date, humanity has in most times relied on a war economy in which there are winners and losers, the country with the biggest army dominates, and where violence is a tactic of economic advantage. When a modern state uses the preparation and use of war production as the engine of its economy, that state is dependent on the war economy. The *guns or butter* zero-sum decision-making process allows modifications in the economy to support one or the other. Consequently, human services suffer when tax dollars and economic production are diverted to producing tools of war.

According to the Institute for Economics and Peace, war expenditures in times of foreign policy crises create a short-term bubble in the economy. When the crisis is over and the bubble bursts, long-term problems are created due to the downturn. The transition from war to peace is difficult not only for those losing but also for the winners, who ramped up their economy with deficit spending and war profiteering.

This up-down cycle may account for the continuous lobbying for more and more weapons even in peacetime. The economic value of war then creates a lobby for the actual use of the weapons stockpiled. This psychology might relate to the *economic instability* theories of economists such as Hyman Minsky, who contended that achieving the progress of economic growth depended on times of instability, even the chaos of recession and collapse, to kick-start a complacent society. To kick-start a complacent military with increased spending and the occasional war, in this frame of reference, is required in order to be fully vigilant.

The report states, "The positive effects of increased military spending were outweighed by longer term unintended negative macroeconomic consequences."[2]

The long-term results of such bubbles are increased public debt and higher inflation, which leads to less purchasing by consumers and less investment. This is certainly taxation without true representation, in that the decisions for a society are made by forces dependent on the need to sustain the industries dependent on a war economy.

Indeed, war investment, even allowing for contributions to economic output, is far less productive than investment in other forms of national defense. Building the infrastructure for commerce, investing in new energy technologies, and providing incentives for technological innovation make an economy strong far into the future. Weapons, on the other hand, are obsolete in a few years, or are used to destroy the infrastructure and youth of other countries.

This divisive economic model also includes the *shadow economy,* which consists of the war profiteers where the opportunity for making a living exists because of the advent of war or violence. Another facet is the *coping economy,* where populations are struggling and surviving, contributing to the war effort by the very nature of agreeing to their wartime conditions.

During the Iraq War of the early twenty-first century, the war economy prospered from the ramp-up to war and the *shock and awe* campaign of Operation Iraqi Freedom all the way through to the withdrawal of troops in 2011. During that time, the shadow war economy also prospered by way of a network of suppliers to the military. While some participants prospered, the coping economy in coalition nations as well as Iraq and neighboring nations suffered a standard of living that came from the *crumbs* of war.

In the wake of the wars on terror and for oil, illicit trade flourished in the regions of conflict. Drugs, guns, and goods and services from occupations flowed within and around borders. During the Afghanistan War, the proliferation of the poppy economy supplied the world with heroin. Petty tribal warlords held peace ransom as they negotiated between the U.S.-led Coalition forces, Afghan president Hamid Karzai's government forces, and the insurgent Taliban.

International assistance in the form of aid flowed with little oversight through the borders. As tales of suitcases and bags of money in the millions became commonplace in the media, the inefficiency of war reparations and winning the "hearts and minds" of the people through building schools and infrastructure was seen as ineffective due to corruption.

Often the solution to the inefficiency and corruption is to call for a stronger centralized state, many times an authoritarian government backed by a military armed by outside influences. Yet the reality in our situation shows that in the twenty-first century, new dynamics are coming into play. Decentralization and collaboration are becoming the rule. The amoral or immoral war economy that supports violence is rapidly turning to the Golden Rule dynamic and the moral economy of innovation and relationships.

What Would a Peace Economy Look Like?

A *peace economy* has been defined in various ways by economists, scholars, politicians, military and social analysts, and pundits and promoters with

various vested interests. The most general definition juxtaposes a peace economy with a war economy in that it features an absence of war. However, that
definition leads to domination models, such as *Pax Romana,* or to dictatorships where the absence of war is built on domination by arms, oppression
by a majority, or intense propaganda using fear.

Other definitions of a peace economy focus on the interacting of institutions, policies, and actions that create systems for conflict resolution. The
means of reducing conflict, either within society or with other societies,
include institutionalizing economic, political, and societal methods of conflict
prevention, resolution, maintenance, and transformation. The essential difference between domination and institutional forms of peace economies is
that the latter addresses the idea of justice for all.

The drive to create a peace economy is certainly the historical urge to
attain *freedom from* and *freedom to.* People also need to see a measurable
economic gain. The Global Peace Index from the Australian-based Institute
for Economics and Peace provides data to show that there would be significant
economic gains if violence were reduced.

"Improvements in peace would result in the realization of substantial
savings for both governments and society," the Index report states. "If the
U.S. reduced its violence to the same levels as Canada then the general community and state governments would collectively save in the region of $89
billion while the same reductions in the level of violence would provide an
economic stimulus of approximately $272 billion. The release of trapped pro-
ductivity through the abatement of violence would create a stimulus that
could generate an additional 2.7 million new jobs, effectively lowering the
U.S. unemployment rate by 20 percent from 8.9 percent to 7.1 percent."[3]

Yet cost containment is only one aspect of a peace economy, which consists of those activities that compose the majority of our lives. The idea of
defining peace economies and war economies gives the impression that there
is a distinct separation between activities that entail violence and those that
entail nonviolence. The activities that promote peace and those that promote
war are parallel in every society, from the tense border between North and
South Korea to the placid shores of Costa Rica, where there is no standing
army.

The ways in which people make their living determines whether or not
they contribute to violence or peace. Economic activity that supports the
perpetuation of war and violence is supported by taxes and social and legal
systems biased toward businesses that support violence. On the other hand,
the peace economy consists of business activity that contributes to safety,
prosperity, and quality of life.

The Peace Index takes into consideration that all societies have a mixed war and peace economy. They are developing expanded frameworks for defining a peace culture within individual states with data that show the level of activity described as the absence of violence. The indicators of violence used in the Survey include violent crimes, including homicide, incarceration, weapons, and police presence.

Several factors contribute to what constitutes a peace culture. One is the power of leaders to make decisions. A functioning system of rule of law is a second factor in a peace economy. Do laws contribute toward justice and fairness? Is everyone equal under the law? Can the police and judges be trusted to uphold the law? What laws contribute to a culture of violence? Is access equal to everyone, no matter what race, creed, color, or social and economic class?

Security is also a major factor in a culture of peace. Can people live their lives free from violence as well as free from the fear of violence? Wellness and health security contributes to lives of peace. Do the citizens have equal access, or even simple access, to health care?

The mission of the Peace Index is to frame peace in a "positive, achievable, and tangible measure of human well-being and progress." The yearly Global Index increases our understanding of the cultural, political, and economic factors that contribute to peacefulness in a particular region. It provides understanding of patterns that contribute to peace. It shows vividly how much violence and war are costing in many communities. It also identifies the benefits that come from improving a community's peace factors. Key findings of the Index include:

- Peace has been on the increase.
- Potential economic benefits from improvement are substantial.
- Peace is linked to opportunity, health, education, and the economy.
- Peace is not related to political affiliation.
- Regions within countries differ in their peacefulness.
- Incarceration is a drag on the economy.

"Our economic institutions," according to Institute's founder, David Korten, "have been designed by Wall Street interests to secure personal economic and political power in the hands of members of a small ruling elite. They do it well. Unfortunately, it is the wrong purpose. We need a top to bottom redesign to put in place the institutions of a new economic system, a New Peace Economy, designed to share power and resources in a world that works for all."[4]

In the end, common definitions of a peace economy, as either domination or institutional models, have limitations due to human nature and the slow development of evolutionary consciousness. Vigilant action is needed to change the cultural story from one that elevates violence and violent heroes to one that heralds the heroes and actions of peacemaking. In the 1950s, the story of civil rights changed the way Americans viewed race. Other movements have been the same: the women's movement, the environmental movement, and the historical Reformation of Christianity.

The peace movement is also changing. We have learned new realities and lessons from the Wall Street crashes, recessions, and economic downturns of the past century. People are finding ways to improve the local economy and rely less on the global economy for ways to make a living. Self-reliance, the local food movement, and off-the-grid energy initiatives have all contributed to making the local economy stronger and less dependent on global networks.

The Main Street economy has provided a counterpoise for the Wall Street economy. Yet such segmentation of the economy contributes to the oppositional economics that have divided and conquered our greatest aspirations. American philosopher William James talked of the "moral equivalent of war." James said, "A permanently successful peace-economy cannot be a simple pleasure-economy. Martial virtues must be the enduring cement; intrepidity, contempt of softness, surrender of private interest, obedience to command, must still remain the rock upon which the states are built."[5]

James called those who endeavored to make a peace economy strong soldiers who do the peaceful "menial tasks of society" in an effort that "is a force equal to war." This idea of actively fostering a peace economy was one of those ideas that become the basis for the Berlin Airlift after World War II and the Peace Corps created by the American president John F. Kennedy. It is the reasoning behind economic aid and nongovernmental organizations that work on food and health issues globally.

Philosophers of the Golden Rule, from Confucius to the modern, have not only taken this practical approach to creating peace but also elevated it to a moral principle. Many acknowledge the stratification of society, the bosses and employees, the leaders and followers, the chiefs and warriors. We play roles in society with a reciprocal respect and cooperation.

However, the unity of a good society depends upon just relationships. At the core of our peaceful economic transactions is empathy and duty to the other as well as to one's self. In Confucianism, the *shu* and *chung*, consideration and loyalty, weave into a trajectory of just relations. A peaceful society depends on these cooperative forms in order to achieve the highest order of personal creativity, which is inspiration—the highest expression of individual and societal purpose.

Chapter 5

From the Golden Mean
to the Golden Rule

*"Geography has made us neighbors. History has made us friends. Eco-
nomics has made us partners, and necessity has made us allies. Those
whom God has so joined together, let no man put asunder."*[1]—John F.
Kennedy

In this era where the difference between the rich and poor is wide and
growing wider, new trends that promote a culture of peace may take a while
to affect the day-to-day lives of everyone on earth. A person living in the
United States or Europe might enjoy more personal time for pursuits that
add to quality of life than many in the developing economies, where survival
is often the priority. Yet peace is not only about personal or national wealth.
The relationships at the base of a Golden Rule society are dependent on the
overall civilization, or cultural environment, within which they form.

A carpenter in Beijing, for instance, may have many of the same needs
and dreams as a carpenter in Chicago, but the society in which they were
born is vastly different. Both are concerned about their health and longevity,
their family and friends, their home and lifestyle. In addition, both must be
concerned with regulations and fees, permits and taxes, union dues and con-
tractor licenses, insurance and bonding, sometimes bribes and corruption.
The relationship with their customers is dependent on middlemen and government intervention by laws that favor one segment or another. The complexity of the work environment seems to rise with the pervasiveness of an
amoral culture, neither moral nor immoral, dependent upon the efficiency
of systems rather than the values at their base.

The trends apparent this century—greater technological advancement,
innovation, globalization, networking, sustainability, transparency, and
empowerment—are quickly affecting the lives of everyday people. These

trends point to an economic system with less bureaucracy and middlemen and more direct access to customers. The repetitive rise and shine for carpenters everywhere will be less burdensome as new technologies and innovations bring efficiency to the daily grind. Smart transportation and communications are creating faster ways to receive and provide the goods and services that make daily life bountiful.

A safe and secure community, supported by Golden Rule education and values, has the potential to enable people to go about their business while worrying less about survival or bodily harm. On a national basis, increased transparency and the use of non-lethal weapons are changing the face of war and crime. With the demise of nation-states and rise of global rule of law, fewer young people will be carried off to war—unless we fail to grasp the opportunity.

As the transition takes place from business cycles and global recessions to a localized economy and exchange rates, prosperity will be less dependent on command and control. The gap between rich and poor will, necessarily, get smaller. The standards of living for carpenters and bakers and for millions of other professions on the planet will, in time, get better. Increased access to education is giving people the opportunity to understand society in ways never before imagined. Many religions are moving from intolerance and proselytizing to tolerance and understanding that faith is a highly personal matter free from the linkage to power.

Lofty predictions, indeed.

Apparent are the issues that could promote or prevent such a life of freedom and prosperity for carpenters of the future, not only in America and China but also in India, Brazil, Egypt, Italy, and other populous areas across the globe. What kind of world will our descendants have in which to live and work? Amoral or moral? Their future is, in many ways, ours to determine. The story of how the human race responds to the challenges and opportunities of the future is not yet fixed.

It will always be a choice to live an immoral, amoral, or moral life. Sometimes we seek justice that is fair to us personally. Sometimes we seek a justice that is as balanced as we can make it within the circumstances. In rare times, we seek a justice that is equal, knowing that what is fair or balanced for the other is the same as what is fair and balanced for us.

It has always been a personal matter to live within the Golden Rule, where in our endeavors we do unto others what we ask they do unto us. Yet the same is true for our societies. So far, the historical choices of the societies we have created is a world where the Golden Rule is not possible within our limitations, so equal justice has been sublimated to the Golden Mean.

And mean it can be. Just as the Golden Rule hails back to Confucius, the Doctrine of the Golden Mean was first presented in the *Analects* and attributed to the Chinese sage's grandson, Zisi. The Golden Mean represents balance and harmony between opposites. At best it represents the virtue of moderation. Nothing in excess is imagined to bring a life of harmony.

Closely associated with the Golden Ratio of mathematics, the Golden Mean is relational. When two quantities create a whole, the whole is split into two measures. The ratio is 1:1 if they are equal. If one quantity is larger, the second quantity is smaller.

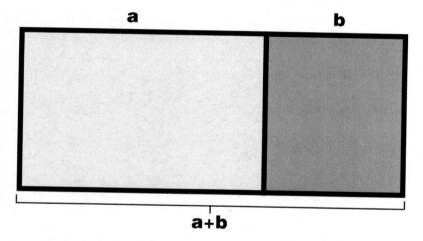

The economic doctrine of zero-sum is based on the idea that there is only one pie to be split between people. One person's gain is another's loss. If the gains and losses are added up, the sum will be zero. This leads to the notion that all economic activity is competitive.

Non-zero-sum theory involves aggregate gains and loses. Such things as collaboration and innovation are factors that expand the overall pie. Competition gives way to working together and finding new ways to live.

In the past, a majority of economic activity was based on competition and a zero-sum psychology. The grand scope of the Golden Mean economy is far too complex to be understood by individual human beings. However, we intuitively know that each of us has the option to simply live in the best way we can. We make decisions based on our character, our individual values, and the resources at our disposal.

For a majority of humans on earth, our personal choices have definitely increased. Greater freedom has come through the safety, prosperity, and quality of life wrought from amoral economies of the past. While one person might take a certain job, another might refuse. Slavery and conscription have declined. Individual decisions are based on whether or not taking a particular job will be advantageous or disadvantageous. Each person weighs the variables and motivations, then acts upon facts and intuition.

This sounds very much like mathematics. Indeed, we add and subtract, multiply and divide our advantages and disadvantages. The factors fall on one side or the other. The eventual solution or decision is a factor of the equation. Such is the natural way we live our lives. The overall economy based on the Golden Mean might be a very elegant diagram (as shown in the Golden Spiral below), but it leaves justice out of the picture. The billions and billions of decisions made each day are essentially dog-eat-dog, where to get a piece of the pie means that you must take it by hook or crook from another.

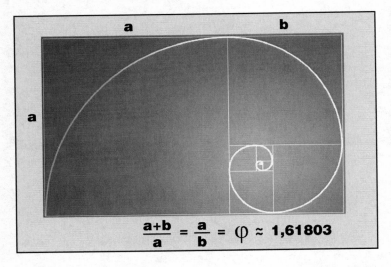

$$\frac{a+b}{a} = \frac{a}{b} = \varphi \approx 1,61803$$

As a species, we have always progressed based on the collective decisions and adaptations of individuals. We are not alone. We have family and friends, neighbors and colleagues. We are tribal when it makes sense. We are collaborative when we need be. The most efficient mode of living is the one that makes the most sense at the time. History is the story of making our living based on what is possible: the system or model reflecting the times.

The History of Economics as the Golden Mean

The history of economic thought tracks the story of individual freedom. From the earliest eras when survival was at the top of our needs structure, the strongest man would necessarily become tribal head, and the tribe's freedom was dependent on the leader's success. The era of the Golden Staff, as we might term it, was the time of tribal rulers, Pharaohs, and the strongest men in council.

As our needs structure shifted from day-to-day survival to the flourishing of agricultural and industrial communities, our economic systems reflected a measure of prosperity. The pie became larger. As history has shown, the slices for the few tribal leaders became much larger than what was left for the vast majority of people. Nature, of course, abhors an imbalance. When one person gets too much, the others rebel or pass taxes or steal until the fortunes of one are not too distant from the fortunes of the other. The zero-sum game of balancing opposites, which has given society a progressive motive of operation, has worked very well, and we have seen progress. From the Golden Staff, our economic systems began to seek moderation of the excesses, or the Golden Mean between the two extremes.

Tribal civilizations segued to slave cultures, which segued to kingdoms and empires. From empires came feudal societies and the advent of democracy. Society has responded to the evolution of our needs and technologies throughout history. We have moved from prehistoric hierarchical "fair justice" to the Greco-Roman legalistic "blind justice" and on to the relational "equal justice" society envisioned by the Enlightenment's awakening of the Golden Rule.

PROGRESSION OF SOCIETAL RULE

GOLDEN STAFF --> GOLDEN MEAN --> GOLDEN RULE

• PREHISTORY; EGYPT	• GRECO-ROMAN	• ENLIGHTENMENT
• HIERARCHICAL	• LEGALISTIC	• RELATIONAL
• FAIR JUSTICE	• BLIND JUSTICE	• EQUAL JUSTICE

The earliest documentation of economic theory dates back to Chanakya and Xenophon. Plato in *The Republic* alluded to specialization of labor and referred to a good society as the domain of philosopher-kings, where important decisions are deferred to a benevolent ruler. In *Politics,* Aristotle analyzed property and differentiated between common and private, taking the position that a measure of private ownership and the competition for it will contribute to progress.

Aristotle's denunciation of accumulation of money, solely for *wealth-getting,* as dishonorable stopped few in antiquity from gaining power. It was left to St. Thomas Aquinas, a member of the Catholic scholarly group called the Schoolmen, to consider economics in terms of the price of goods and services. There was a *just price* that covered the cost of production. Anything over this just price was immoral. The Golden Mean, the process of determining a balanced price, could be augmented by moral choice.

In the Middle Ages, as communication and transportation increased, the great economic *systems* began to take shape. Mercantilism, a term coined in 1763 but a concept that developed centuries before, came in the wake of the great military and seafaring power to open new markets and plunder colonial acquisitions. Such international trade soon moved from chaos to stability and concepts such as balance of trade and export and import tariffs.

The rise of nation-states inevitably gave impetus to wars for territory and resources. The rise of England as a seafaring power came after the defeat of the Spanish Armada and the quick rise and decline of the Dutch fleet, which was focused on commercial rather than martial goals. The Dutch East India company became a nation unto itself and was commandeered by the East India Company, a wholly owned subsidiary of the English Crown.

Meanwhile, Jean-Baptiste Colbert, Minister of Finance for the Sun King, Louis XIV, began the obsession of national governments to regulate the economy. The search for the balance between two extremes could be found best through intervention. Colbert set up a system of national guilds for the manufacture of goods such as linens and furniture. State power, it was determined, depended on the accumulation of wealth within its borders.

The Pre-Enlightenment period spurred many late Age of Reason philosophers of economics, including John Locke, who wrote of the social contract that would be elevated as an icon of revolution by Rousseau. Locke's *Second Treatise on Civil Government* institutionalized the right of humans to acquire private property, which was a combination of labor and the raw materials found in nature. The state, in his view, should have little interference other than ensuring the "lives, liberties and estates" of its citizens. The market, or price for goods, would do very well on its own by virtue of the Golden Mean.

The Rise of Capitalism and Socialism

In the eighteenth century a group of economic thinkers called the Physiocrats took Locke further and promoted *laissez faire,* or trade free of government interference. From Frenchman Francois Quesnay to the American president Thomas Jefferson, this new philosophy of economics focused on an agrarian economy mostly of farmers and the natural flow of producer, distributor, and consumer.

The rise of modern economic theory is dated to Adam Smith and his 1776 publication *Wealth of Nations*. Smith's first book is little remembered. *The Theory of Moral Sentiments* contended that our ethics and indeed our economic activity are developed through personal relations. Others react to our behavior, which determines our reaction to theirs. The result of these relationships determines our sense of right and wrong, which determines all the activities in our lives.

Beyond Smith's allusion to a relational economy, his book *An Inquiry into the Nature and Causes of the Wealth of Nations* had specific processes that those in power were keen to notice. Smith advocated free markets and the invisible hand of capitalism as a more efficient system than government intervention. Smith is a hero of free enterprise and the predecessor of modern free market theorists such as Ayn Rand and Milton Freidman.

The counterbalance to classical economists and capitalist theory came through history in a dependence on nations to provide for the general good through socialist policies. Though firmly fixed in the sum-zero game and the Golden Mean, socialists sought a better society through concentration of resources and the decision-making rationality of centralized organization.

Social thinkers such as Jeremy Bentham advocated utilitarianism with free speech, free trade, and universal suffrage and health insurance. The mission of government is to ensure the greatest well-being for the greatest number.

The icon of socialist theory is Karl Marx, who might not have considered himself a Marxist in the modern connotation. Marx was simply an intellectual economist who determined that a human's labor was a power in and of itself. In the search for the Golden Mean of justice, labor had a primary power to keep the entrenched wealthy *bourgeoisie* from keeping all of the pie.

Zero-sum economists such as Thomas Malthus and John Stewart Mill debated whether there would be depletion or plenty. Stock trader David Ricardo separated the worker's wage and the landowner's rent from the capitalist who receives profit simply by ownership of the means of production.

Excess profit and accumulation of wealth from the capitalist system gave rise to the modernized notion of a communal economy, or communism. Set forward in his book *Das Kapital*, Karl Marx illuminated the inherent contradictions in the drive for wealth in a system that alienated the worker from the product and tilted power toward the capitalists who owned the means of production.

In the *Communist Manifesto,* Marx and compatriot Frederick Engels made the search for a just economic system a revolutionary endeavor with the call to action, "Workers of the world unite!" In the hands of Vladimir Lenin and Mao Zedong and others, communism was institutionalized by nations such as Russia and China, and presumed just economic activity became the domain of the state.

The Modern Age of Intervention

Most modern economic theory revolves around the debate over government intervention in the markets. In the twentieth century, the most influential proponent of government deficit spending to kick-start the economy was British economist John Maynard Keynes. One of the major influences on the free market side was Milton Friedman of the Chicago School, which focused on the role of the money supply in generating economic activity.

The debate goes on between Keynsian and monetary activism. Yet the zero-sum game of the Golden Mean is even more institutionalized, with centralized banks and deficit spending all controlled by bankers who use the Golden Mean as the mantra of economic life.

There have been few radical ideas about economic theory since Marx. Today, the main debate beyond the role of government comes from discussions about the business cycle, the entrepreneurial spirit, and the function of corporations.

Joseph E. Stiglitz, who received the Nobel Prize for Economics in 2001, has focused on the information world. In his book, *In Making Globalization Work,* Stiglitz wrote, "The fundamental problem with the neoclassical model and the corresponding model under market socialism is that they fail to take into account a variety of problems that arise from the absence of perfect information and the costs of acquiring information, as well as the absence or imperfections in certain key risk and capital markets. The absence or imperfection can, in turn, to a large extent be explained by problems of information."[2]

At each stage in the development of our economic theory, human beings have chosen to utilize the most efficient way to prosper. Stiglitz pointed out the cost to our economy of non-transparency, misinformation, and lack of information. When inefficiencies develop, our economic models factor in the challenges and evolve to achieve new efficiencies. The Golden Mean is a mathematical model based on the mystery we see surrounding the economy. Most don't understand it. Most don't trust it. Just ask what people think about economists.

Yet mathematics is becoming central in the new economy. Using numbers, algorithms, and statistics is becoming more accepted. It is now standard practice for the Nobel Prize in Economics to be given to a theorist who has come up with a new way of explaining economic activity through mathematic properties.

For a peaceful economy to develop, mathematical models that achieve justice are essential. Golden Mean economies are obsolete. The Golden Rule provides an equality process based on mathematical certainty.

Case Studies of the New Peace Economy

Just as societal conditions tell us about economic systems of the past, present conditions tell us about the future. Particular trends are harbingers of the new general course for the economy of tomorrow.

For the purposes of clarity, the next two sections of this book interleave two different types of chapters. Particular chapters will communicate the basic processes for both relational economic and judicial governance systems. The chapters that separate the specific processes will focus on ten sectors of our economy using specific case studies of organizations that exemplify the trends and responses.

Each case study shows the ways that innovation and collaboration are becoming the new "way of doing business" for the most successful organizations. Each example, which is pulled from a particular sector of the rising global peace economy, focuses on an industry or organizational leader that is showing the way toward a peace economy of the future, sometimes by design, sometimes inadvertently, by utilizing Golden Rule dynamics.

As we will see from these case studies of contemporary innovative organizations, the seeds of a new economy are already in place. From the connectivity cloud of Salesforce.com to the customer-focused innovations of Apple, relationships are driving the global economy. Of course, good relations have always been important in economic activity, but today there is a new dynamic afoot. The new economy has a moral base. The reciprocal relationships of commerce are taking advantage of the practical generosity inherent in the Golden Rule.

- **The Service Sector** has grown up from our individual and collective sense of duty to others. To have the freedom to help others is not as easy as it sounds. Our case study, Rotary International, has bounded past international borders and legal restrictions on pharmaceuticals to do wonders for millions. Rotary International has moved the service sector into broader peacemaking efforts by leveraging the power of private enterprise to work for human needs.

- **The Faith-based Sector** speaks to our instinct for compassion. The freedom to do good works, a core belief of all spiritual traditions, continues a legacy that offers help to the hungry and despondent. The St. Luke Foundation, winner of the Opus Prize, is using entrepreneurial methods of collaboration to help the disenfranchised and suffering in the ravaged population of Haiti. The faith sector is fully embracing the "good works" part of religious and spiritual practice.
- **The Arts Sector** is available to all of us as a choice of meditative practices. The freedom to create has been at odds over time with another societal need, that of the status quo. However, times have changed, and companies like Apple have blown the doors off self-expression. The arts sector as a whole is expanding its definition and tools to enable creativity for all human beings.
- **The Environmental Sector** endeavors toward a more positive and symbiotic unity with nature. The freedom to commune with the earth, water, air, and creatures other than humans is essential to our welfare as a cohabitating species. With water and wellness programs, Hindustan Unilever has taken great strides in linking commerce with attention to the needs of the environment in which they trade. The environmental sector is being integrated into every action even in remote corners of the earth.
- **The Recreational Sector** is about leisure time and how we interact with our fellow humans. The freedom to celebrate has given rise to a cacophony of sports and entertainment venues and activities. Sports as exemplified by the Olympic Spirit are a majestic mixture of intense competition with generosity and respect for the others involved in the contest. The recreational sector is moving from a competitive motive to an enervating celebration of the human spirit.
- **The Civic Sector** keeps our society rolling smoothly along with good roads, bridges, and other community needs that have historically fallen between the cracks of private enterprise. The freedom to contribute is based on a social contract among members of a society for mutual benefit. The High Line Park in New York City was a collaboration of citizens and government to turn an eyesore elevated train track into a beautiful community park. The civic sector is mimicking the relationships of the family, where the needs of the whole become the drive to vitalization.

- **The Wellness Sector** ensures the health of our families. The freedom to live is the most basic human right and, as a testament to progress, our life expectancy has skyrocketed. Intuitive Surgical is a leading edge company putting robotic technology to work for less intrusive surgeries, contributing to a greater quality of life. The wellness sector is combining technology and the Hippocratic Oath to anticipate and respond to medical needs.
- **The Academic Sector** contributes to our understanding as individuals and as a society. The freedom to learn is a necessity in a democracy. Our example of how innovation and collaboration have come together in the academic sector is the Khan Academy, which provides free video lectures on thousands of topics. The Khan Academy has fine-tuned the relationship between the teacher and student.
- **The Commerce Sector** has to do with filling our needs through the ways we make our livings. The freedom to trade is essential for a healthy society. Innovations by companies such as Salesforce.com have burst through the regulations and status quo to imagine a new world where producer and customer are intimately connected for greater benefit. As more and more data becomes available, the commerce sector is expanding their view of customer as communicative "users" of beneficial products and services.
- **The Security Sector** provides a calmer world in which we can live and work to fulfill our needs and purposes. The freedom from fear is necessary for people to raise families and live life without threat to life and prosperity. The company iRobot is using low-profile robotic technology for such dangerous necessities as removing land mines, sweeping up oil spills, and increasing the transparency that can prevent conflict and wars. The security sector has begun to move from lethal to non-lethal technologies that preserve human life while ensuring our safety.

The case studies presented in the next section were the result of research into how each organization has succeeded by utilizing innovation and collaboration. These for-profit and not-for-profit companies have flourished in the technological and evolutionary changes apparent in these latter decades. They exhibit creativity and the ability to form alliances in order to achieve their goals where others either failed to succeed or failed to envision. Though none are perfect and change will forever challenge their status quo, these companies have achieved a moral quality in their pursuit of success.

A Moral Economy

"History shows that where ethics and economics come in conflict, victory is always with economics. Vested interests have never been known to have willingly divested themselves unless there was sufficient force to compel them."[1]—B. R. Ambedkar

A relational economy is the natural evolution of humankind's historical search to form associations that have reciprocal benefits for individuals within society. The Golden Rule is the moral principle that necessitates an empathic evaluation of current problems and allows us to propose compassionate solutions for future economic and governance systems. With that evaluation and proposal in mind, Chapter 6 gives an overview of a relational economy. Chapters 8, 10, 12 and 14 detail the four imperatives of a relational economy and are arranged with the following subsections:

1. Core Problem: Why change is important
2. Background: The history of the challenge
3. Solution: The Relational approach
4. Prototypes: Current indicators
5. Result: Visualization of progress
6. Challenges: Main objections

Chapters 7, 9, 11, 13 and 15 are case studies. The organizations highlighted in the case studies included in this book were not asked to condone and are in no way associated with the author or the ideas expressed herein. The information included about the organizations was derived from a combination of interviews and research.

Chapter 6

The Relational Economic System

The trends of current economic activity foreshadow a profound change in how we make our livings. Humankind is emerging from the ancient fear that there is just one small pie to go around and is embracing alternatives to the zero-sum game of competing tooth and nail. Innovative companies, technological discoveries, collaborative enterprises, and a new generation of social entrepreneurs are constantly finding a larger and larger pie.

The economies of our history were primarily survivalist systems that often benefited from aggressive organizational, even nationalistic strategies. In the absence of expansive technologies and intense innovation, winning market share or plundering the resources of a neighboring country were seen as great ways to keep an economy moving forward. The customer base of industry leaders was a Golden Fleece that could be captured by entrepreneurial Argonauts who exhibited competitive prowess and, at times, immoral guile.

While our capabilities developed and our consciousness evolved, people did whatever they could to provide safety and prosperity for the good of the tribe. To feed their children and keep their families safe from harm was held, understandably, high above individual quality of life. The economies of the Golden Mean were simply expressions of limitations and fears.

The Golden Rule, on the other hand, requires higher levels of morality-based freedoms. As we progress beyond fear as the main motivator in our economy, we find Golden Rule consciousness requires putting into practice the virtues and expansive power of reciprocal exchange. The Golden Rule has been a central thesis in all religions and philosophies, but values such as compassion and fair play have often been belittled in the quest for tribal winner-take-all safety and prosperity.

The question has always been: Why would someone care about others outside the tribe?

The answer to why people might do "good" for others is embedded in a simple yet profound idea—do unto others as you would have them do unto you. The Golden Rule lets us emerge from tribal consciousness into a relational ethic. The Golden Rule reveals the magic words that can lead to universal peace. Look to the heroes that fill our history books, or to those whose authentic smiles are expressed internally. Heroes don't need to be saints or kings. The Golden Rule is available to everyone, however flawed. The Golden Rule is the key to a peaceful existence, the *abracadabra* that opens the door to deep riches and mutual respect.

Unfortunately, an economy based on the Golden Rule is considered by society a dreamer's delusion. With irony and satire, Voltaire's Dr. Pangloss put idealism in a useless light: "All is for the best in the best of all possible worlds."[1] Ridicule is often the result for those who would offer a path of positive reciprocity. Idealists, optimists, romantics, whatever names we have for those who hold space for the virtue of reciprocity are often heckled, sometimes despised. With fearful nature, many discard the virtue of reciprocity as an impractical strategy in the context of reality of the human condition.

Yet today, the idealists have new cause for optimism. The dreamers of history are beginning to be lauded for practical, innovative ideas, strategies, and products that are changing the world. The Agricultural Revolution, the Industrial and Technological Revolutions, the Communications Revolution, even the Globalization of Consciousness, have in a very few centuries released us from many limitations. The evolution of consciousness has enabled our bigger brains to fathom the nature of empathy, compassion, engagement, and unity for their potential in delivering a thriving economy and the potential for peace.

A relational Golden Rule economy is, indeed, part of the natural progression of human history. As our innovations transcend limitations, it is only our backward thinking that gets in the way of making food and housing available to all, of reducing war, and of enabling the creative spirit to be unleashed through universal education. The balancing act of limitation within the Golden Mean is grandfathered into our consciousness as a potent but unnecessary barrier to realizing an amazing future. Like a mental appendix, a body part that has lost its ancient function, the ethic of zero-sum consciousness prevents us from visualizing a shift to a world where we are free as never before.

Evolving away from the Golden Mean and moving beyond limitation consciousness has been foretold by prophets and bards since the beginning of the written word. The transition from the Golden Mean to Golden Rule is the subtext of our economic evolution from the amoral fight for survival toward a moral collaboration of plenty. Where all of our previous economic systems have been based on one pie to be divided by all, the new basis is a moral act that expands our possibilities to a nearly limitless future but for the limitations of our minds.

The Golden Rule lies patiently waiting in our consciousness. It is the ascendant and expansive principle of an economics of peace. Morality as the basis of economic activity is absolutely necessary to achieve greater safety, prosperity, and quality of life in a world currently wracked with untransformed conflict. Without a moral basis, the actions we take to provide food and other needs for our families will, necessarily, include violence. There is no effective restraint in an amoral society where ethics, religion, and philosophy are considered impractical in the real world. Where power trumps compassion, it is *us against them.* Scraping for limited resources inevitably encroaches upon the scraping of others, which leads to unending conflict. With no moral center to bring in the benefits of reciprocity, conflicts necessarily lead to violence and war.

As the Golden Mean wanes and the Golden Rule rises, there are parallels in their processes. The Golden Mean was mathematical in its efficiency. The formulas of limitation, the balancing act of the Golden Ratio whereby the sum of two parts can only equal the total, gave rhyme and reason to moderating the economies of violent extremes. From there, the parallels begin to fade. With the Golden Mean there was no significant *other.* There was only the pie and the bigger the piece the better, regardless of how it was served.

The Golden Rule is much the opposite. It fully utilizes the mathematics of gain. It entails the properties of association, permutation, distribution, and commutation. The Golden Rule's win-win ratio, where the other person is considered important along with one's self, comes with the efficiencies of a mathematical morality for the post–Capitalist, post–Socialist economic system of the future.

Though it has never been fully honored as the true consensus ethic of humanity, the Golden Rule is constantly being applied, time and again, by the poor and the powerful, by the victors and the losers. Our ancient moral principle has always been with us to chide and shame the most adamant of *takers* and give hope to those *taken.* The truth in the ancient axiom is undeniable in its longevity and usefulness. As society, we pass laws and render judgments based on reciprocity. Our greatest challenge is the search for equal justice.

Often the Golden Rule seems to lie nearly dormant in our subconscious, rendered useless by a narrow view of practicality. It is as if we are waiting for proof that reciprocity has a power over avarice and ambition. "Aristocracy degenerates into oligarchy," the Greek philosopher Aristotle wrote over 2,000 years ago, "when the few, who are rich, govern the state as benefits the interests of their avarice and ambition: and a republic degenerates into a democracy, when the many, who are poor, make the gratification of their own passions the only rule of their administration."[2]

Such is the weakness of the amoral state, no matter whether it is a dictatorship or democracy. Yet the proof of the power of a moral economy and governance has lately come to the forefront. The past few decades have seen a rise in new economic activity based on forming associations and collaborations with regard to the *other*. The circumference of the pie is not set in stone. Examples abound. Apple has created entirely new markets and needs based on empathy with the other. Companies such as iRobot, Unilever, and others are fully engaged in finding solutions for society's ills with new technologies for communications, resource acquisition, and energy. A new agricultural revolution is upon us, and medical breakthroughs as well as global distribution have cut through the barriers that, just a few years ago, were hindering progress.

We are seeing the effects of a rise in economic morality. Through millennia of war and pillage, the Golden Rule is still with us. Reciprocity is taking its place among the great virtues of the world, such as courage, responsibility, and forgiveness. And when the economy is set firmly on morality, a system of fair, balanced, and equal justice cannot be far behind.

Steiner and the Associative Economy

The idea of combining morality and economics is ancient, as the work of Aristotle and other philosophers attest. Yet awareness of the globalization of consciousness is a recent phenomenon. For instance, only in the last century did it become clear that it was counterproductive to our interests to consider the earth's resources a part of the Golden Mean, to be cut and split like a piece of pie into parts.

To succeed in a global economy, organizations have found that partnerships and collaborations are essential. One size does not fit all. One culture is not like another. For global companies to sell their wares into other lands, associations with local residents have become a necessary part of doing business. In fact, to succeed in any market, whether local or international, requires associations at every level of economic activity.

The idea of associative economics—an economy based on the conscious coordination of producers, distributors, and consumers—was proposed in the modern context by Austrian philosopher Rudolf Steiner. In a series of lectures on globalization in 1922, Steiner contended that the world was becoming more integrated and economic properties more scientific.

When considering this integration, Steiner's associative economy focused on a conscious coordination of all parties to an economic transaction. Producers, distributors, and consumers are a closed loop for the purpose of meeting everyone's needs. There is a conscious coordination between the members of the economy, which is different from the invisible hand of capitalism or the command economy of socialism.

"You create something real," Steiner said, "if you regulate the Labour— that is to say, the number of people engaged on a certain kind of work. For the price depends on the number of workers engaged in a given field of work. To try to regulate these things bureaucratically, through the State, would be the worst form of tyranny; but to regulate it by free 'Associations,' which arise within the social spheres, where everyone can see what is going on—either as a member, or because his representative sits on the Association, or he is told what is going on, or he sees for himself and realises what is required— that is what we must aim at."[3]

Steiner also brought morality into the discussion of economics. His *threefold social organism* included three realms: the economic life, the rights life of politics and law, and the spiritual-cultural life. This threefold approach is similar to many theses throughout history, including the French Revolution's *liberté, égalité, fraternité,* Jefferson's *life, liberty, and the pursuit of happiness,* as well as this book's use of *safety, prosperity, and quality of life.*

For Steiner, society could only function when each realm was considered independently important. In this social model, freedom was essential. When human beings come together for the purpose of making their living, there needs to be a sense of equality and self-determination just as in the rights and cultural realms.

"Something else must be contained in the Associations," he said, "and will be contained in them once the necessity of such Associations is recognized. There must be in them the community-spirit—the sense of community, the sense for the economic process as a whole."[4]

There is no evidence that Steiner started with mathematics to create the social order, but it gives a glimpse into the thought process of his Associative Economy. To increase our understanding, we consider the associative property:

$$(a + b) + c = a + (b + c)$$
Example: $(5 + 2) + 1 = 5 + (2 + 1) = 8$

$$a \,(b \times c) = (a \times b) \,c$$
Example: $5 \,(5 \times 3) = (5 \times 5) \,3 = 75$

The associative property states that, for addition and multiplication, the rearrangement of the factors does not change the final value. There are other factors that could be put into the equation that would, indeed, change the final outcome. Yet the associative property itself is only a relation between factors.

We can immediately see that economic activity, especially the associations and relations among participants, can be described through mathematics. In a transaction, the association of the supplier and the customer is the basis of distribution and exchange. There is a mathematical association among members of a Steiner associative economy.

Yet with a pure associative economy, as the mathematics suggests, the

Rudolf Steiner (1861–1925), Austrian philosopher and social reformer who conceived of an associative economy as an expression of the Threefold Social Order (photograph by Otto Rietmann © Dokumentation Goetheanum, courtesy of Rudolph Steiner Institute).

rearrangement of producers, distributors, and consumers does little for progress. True progress would depend on a compounding relationship between the three. For instance, with innovation, a producer and distributor can offer more to the three-part producer-distributor-consumer value. The mathematical model becomes algebraic in form:

$$a + b + c + i \geq a + b + c$$
$$(a + b)^i + c \geq (a + b) + c$$

The factor "i" represents an innovation, which results in something greater than the original expression. In the first example, innovation becomes an additive factor for the whole economy. In the second, innovative collaboration of two parts of the economy supplies the consumer with a multiplicative value. The innovation can be as game-changing as the iPhone or as simple as a line extension for a Procter & Gamble soap product. It can also be the addition of a new market or the multiplication of a collaboration between two companies in the same industry. The possibilities of innovation are endless.

In an associative economy, the relationship between the producer and innovation is a conscious action. As an act of consciousness, it is a moral action. In fact, the drive toward innovation and progress is a moral imperative of Kantian perspective. The innovation comes in and of itself. It is spontaneous. It is a creative act that is *a priori* to further action in the economic process.

A productive economy comes through the relationship between the producer and the product, the producer and the distributor, the producer and the customer, and all the reciprocal actions that produce healthy economic activity. These multiple microassociations combine to create a macro relational economic system that takes into consideration the morality in the action of creative production. A highly creative economy, one where moral action gives us *freedom to* and *freedom from,* provides a profound sense of purpose and unity.

A Relational Economic System

The threefold associative economics Steiner proposed provides a precedent, or path, for the global relational economic system necessary for any future economy of peace. At both the beginning and end, at the core and result of associations are the relationships that form. A Relational Economic system naturally occurs as the culmination of individuals and groups freely forming associations. In the Golden Rule, the ancient moral basis for the relational economy is established. The Golden Rule is the guiding principle of reciprocal relationships that actively drive our associations, innovations, distributions, and rewards.

As we move toward a society free from the amoral and immoral accumulation of power, which are driven by laws that cause unfair competition, the relational economic system provides a highly productive, low-conflict, intentional and purposeful means of making a living. The benefits resulting from the combination of collaboration and innovation are all around. Examples of the modern moral economic potential are detailed in later chapters of this book. Trade is becoming a moral function, facilitated by digital and hard money exchanges based on regional valuation of goods.

The freedom resulting from a relational economy will necessitate the same Golden Rule dynamic in an evolving governing system. The associations, innovations, collaborations, and distribution flow of an economy have a parallel in the way we organize, maintain order, and ensure safety. The trends toward a Golden Rule governing system are present. Contracts and disputes between individuals and associations are being adjudicated by a global judiciary and enforced by a global policing system. The right of appeal has been institutionalized in articles, statutes, and constitutions around the world. A just governance system with the dominance of a relational judicial system is taking form.

Later chapters will investigate the practices currently in place to foretell this necessary arrangement between just governance and the developing economy. The relational economy of free associations subject to adjudication by an expanding judiciary is now facilitating the flow of goods and services while limiting the inequities resulting from the legislated entrenchment of power.

Collaboration among and between organizations is increasing mutual assets and capabilities in order to meet the challenges of a changing world. Cooperatives, collectives, and other freely forming associations have always been a part of the world economy, yet their influence is growing. Some collaborations are simply evolutions of the formal economy; others are developing informally, sometimes illegally or at least below the radar. Bartering alone, for instance, accounts for an estimated fifteen percent of the global economy, yet that tally is not included in the $60 trillion Gross World Product (GWP).[5]

The evolution to a relational economy for the next century will come by reversing the legislative establishment of obsolete economic laws, including agenda-driven taxes, regulations, and supports. As a replacement for legislated government, the criminal and civil laws that bring stability to society are firmly established through precedent and constantly being changed through judgments and mediated agreements by a system of local and international courts.

Tremendous technological advances and the rise of innovation instead of competition as the motivation of commerce have made a pervasive, worldwide relational economic system practical for the first time in history. "The conventional top-down organization of society," noted Jeremy Rifkin in *The Third Industrial Revolution,* "that characterized much of the economic, social, and political life of the fossil fuel-based industrial revolutions is giving way to distributed and collaborative relationships in the emerging green industrial era."[6]

The relational economy, like all systems, has fundamental processes of action or conduct. These four general *rules of the road* are the guiding requirements and obligations through which a relational economy flows. The standard model for any economic system is centuries old and includes the organizing elements of producers, innovators, distributors, and customers.

However, the new dynamic of a relational economic system is in its associative relationships. Through the associations of all stakeholders in the trans-

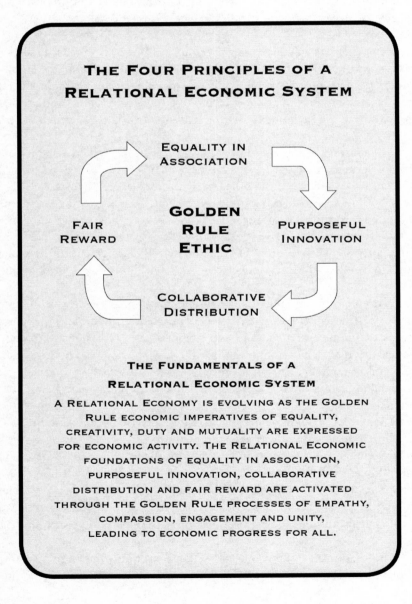

THE FOUR PRINCIPLES OF A RELATIONAL ECONOMIC SYSTEM

EQUALITY IN
ASSOCIATION

GOLDEN
RULE
ETHIC

FAIR
REWARD

PURPOSEFUL
INNOVATION

COLLABORATIVE
DISTRIBUTION

THE FUNDAMENTALS OF A RELATIONAL ECONOMIC SYSTEM

A RELATIONAL ECONOMY IS EVOLVING AS THE GOLDEN RULE ECONOMIC IMPERATIVES OF EQUALITY, CREATIVITY, DUTY AND MUTUALITY ARE EXPRESSED FOR ECONOMIC ACTIVITY. THE RELATIONAL ECONOMIC FOUNDATIONS OF EQUALITY IN ASSOCIATION, PURPOSEFUL INNOVATION, COLLABORATIVE DISTRIBUTION AND FAIR REWARD ARE ACTIVATED THROUGH THE GOLDEN RULE PROCESSES OF EMPATHY, COMPASSION, ENGAGEMENT AND UNITY, LEADING TO ECONOMIC PROGRESS FOR ALL.

action of a good or service comes innovation and collaboration. Fair reward comes from a reciprocal valuation and exchange, which begins another productive cycle of associative relationships, leading to more collaboration, innovation, and reward.

1. **Equality in Association (Associative Property)**
   Individuals freely and equally form informal and formal contractual relationships, or associations, in order to organize their lives in a purposeful manner. The mathematical nature of a relational ethic is described by the sequential logic of the associative property where even though the order is changed, the object of the association remains the same.

2. **Purposeful Innovation (Variable Expressions)**
   Innovation transforms the actions of individuals and associations into creative processes that increase the benefits of production and maximize the reward. In economics, as in mathematics, a variable expression such as innovation may change the entire system to increase value.

3. **Collaborative Distribution (Distributive Property)**
   Collaborations are freely formed through contractual relationships that maximize sustainable distribution of products and services. As an advantage over simple repetition, the distributive property creates efficiencies and opportunities when work is distributed among variables.

4. **Fair Reward (Commutative Property)**
   Reciprocal exchanges are influenced by the comparison dynamic of the Golden Rule to result in a fair reward. The commutative property allows for changing the order in an expression without changing the value.

To ensure that the relational economy is a freely flowing system will require the evolution of the way we settle the natural conflicts that are a part of economic life. Just as in the evolution of the economy toward a Golden Rule ethic, broad changes are occurring in modern systems of governance.

5. **Judicial Governance**
   A growing global network of courts and judges, supported by collaborative and integrative law innovations, are settling disputes, adjudicating cases, and making new laws based on a relational approach to governing.

6. **Global Policing**
   Global policing organizations, with responsibilities for specific geo-

graphical jurisdictions, are becoming more important in enforcing trans-national laws based on international precedent and evolving rulings.

To enjoy the freedom expressed in a relational economy with judicial governance is an evolutionary opportunity, but it will not require a person to have an associative sensibility. Indeed, the freedom of the hermit who tends toward an economy of one is preserved. Yet attention to cooperative efforts, understood implicitly and explicitly, in order to create innovations is valued and esteemed.

"As long as men are free to ask what they must," wrote physicist J. Robert Oppenheimer, "free to say what they think, free to think what they will, freedom can never be lost and science can never regress."[7]

Chapter 7

Case Study—
The Service Sector

*Rotary International and
the Freedom to Contribute*

The practical wisdom of the Golden Rule is at the root of our desire to help others as we wish to be helped. The oft-quoted common axiom of empathy states the motive of reasoned reciprocity: *There, but for the grace of God, go I.*

Humanitarianism is active compassion toward other human beings expressed through kindness, benevolent treatment, and assistance. Complementary to humanitarianism is service, or contributions to aid people in need by providing emotional, educational, and physical support. Service is an act of helpful activity, which can mean providing water and electricity or academic and job training. Service to humanity within the global consciousness is in recognition that each person's duty is to promote universal human welfare.

A relational economy is made possible by the Golden Rule's relational ethic, which is most obvious in humanitarians whose daily activity is dedicated to the service of others. Yet service to others has its headaches. The freedom to contribute is often hard-won, with reams of red tape, national boundaries, tax implications, and organizational difficulties to overcome before the giving can be done.

Rotary International is one such relational organization that has found innovative ways around the bureaucratic barriers of the Golden Mean. As one of the largest and most successful humanitarian organizations, the civic group fosters the idea of service as a worthy objective. In addition to attending a networking lunch once a month, members are encouraged to do service

Rotary Peace Fellows from a class at International Christian University are a good indication of the new relational economy. These individuals are working toward professional development certificates in peace and conflict studies or a master's degree in international relations, sustainable development, peace studies, conflict resolution, or a related field (Rotary International).

that promotes understanding, goodwill, and peace. The Rotary's Four-Way Test gives members a high ethical standard.[1]

- When you say something, is it the truth?
- Is it fair?
- Will it bring goodwill and friendship?
- Is it beneficial to all concerned?

To Rotary International, the ideal of service dignifies all occupations to the level of providing a service to society. Whether it's in a member's personal, business, or community life, actions should be worthy of humanity. With over a million members in over thirty thousand clubs around the world, the organization is committed to some very serious work.

The group is on its way, for instance, to contributing largely to the eradication of polio, which is an infectious disease that cripples youngsters, usually under the age of five. There is no cure for poliomyelitis (polio) so prevention is the only way to combat the ravages that can paralyze victims within hours. The disease, which affects the neurons in the brain, has been rampant globally, but now, due to the efforts of Rotary and its partners in the Global Polio Eradication Initiative, it remains endemic in only Pakistan, Afghanistan, and Nigeria. The vaccine, which protects a child for a lifetime, costs a little over half a dollar. The group's PolioPlus program is a volunteer initiative that has raised over a billion dollars to make the world polio-free.

Rotary started immunizing children against polio in the late 1970s through a pilot project in the Philippines. Its PolioPlus program was launched in 1985, and three years later Rotary became a spearheading partner in the launch of the Global Polio Initiative. Today, the group organizes distribution to localities, monitors efforts, and ensures that every child has a chance to take advantage of Immunization Days.

Besides raising funds, over one million men and women of Rotary have donated their time and personal resources to help protect nearly two billion children against polio. Rotarians work with partners including UNICEF to prepare and distribute mass communication tools to share the message with those isolated by conflict, geography, or poverty. Rotary members also recruit fellow volunteers, work alongside health workers to administer the vaccine, assist with transporting the vaccine, and provide logistical support. The group has associated with other organizations, including the Bill & Melinda Gates Foundation, to bring high technology into the eradication effort.

Rotary International also has a long history of supporting peace education. In 1999, the Rotary Center for International Studies in peace and conflict resolution was established to help peacemakers achieve a master's degree in peace studies, international relations, public administration, sustainable development, or a related discipline. Hundreds of Peace Fellows tour the world for national and international cooperation, peace, and the successful resolution of conflict.

"To a significant degree," the organization states, "the failure to provide for these needs—food, water, shelter, healthcare, literacy, jobs and human rights—is the root cause of conflict. Left unresolved, conflicts intensify and expand, in turn generating greater needs. Trained peacemakers are critical to breaking this cycle of devastation and despair."[2]

The Rotary Peace Centers have been established at eight universities around the world with over one hundred Peace Fellows receiving training and education in conflict resolution studies. In 2012, then Rotary president Sakuji Tanaka established *Peace Through Service* as the theme for his term. During that time, Rotary sponsored three Global Peace Forums to engage and inspire Rotarians to work for peace.

"Rotary Peace Fellows are leaders promoting national and international cooperation, peace and the successful resolution of conflict throughout their lives, in their careers and through service activities. Fellows can earn either a master's degree in international relations, public administration, sustainable development, peace studies, conflict resolution or a related field, or a professional development certificate in peace and conflict resolution."[3]

Help Others and They Will Help You: The Golden Rule as the Moral Drive for Humanitarians

Whether the call is to deliver the Word of God or soup for the homeless, tutoring for children or help for someone to start a business, the gifted person who does for others out of the bottom of the heart lifts us all to a better world. In many ways, the drive to provide goods and services to others has been reduced to a one-dimensional motive to make money. Yet the very fact that many are drawn to service by the goodness of their hearts is testament to the fact that the financial impetus is only one of the benefits we derive from supplying services to others.

Generosity is a profound societal virtue. The billions of dollars in aid that have gone to serve people suffering from disaster, hunger, and disease are a testament to human progress. The way this aid was distributed in the late twentieth century into the twenty-first was through a combination of private and public funds. In addition to direct aid from national budgets, the World Bank and the International Monetary Fund have been used by member nations to distribute billions of dollars in loans. These funds are given under tight restrictions on how the money is used and what payment schedule is part of the agreement. The availability of World Bank and IMF loans has changed the world forever: hydroelectric dams, railroads, reservoirs, commercial enterprises as well as food, water, and necessities have resulted in raising the world's standard of living.

However, the loan repayments quickly became burdensome to the emerging nations, hampering further progress and miring people in debt. Public funding through national budgets has always been a contentious political issue, one side urging unfettered humanitarianism, the other side demanding an interest-based allocation. Mandates on how the money is used and what return may be accounted has mired humanitarianism in what many times has become a political muck. The idea that governments and corporations manipulate the flow of food to enable foreign policy objectives or higher profits is not a new idea. From the French Revolution to the Arab Spring, people have opposed this one-dimensional expression of humanity and risen up to take the power away from government and bureaucrats to reduce food prices and facilitate life-giving sustenance.

Charitable organizations have lately proliferated. As of 2008, there were more than 1.5 million charities registered in the United States alone. They do work in a variety of religious, educational, and humanitarian disciplines. Whether giving to those in need is individual in nature or part of a larger group, the act comes from the heart. "I slept and dreamt that life was joy," said Bengali writer and musician Rabindranath Tagor. "I awoke and saw that life was service. I acted and behold, service was joy."[4]

There have undoubtedly always been acts of service regarding the giving of food. Throughout history, groups have formed to enable greater reach to these acts of charity. In addition to governmental and secular NGOs, thousands of faith-based organizations have endeavored to feed the hungry. These benevolent efforts make the connection between physical wellness and spiritual development.

The St. Mary's Food Bank Alliance may have been the first food bank, established in 1967 in Arizona. Founder John van Hengel saw that food in a community dining room where he was working was going to waste. He began gathering damaged packages, canned goods with expired usage dates, and other food that had been deemed unacceptable by the organization's rules. He realized he needed a central distribution area, so enlisted the help of the local basilica.

The idea quickly spread on a local, national, and international basis. Today, the work of food banks includes food rescue and salvage as well as sometimes sophisticated development programs that generate millions in monetary donations. Whether it's called a food pantry, soup kitchen, or homeless shelter, organizations find ways to distribute food in the areas where populations are at risk. Feeding America, for instance, has a network of over two hundred food banks that support over 90,000 projects. Ample Harvest is another group, with over 30,000 food pantries.

The loosely federated Food Not Bombs organization negotiates surplus food from grocery stores, restaurants, and bakeries that would go to waste. As franchises, the Food Not Bombs groups have the flexibility and independence to balance local needs with local supplies. The group may have a political ideology, but their efforts are wholly practical. In their view, providing vegan or vegetarian food to the poor is an act of protest against poverty, hunger, and war. Their organizational structure of loosely franchised collectives is a form of cooperative activism that fulfills their philosophy of nonviolent action. Today, the group has organizations in over 1,000 cities. The central organization, founded by Keith McHenry, provides resources for start-up groups, including a cookbook on how to prepare vegan meals for one hundred people.

St. Mary's Food Bank Alliance, Food Not Bombs, and Rotary International represent a part of our relational economy driven by the Golden Rule ethic. Those who help others find that both parties in the transaction benefit richly. Thousands of organizations and millions of individuals in the service sector of our economy are putting into practice the virtues and expansive power of reciprocity. To make a living from such humanitarian efforts requires a morality-based freedom that allows us to emerge from tribal, limitation consciousness toward unfettered innovation and collaboration that moves the heart to action.

Chapter 8

Equality in Association

The history of freedom is sometimes considered in context of the individual as opposed to the collective. Some believe in the primary importance of personal independence. Others consider practical freedom in a populated world to be found in making decisions that benefit the collective. This chicken-or-egg conundrum is solved handily by the Golden Rule's formula for the oneness of humanity. Treat others as you would yourself. The empathy inherent in the Golden Rule cuts through the separation between good of the many and good of the self toward a societal ethic of equality.

The reciprocating relationships that are core to the Golden Rule are expressed in economic activity through people finding common ground. These associative connections combine our unique assets and abilities with others to create a partnership strategy for accomplishing a joint purpose. In effect, all being equal, the sum is greater than the parts.

Associations can be entered into for purposes of business or to foster a social relationship. Associations are simply arrangements, nothing more than people coming together for a mutual purpose, yet the associative principle is deep in our genetic makeup. As educator Salman Khan puts it, "Adults seem to be better at learning by association ... [they are] more likely to grasp new concepts by way of their connections to ideas already known."[1] When associations are entered into freely, the relationship is not obstructed or corrupted by coercion. When associations become forced or restrictive, individuals will endeavor to abandon the connection. Sometimes people are free to make this decision. At other times, especially in light of the need to make a living, people remain in relationships that are counter to their long-term needs.

Associations are formed by many means, including legal structures such as corporations, unions, and the governmental structures of nations and cities. There are also associations less formal, such as friendships, faith-based networking, personal relationships such as marriage, and volunteer associations for the benefit of service.

Instead of going it alone, our associations are how we put many hands to work for efficiency and mutual benefit. The contractual methods of association can be informal or formal. Contracts are explicit or implicit (written or non-written). Each associated person expects to receive benefits. The duties and responsibilities can be simple or complex. All relationships depend on the time or duration the participants agree to give; therefore associations are by nature temporary.

People form thousands of associations throughout their lifetimes. The earliest associations are with family, mothers and fathers, brothers and sisters, aunts, uncles, and cousins. Other associations include faith-based centers: churches, mosques, and synagogues. Associations are formed with schoolmates and working colleagues as well as the schools and companies where individuals come together for a common purpose. The examples are endless. Most people pay taxes for governments to pave highways. Many give consent for our governments to go to war. Research teams are formed to find resources such as oil and natural gas.

The associations of our lives are astounding in their complexity: spouses, friendships, colleagues, and identities such as affiliations with political parties, sports teams, and ideological compatriots. When associations go wrong, the members may end up in conflict and the assets distributed by the ruling of the court. In many cases, a judge's action may endeavor toward justice by preventing the disputants from doing each other further harm. In marriages, for instance, the assets can be considered in a divorce case, yet the harm in the relationship goes far beyond the material. The benefits and risks of associations are inherent in the action of forming bonds.

Core Problem

In terms of the overall economy, associations can be set on an immoral, amoral, or moral basis. With our current governmental and economic institutions, especially with the structural systems of capitalism and socialism, the unequal accumulation of power and wealth in the hands of a few point to an immoral or, at best, amoral basis. Contrary to the reciprocal intent of the Golden Rule, accumulated power is the by-product of the amoral structures of survivalist individual competition or promotion of the collective that subjugates the individual. The result is associations that constrain or obligate people, limiting their freedom and creativity to thrive and find purpose.

Most associations are social in nature, but social contracts have been created to form governments that have extensive duties as well as great powers. These governmental associations are subject to powerful interests that, throughout history, have necessitated the use of protest and rebellion to temper their misuse of authority.

In addition, legislated corporate laws passed by governments have created long-term institutions that, in many cases, accumulate vast power. In the United States, associative corporate law includes both federal and state laws. The mechanics of corporations are handled under state law. Under federal law, the Securities and Exchange Acts of 1934 and 1935 passed rules for trading of stocks, bonds, and debentures. Companies commonly raise money through the issue of these securities. Corporate boards are responsible for the health of the corporations and are focused firstly on the survival of the institution, secondly on wealth accumulation, and lastly on the welfare of workers. To limit personal liability, "corporate veil" laws and insurance programs protect individual board members, who are usually stockholders in the companies.

Congress and the Securities and Exchange Commission under the executive branch create the rules, limitations, and special privileges for corporations. However, the courts may also change the nature of the rules and establish new precedent under which corporations are structured. At best, government can be the great leveler by creating laws that are fair and benefit society. Unfortunately, the power of a few individuals and groups in control of the flow of money greatly influences those making and executing the laws. This often results in an unfair society with a huge gap between the rich and poor. As long as government is structured to allow for inequality and for pockets of power, there will be manipulation, and the efficient and just utilization of resources will be obstructed.

Background

In all economic systems, people develop economic relationships in order to combine their ideas, labors, and resources for personal, family, and community gain. These relationships are constantly forming, dissolving, and reforming depending on the circumstances and potential.

Currently, many of these organizations of common purpose are incorporated by legislation into for-profit and not-for-profit corporations. As such, they are legal entities with bank accounts and, in for-profit cases, stock whereby they accumulate wealth, develop cultures, and wield powerful influence. As people come into the workforce, corporations have the power to limit personal choices and influence national policy. Global expansion of these legalized blocks of accumulated power has evolved beyond local control as well as control by nation-states.

At the basis of associations, including corporations, are contracts, which have their roots at the beginning of human history. Most contracts are verbal, whereby a relationship is sealed by a person's word, sometimes with a nod or handshake. More formal contracts are formed by a written agreement. Contractual common law is established over time and creates precedent through rulings by civil courts. On the other hand, contractual legislative and executive laws are established by legislatures or executive orders, usually under some influence by powerful constituencies.

Contracts are entered into with the intention of forming a legal obligation. Contractual agreements can also be specified or implied by the actions of one or more parties. The citizens of a geographical location can enter into a social contract that pertains to utilization of natural resources, land, or improvements. The French philosopher Rousseau pointed out that a "social contract" between citizens and their governing bodies outlines the responsibilities of both. In exchange for the protection of some rights, the people in a social contract consent to submit some of their self-sovereignty to authority.

Formal and informal contracts forming economic associations are created by desire or necessity. When there is value at stake in a relationship, contracts can be formed by mutual assent or by offering a form of consideration, such as currency or promise of labor or other duties. Contracts provide information on the responsibilities and operation of the relationship. These contracts involve the means of production, whereby inputs and outputs are defined by work done, resources provided, and profit rendered.

Social contracts also include areas where there is a responsibility or monetary value involved in personal relationships, including such documents as birth certificates, diplomas, marriages, and wills. Personal innovation forms its own contract. The creator of an innovation owns the rights but is free to form contracts with other parties to fully develop or exploit its potential.

Contractual agreements regarding private property involve personal belongings and forms of innovation. The exploitive focus on private land property, where the property is used as part of a personal production cycle, restricts our understanding of the universal responsibilities for the mutual care of the earth's resources. Land is only one aspect of nature that includes far more in a social context, including air, water, plant life, minerals, access, productivity, sunlight, historical renewal, and potential for reward. In many civilizations, public land, or the *commons* in a community, may have no physical boundary, but people have rights to the land based on precedent and community agreements. According to Plato in his *Laws,* "if I am a man of reason, I must treat the property of others in the same way."[2]

Solution

The first imperative of a relational economy is the right freely and without coercion to form relationships, or associations. We enter into our associations by informal agreement or by formal contracts subject to civil law based on legal precedent. Contractual documents include agreements among members of the association for a specific time frame and purpose. In order to form an association, individuals need to cooperate, or collaborate, with others.

When forming mutually beneficial associations, the individuals and groups involved must consider the other parties. The Golden Rule necessitates an empathic recognition of the other. The process of empathy entails identifying with the feelings, ideas, and experiences of others. A mutually beneficial relationship, or association, depends on a clear understanding of the needs and wants of others. Otherwise, the members of a relationship will not be able to cooperate in the most constructive ways to achieve the common purpose.

The benefit of cooperation, of course, is achieving greater results from collective actions than those available to individuals. With the group larger than the sum of its parts, the benefits of association include positive social and cultural affirmations between and among members. Economic examples of benefits include utilizing extra resources to reduce costs or increasing efficiencies of production and distribution of goods and services.

The Declaration of Human Rights, Article 20, attests that "everyone has the right to freedom of peaceful assembly and association." In addition, it contends that "no one may be compelled to belong to an association."[3]

To ensure that concentrations of power would be avoided, the contract has time limits. The association would be nullified upon the withdrawal or death of the parties. Continuing the contractual association would simply be a matter of reforming under the same or adjusted agreements.

The Rochdale Principles of Cooperation, devised in 1937 at the International Cooperative Alliance in London and revised in 1966, include as its principles[4]:

- Open, voluntary membership and democratic governance
- Limited return on equity; surplus belongs to members
- Education of members and public in cooperative principles
- Cooperation between cooperatives; concern for community

The associative property of a relational economic system is one of four necessary facets of a Golden Rule moral economy. The reciprocal nature of associations is the basis for finding mutual benefit without the negative results of an immoral or amoral economy, where the structure of the system encourages the accumulation of power at the expense of other individuals.

The associative property states that for addition and multiplication, the rearrangement of the factors does not change the final value. The variables and their interactions are all equal in importance. In a relational economy, individuals freely form informal and formal contractual associations in order to organize for ensuring their livelihood. We can immediately see that economic activity, especially the associations and relations among participants, can be described through mathematics.

$$(a + b) + c = a + (b + c)$$
$$(5 + 2) + 1 = 5 + (2 + 1) = 8$$

$$a\,(b \times c) = (a \times b)\,c$$
$$5\,(5 \times 3) = (5 \times 5)\,3 = 75$$

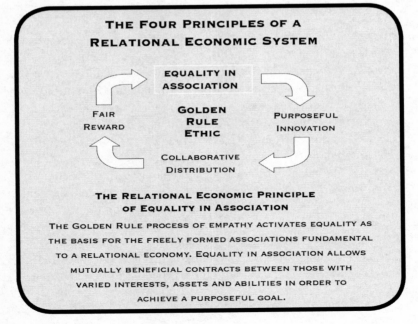

THE FOUR PRINCIPLES OF A RELATIONAL ECONOMIC SYSTEM

EQUALITY IN ASSOCIATION

FAIR REWARD

GOLDEN RULE ETHIC

PURPOSEFUL INNOVATION

COLLABORATIVE DISTRIBUTION

THE RELATIONAL ECONOMIC PRINCIPLE OF EQUALITY IN ASSOCIATION

THE GOLDEN RULE PROCESS OF EMPATHY ACTIVATES EQUALITY AS THE BASIS FOR THE FREELY FORMED ASSOCIATIONS FUNDAMENTAL TO A RELATIONAL ECONOMY. EQUALITY IN ASSOCIATION ALLOWS MUTUALLY BENEFICIAL CONTRACTS BETWEEN THOSE WITH VARIED INTERESTS, ASSETS AND ABILITIES IN ORDER TO ACHIEVE A PURPOSEFUL GOAL.

With the associative property, even though the order is changed, the object of the association remains the same. There are positive and negative factors that could be put into the equation that would, indeed, change the final outcome. Yet the association itself, done freely and without coercion, is focused on the final proof.

Attention to the Golden Rule as an evolutionary morality is essential to determining fair and equitable relations. Understanding the circumstances of others, having empathy for their fears, needs, and desires—many times as reflections of our own—is the fundamental driving force for entering into an association with equality at its core. Associations can achieve common goals much more efficiently than either coercive relationships or going it alone. The Golden Rule provides the imperative of reciprocal equality that allows the formation of associations that benefit all.

Prototypes

In modern history, there are many precedents, or prototypes, for associations that have benefited both the individual and the collective. Most of these prototypes have one aspect in common: consideration of the moral dimension of the relationship. A partial listing of types of such contemporary associations is below:

- Cooperatives and voluntary cluster organizations such as credit unions and labor unions
- Collectives, such as artist collectives, focused on working together as well as economic benefits
- Food-buying Co-ops for crowd buying and distribution
- Social welfare organizations, usually faith-based
- Nongovernmental organizations (NGOs) for social or charitable purposes
- Microcredit or microloan organizations to encourage entrepreneurial solutions to poverty
- Volunteer and community groups for a shared purpose
- Industry and trade associations for promotion and/or standardization of best practices
- Social networking and affiliations forming energy-building dyadic ties
- Community-supported agriculture subscription association to grow and distribute local foods
- Regional economic cooperatives: ASEAN, NAFTA, EU, and the African Union

- Private law contracts in the *jurs commune* between private individuals instead of public law contracts with governments
- Private relationship contracts, such as some wills, marriage, and separation agreements
- Gentleman's agreements for informal spoken understandings
- Memorandum of understanding for more formal agreements than a gentlemen's agreement
- Corporate social responsibility (CSR) and sustainability practices to increase organizational ethics and governance

These examples of how individuals enter into both written and non-written contracts are the tip of the iceberg of our emerging and burgeoning relational society and economy. The breadth and reach of associations that are regulated only marginally by governments parallel the black market in one way: the economic impact is little measured or realized. For instance, there are over 1.5 million nongovernmental organizations in the United States alone, with many millions more in Africa, India, and around the world.[5] With volunteer activities mostly undocumented, the productivity added to the global economy could only be understood in terms of social impact if those efforts were suddenly removed.

Result

In 2012, the United Nations declared the "International Year of the Cooperative," finding that one billion people are co-op members and owners.[6] Such worker-owned cooperatives are predicted to be the fastest-growing business model by 2025. Cooperatives along with other forms of collaborative associations are replacing the purely competitive, amoral models and transforming society through the Golden Rule ethic of giving and receiving in equal measure.

These relationships are also providing people with individual benefits beyond a standard measurable reward. By freely forming social and economic associations, without the corruption of power or the intrusion of coercion, each individual regains creative needs-based control over her or his life and livelihood. An economy based on temporary contracts, without the institutionalization or control by legislated laws, can prevent power from accumulating and allow freedom and creativity to take their natural courses in human relations.

Challenges for Equality in Association

First, is empathy strong enough to affect economic decision-making? The alternative, used with great enthusiasm today, is indifference. Yet as modern businesses are learning, empathy trumps both greed and unbridled ambition as the values that assure reciprocal progress.

Second, if freely formed associations are the basis of human activity, what is the role of government in economic activity? Can associations flourish without the consent of legislated laws?

The human ability to work cooperatively without statutory dictate is attested to by prototypes and examples of relationships that have low or no involvement of government. The economy is a combination of all the written and unwritten contracts needed for maintaining individual and collective prosperity. Many of these contracts are naturally headed for disputes. The judiciary was conceived as an institution best suited for weighing the facts and rendering judgments based on equality among people as expressed in the Golden Rule ethic. The establishment of precedent and evolving civil and criminal law ensures that the relations among people are maintained as equal and just.

Third, with less need for legislated laws to govern our associations, what happens to the fundamental duties and responsibilities that citizens expect from government?

Government is a contractual association, nothing more. Governmental duties have changed over time and are changing now. Constitutions, declarations, and legislated laws are the contracts, as Rousseau declared nearly 300 years ago, that have institutionalized society's evolutionary means of achieving collective goals. Citizens give consent through a social contract that can be withdrawn at any time.

Bureaucratically and politically controlled governing bodies are easily dominated by powerful individuals and interest groups. The necessary and responsible duties usually attributed to government, such as building roads and providing security, are contractual in nature. For thousands of years, these duties were the responsibilities of local associations. In a relational economy, these needs will continue to be duly acted upon as contracts between groups with larger goals in mind.

Government is not what gives these contractual groups their impetus to form. Rather, the impetus lies in the necessity of their creation. By simple and straightforward contract, such necessities as paving roads and building bridges will be negotiated by local citizens, just as they have been in many societies for thousands of years. Disputes in the delivery of these duties will be arbitrated, just as they are now, by the local magistrates.

Though the developing relational economy seems a dramatic and fearful evolution away from centralized control, most of human activity is accomplished simply by people working together freely in community. The evolution, of course, will come slowly as society adapts to new circumstances and realities that drive us toward the possibilities of more freedom in our relations. When inefficiencies arise, the judiciary will be more and more utilized to glean the justice and provide a path to accomplish the most basic or complex of societal needs.

Chapter 9

Case Study—
The Faith-Based Sector

*St. Luke Foundation and
the Freedom to Love*

The primary commandment of all religions is to form an association between one's spirit and the essence of love. To find love in family, in community, in the universe, to love God or Allah, to love Nature, the Divinity, or other spiritual forms provides people with a deep sense of meaning in their lives. From that overarching love springs the essence of human-to-human relations. As Jesus is said to have urged his followers, love others as yourself.

Love is an emotion that connects us to other people, and a connection is a relational experience: in effect, an association. Human kindness, empathy, compassion, and the actions of service are expressions of love's associations. Love's evolutionary rise as a survival tool is expressed in the love of our children and the love of our tribes. Reciprocal love comes from religious and secular concepts of equality. We are all deserving of love in God's eyes. We are all equal under the law. Golden Rule reciprocity is fundamental to the associations of equals in the society of humankind.

The most overt expression of associations dedicated to love may be found in religious orders that endeavor to feed and care for the poor. The call to love others is rooted in ancient spiritual and religious teachings that provide the impetus for action through a specific code of ethics. As Mahatma Gandhi said, "Recall in the face of the poorest and most helpless person who you may have seen and ask yourself if the step you contemplate is going to be of any use to him."[1]

The Golden Rule is the common thread that runs through all spiritual

Founder of the St. Luke Foundation, Father Rick Frechette has formed associations with many organizations, including the Mayo Clinic, to increase the service level for humanitarian support for the mission in Haiti (St. Luke's Mission).

traditions. Some who practice this code do so in deeply personal ways; others are driven outside their immediate surroundings to take responsibility for the welfare of brothers and sisters of a common humanity.

One such endeavor toward human love is The Opus Prize. Initiated by Opus Group founder Gerald Rauenhorst, the Opus Prize recognizes the peace heroes of all faiths in every part of the world. With prize money of over a million dollars, the annual award represents the largest faith-based humanitarian award for social innovation. Winners must hold an abiding faith in the hope that we can combat the world's most intractable problems. These heroes work under extremely difficult conditions to alleviate hunger and disease, poverty and illiteracy, injustice and oppression.

The Opus Prize is different in that it considers faith-based work that is entrepreneurial in approach. The work must empower the poor and inspire the disenfranchised to pursue lives of service. One recipient of the Opus prize is social innovator Father Rick Frechette, an American priest and doctor. Father Frechette founded the St. Luke Foundation in response to the wishes of the orphans he raised in Haiti, who wanted to help their people. Receiving the $1 million prize in 2012 for transformational leadership, Father Frechette has worked closely with this group of energetic Haitian young people, who are working to find a better future for their country. The St. Luke mission is a contractual association with other humanitarian organizations, such as the Mayo Clinic, that has delivered to over 150,000 people the basics of health care and education.

"Works of justice are works of peace"

The St. Luke Foundation for Haiti is, indeed, entrepreneurial in its approach to faith-based service. Its goal of providing food, water, medical support, education, employment, and many other essential services is based on the belief that the Haitians must have the chance to create their own sustainable society. Of their over 1,000 staff members, one hundred percent are Haitians.

As one of a new generation of entrepreneurial faith-based visionaries, Father Frechette merges compassion with business practices that can make a long-term difference. With a vast on-the-ground network of professionals and volunteers, St. Luke has two hospitals, a maternity clinic, 29 primary schools, a trade school, a high school, and outreach programs for psychological and social services.

Established in 2001, the St. Luke Mission had begun over a decade earlier with the *Nos Petits Frerers et Soeurs,* a program also started by Father Frechette. His mantra, "If not us—who? If not now—when?" is an expression of his faith in the practical actions of love. "The courage, strength, and capacity of the Haitian people is limitless,"[2] he says.

The group's mobile disaster response units have contributed to limiting the impact of hurricanes, an earthquake, and other natural disasters that have devastated Haiti. These units are equipped with sophisticated medical equipment and nurses and doctors and are in close contact with their newest facility, St. Mary's Hospital in *Cite Soleil*, and their partners in the United States.

During the recent cholera outbreaks, the mobile units of St. Luke and their partners set up clinics and provided on-site services and information to victims and the general population. Amazingly, over 40,000 cholera patients received essential medical services, which contributed to saving thousands of lives.

St. Luke's educational outreach program is perhaps its greatest legacy. An army of volunteers endeavors to communicate healthy practices through printed material, teaching platforms, and other means of getting the word out to average Haitians. The St. Francisville Production and Training Center, in coordination with the Francesca Rava Foundation of Italy, provides jobs with purpose. Its motto of "Works of Justice are Works of Peace" is expressed in over a million loaves of bread each year, a peanut butter and pasta operation, oxygen units for hospitals, and cinder block production for housing.

Father Frechette's innovative business and humanitarian approach has become a model for such efforts. The Foundation is committed to training Haitians on how daily wellness practices can bring peace to their community. Such is the truth in the adage, "Give a person a fish, and you have fed him for a day. Teach a person to fish, and you have fed him for a lifetime."[3]

Love Others and They Will Love You: The Golden Rule as the Moral Drive for Faith

There are thousands of faith-based associations created to do the work of love. As an example, Caritas Internationalis is a confederation of Roman Catholic relief, development, and service organizations. These diverse Catholic groups bring relief to the poor in over 200 countries and territories.

Founded by Lorenz Werthmann in 1897, Caritas took a leap forward with a 1924 conference in Lucerne, where sixty organizations dedicated their work to helping the poor and oppressed. This international conference has continued today and has become one of the largest humanitarian networks in the world. One of its associated organizations, Catholic Relief Services, began during World War II when war refugees from Europe needed physical and emotional assistance as well as help in settlement. Several bishops in the United States established the organization based on what they considered a mandate from Jesus Christ.

In later decades, as Europe began to recover, Catholic Relief Services expanded operations, setting up agencies in Asia, Africa, and Latin America. The expansion took place not only in geography, but also in its mission. Long-term solutions began to be focused on breaking the cycle of poverty in developing countries.

Community-based initiatives, including setting up health education services, initiating clean water projects, and forming community banks and agricultural projects, all led to increased quality of life in many regions of the world. Natural disasters, such as hurricanes and tsunamis, have taxed the resources of the Catholic organization. The organization has partners and worked alongside NGOs around the world.

Peacebuilding is a core tradition of Catholic Services. After the World Summit of 2000 and the genocide in Rwanda, the organization committed to a more expansive view of working in communities. Three key objectives have resulted from that commitment:

- Improve cohesion in society
- Work to attain justice for marginalized people
- Increase interfaith engagement

At their World Summit in 2000, Catholic Relief Services established a visionary statement: "Build a culture of peace throughout the world based on a foundation of justice and reconciliation."[4] By 2008, Catholic Relief Services was involved in fifty-three counties and 112 projects.

"Our one human family," states its 2006 strategy, "in solidarity with its poor and vulnerable members outside the U.S., transforms conflict nonviolently and advances justice and reconciliation."[5] Innovation and sustainability are at the core of these programs. Training, curricula development, manuals, and assessment development, as well as alliances with universities in each location, ensure that programs will continue to help in the long term.

Global Communities of Charity

Faith-based peacebuilding is the historical root for many religions and spiritual associations. The Abrahamic religions, consisting of Christianity,

Islam, Judaism, and the Baháí Faith, have the most worldwide adherents. Indian and Asian spiritual practices such as Buddhism, Jainism, Hinduism, and Sikhism, as well as East Asian traditions such as Taoism and Confucianism, and many other local traditions, all have charity and service as a core practice.

Many of these religious traditions have formed organizations, or religious orders, to provide service through acts of charity. The communities often live in communal living groups. The Franciscans, for instance, are devout followers of St. Francis. Those in the order are called to be "bearers of peace" in both their family and their community. They accept poverty and the simple life as conditions for following the example of St. Francis and serving Jesus Christ and fellow humans.

The Franciscan Order has renounced violence, though it affirms the right to self-defense. No matter if an individual chooses nonviolence or whether he becomes a soldier, the actions of the Franciscans should be motivated solely by Christ's love. Such selfless dedication has resulted in millions finding solace and practical help and support.

In the engaged Buddhist tradition, the Zen Therapy Center provides educational and training services in applying the practices of Buddhist philosophy in daily life. A program of the London-based Amida Trust is a Buddhist charity that provides support for outreach groups grounded in Buddhist philosophy.

The Institute for Zen Therapy has many partners who extend the teachings to a wider community, especially in Europe. The group offers psychotherapy, counseling, professional training, and a global network of resources for therapeutic practitioners. Affiliated groups and individuals do not need to be Buddhists but are welcomed into an interfaith atmosphere where innovation in providing help to people is foremost.

The Reciprocal Benefits of Faith

The guiding principles of Catholic Relief Services have emerged from the social teachings of the Church. They are common to all religious associations that seek to promote and work towards justice and peace.

- Sacredness of the human person
- Dignity as a basic right
- Responsibility to work for the common good
- Community as expressed by our social nature
- The common good supported by our social fabric

- Effective organization at the grassroots level
- Solidarity with the human family
- Concern for the needs of the poor and vulnerable
- Stewardship of creation

Doctrines, proselytizing, cultural differences, and land disputes aside, the love at the core of all religions has always been the clarion call after all conflicts have worn themselves out in defeat. We find that the freedom to love is essential as we live together on our small planet and endeavor toward peace. Associations of interfaith and reconciliation are finding common ground in the meditative act of worshiping. Rather than requiring a synthesis of doctrines and practices, interfaith promotes dialogue and understanding, prerequisites for the full expression of our essential equality and the reciprocity of love.

To love others, no matter how we pray or give to others, is to receive the benefits of that love in equal or greater proportion. "The life of a man consists not in seeing visions and in dreaming dreams," said Henry Wadsworth Longfellow, "but in active charity and in willing service."[6]

Chapter 10

Purposeful Innovation

Innovation has become the essential economic driver for the new economy. Awards are given to the innovator. Market share is the boon of the innovative organization. A product or service that gives to the other what we would want to give to ourselves has been, since ancient times, the motive of craftsmanship and artistry.

Through innovation, we create the new services and products, the methods and technologies of the future, the ideas and strategies that offer new solutions for everyday living. The end result may be a specific invention, but the process has a much greater dynamic. The act or process of creating something new and different not only has an inherent value to the way we make our livings but also feeds what many call our souls. The personal journey of innovation gives us purpose.

Experiencing the insights and epiphanies of innovation is one of the highest forms of human existence. The creativity we put into our jobs gives us a high sense of self-worth and accomplishment. Arising spontaneously in and of our own selves, forming from our unique imaginations and experience, our innovations can determine and fulfill our reason for being. Innovation, beyond its economic benefits, has an inherent transformative dynamic that gives us meaning.

The natural moral principle of the Golden Rule speaks directly to the individual's need to have greater meaning in life. The empathy we develop with others gives us understanding and insight into their needs and desires. We find that on the most common level, their needs and desires are much like our own. From our family and spouses, to our neighbors and community, we find commonality, mutuality. With empathy, we hold the other's hopes and suffer with their troubles.

After empathy, compassion is the next step in the process that drives us toward action. At the core of innovation is a problem: a challenge. In many cases, it arises from an identified frustration or need. Empathy identifies the challenge; compassion gives us the urge to solve it with a better way, a new process, or more efficient device. The need to alleviate a concern rises with passion to drive our sense of purpose. The resulting engagement, or compassionate action of providing to others, is the giving part of the reciprocal ethics of giving and receiving.

Innovation as a term is derived from *innovatus*, the Latin for renew. To go into the "new," to create, is our opportunity to live, to thrive. To find our contribution is our greatest challenge. Our purpose is individual, but it is intimately connected to the purpose of our fellow human beings. The collective is made of people, each seeking their purpose among the many.

To ensure that billions of people have adequate opportunity to achieve their purposes, our global economy is always changing, always undergoing a renewal. We struggle not to make ends meet but to extend the advantages of the few to the many. At times, this has taken the form of global mass production. At other times, we find it benefits our local economy through innovations in resource acquisition and distributed technologies.

Over the last few centuries, innovation is beginning to replace competition as the way people succeed in outpacing their peers. Recalling the nineteenth-century French economist Jean-Baptiste Say, Jeremy Rifkin points out that innovation is like a "perpetual motion machine." Say wrote that "a product is no sooner created than it, from that instant, affords a market for other products to the full extent of its own value.... The creation of one product immediately opens up a vent for other products."[1]

Rifkin writes, "Lower prices from technological innovations and rising productivity will mean consumers have extra money left over to buy other products, further stimulating productivity and increased employment in other parts of the economy."[2]

This perpetual motion machine has caused concern for many that the craftsmanship honed in previous centuries is being lost. Often a focus on the newness of our material possessions is seen as a detriment to the benefits of the "old" quality. The new has threatened to overwhelm the tried-and-true.

As we emerge from the unrelenting changes of the later twentieth century, innovation is the evolutionary heir to craftsmanship. The best way to gain market share in a competitive environment is now through creativity, skill, and ingenuity, i.e. innovation. Better formulations, more for your money, even different colors and sizes are stock characteristics of innovation, yet those superficial qualities have given way to the reign of substantial changes. The better, faster, and cheaper of the metaphorical mousetrap have become attainable goals of the innovators, and "innovation," as Michael Porter wrote, "is the central issue in economic prosperity."[3]

The purposeful innovation principle of the relational economic system is the second of the four imperatives of a Golden Rule moral economy. Continuous innovation transforms associations into organized purpose. Through innovation, an individual or organization can increase the internal and external efficiency of design and operation.

The importance we place on creativity in economic innovation establishes, by way of the Golden Rule, a reciprocal relationship of purpose that drives economic activity and maximizes the rewards of the collective. The nature of creative innovation transforms our daily work into unique expressions of our humanity. Innovation is, in essence, moral in nature.

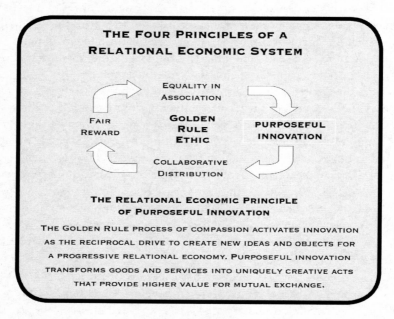

Innovation may completely change the dynamics of any system. The mathematical expression of innovation attests to the addition of an extra factor for a greater associative collaboration.

$$a + b + c + i \geq a + b + c$$

The process of positive innovation offers a continuous means of modifying the system so that it flows freely either from within the system or from without the system. Changes naturally offer the potential for increased productivity, quality, reward, and personal fulfillment.

Core Problem

As the main drivers of economic growth, capitalistic competition as well as the socialistic emphasis on the collective have inherent contradictions. Conflicts arise as power is accumulated in the hands of those holding the reins of power, whether as individuals or collectives.

The capitalistic structure puts emphasis on conflict rather than a sense of human accomplishment. Competition dwells in the domain of the disconnected universe and ignores the oneness of humanity. Decisions are made with little concern for cooperation, collaboration, or community welfare. Compassion, the raw motivator of a passionate innovation, is lost in the drive for reward. Competition is an amoral mechanism that creates winners and losers, thus decreasing the efficiency of the whole.

In socialist or state capitalist nations, the collective dominance of command economies debases the individual. Touted from the beginning of its first conscious use in the 1800s, socialism relies on collective ownership and cooperative management. In practice, socialism elevates decision-making to a small, centralized group that attempts to aggregate information and command the economy. Some would say the attention to societal needs is expressive of the Golden Rule, yet when moral action is institutionalized, innovation is not possible. Society stagnates and conflicts result.

Generally, of course, conflict is natural. It arises when two people want the same things, the same goal. The win-lose dynamic of competitive and command economies naturally leads to increased conflict. When the individual is relegated to a cog in the political economy, one's sense of uniqueness seems contrary to the collective. When competition is ascendant in a society, conflict becomes the dynamic of progress in a zero-sum game where personal power is the goal. Economies based on competition and/or command are the antitheses to an economy of the Golden Rule, whereby decisions are made in the moral context of empathic reciprocity.

Background

In the past, market-based competitive economies as well as command economies were used to gain advantage over others. While there has been historical success of such systems in wealth accumulation and lifting masses of humanity out of poverty, these economies have begun to be superseded as technology and new thinking take advantage of collaboration and networking to release creativity.

Command economies put emphasis on controlling prices and resources as well as influencing public opinion, which limits true advancement, manipulates people, and encourages over-consumption. Competition necessarily pits people against people as well as nature and creates a society of contention.

As noted in *The Third Industrial Revolution:* "While ICT (Information and Communication Technology) enhanced productivity, streamlined practices, and created some new business opportunities and jobs—which probably extended the useful life of an aging industrial mode—it could never achieve its full distributed communications potential because of the inherent constraints that come with being attached to a centralized energy regime and commercial infrastructure."[4]

Solution

From the British Industrial Revolution to the American Technology Revolution, innovation has slowly become the prime mover in an unprecedented historical growth of output and wealth. "Conformity is the jailer of freedom," said John F. Kennedy, "and the enemy of growth."[5]

With the advent of Internet communications and networking, innovations now happen more rapidly and are implemented on a wider geographical scale. The accelerated flow of information enables people to use computers and advanced materials to creatively add quality to their lives even before industry provides greater distribution.

Today, innovation is increasingly at the center of economic activity, providing motivation without the need for competition and centralized command. As the catalyst for growth in many industries and markets, incremental and/or major innovations provide advantages that are reflected in increased revenue and market share as well as creating new markets.

Though most often associated with breakthroughs or world-changing inventions, innovation is a common experience when someone thinks of a new process or product. Innovation drives productivity, differentiates products, increases quality, lowers costs, opens new markets, changes organizations, and revolutionizes the way people live. People pay more for innovation. It generates attention and has higher potential to make people's lives better.

Innovation is also an expression of the spontaneous creativity of the individual as well as the collective. When a person comes up with a small enhancement to a service or, indeed, a completely new product, the moral drive toward the compassionate Golden Rule is in play. To find new ways of operating or better ways to do a job requires putting oneself in the other's shoes, to suffer with, to rise with hope to alleviate the challenge. An innovation may begin with making things easier for one's self, but it has immediate practical importance for the other. Such a meaningful action transforms work into purpose.

Prototypes

The concept of innovation is now being applied to every aspect of economic and social activity. Many strategies and management organizations are prototypes for the wide-reaching effects and definition of modern innovation.

- The business cycle is driven by innovation. From Nikolai Kondratiev's fifty-year cycle to Joseph Schumpter's waves that vary in purpose and time, the business cycle depends on the creative entrepreneurial spirit that expresses itself with innovations.
- The results of the innovation process are the inventions that have changed our world, such as the train, automobile, airplane, radio, phonograph, electric light, washing machine, dishwasher, microwave oven, transistor, integrated circuit, and computer.
- Think tanks that perform research and advocate innovation.
- Research grants that fund innovative strategies.
- Research and development (R&D) organizations that form collaborations for new products and technologies.
- Business incubators that provide a cooperative environment for start-up businesses.
- Patent and copyright protection that offer public exposure with special rights to the innovator.
- Open-source technologies that allow access and encourage improvements by multiple innovators.
- Early adopters who make a conscious and moral decision to encourage new technologies and products.

Result

Purposeful innovations result in better ideas, advanced technologies, and more efficient processes that emerge from creative thinking. A society that puts emphasis on innovation is one that chooses to change the status quo and find new ways to extend safety, prosperity, and quality of life.

Personal and associative creativity is at the base of the innovative process. Through innovation, we seek higher levels of peace for ourselves and for others and express our need and desire for a meaningful, highly creative life. The dynamic of innovation allows the Golden Rule to flourish even in our smallest and least significant endeavors. "People acting in their own self-interest," said John Stossel, "is the fuel for all the discovery, innovation, and prosperity that powers the world."[6]

With innovation, each way of making a living takes on the aura of excitement and discovery. From empathy arises compassion, whereby the drive for innovation transforms us to give purpose. With purposeful innovation, the economy bursts with advances and progress on every front.

Challenges for Purposeful Innovation

First, how can people use compassion in their economic decisions? From empathy, a manufacturer or service provider determines the needs of its customers. From compassion arises quality. Profit is two steps beyond the economic decision to create the products and services someone hopes, within the Golden Rule ethic, would be created for them.

Second, is innovation necessary to infuse an economy with compassion? Innovation as compassion comes in many forms. The standard product is still the mainstay of any economy. Though beginning its life cycle as an innovation, many standard products meet a need and continue their existence with little change. Most activity is a repetitive experience that, when infused with compassion, becomes akin to innovation as craftsmanship and customer service.

With workers experiencing the transformative nature of compassionate creativity, each product that comes off the manufacturing line is, in essence, a new product. Though it might not be an innovation, *per se,* the output of each worker achieves its highest goal by way of the quality that goes into its creation.

To make an automobile, for instance, is a process that constantly benefits from craftsmanship. In the manufacturing line, the quality control method of decreasing specified tolerances of nuts and bolts can make stronger bonds that will benefit customers. Another creative process might entail finding the right temperature to spray paint for the best adhesion. Are these simply standard processes and instances of continuous improvements, or are they innovations that can give purpose to the innovator?

Purposeful innovation, the realm of craftsmanship and customer service as quality and creativity, is within the capability of each individual. From the person on the line to the sales person hawking its benefits, from the accountant who keeps the books to the supervisor who makes sure the line is productive, each process entails creative expression. Every product and service in the economy is an opportunity for us to find our purpose with the processes of the Golden Rule. The measure of innovation is the continuous expression of actively serving others as we would have them serve us.

Chapter 11

Case Study—The Arts Sector

Apple Computer and the Freedom to Create

In 1997, Bill Gates, a founder of major Apple competitor Microsoft, made a $150 million investment in the company that had been a thorn in his competitive side since the early 1980s. The financial markets and computer world analysts looked on in disbelief. Steve Jobs, who had returned to Apple after being forced out a decade earlier, said that the firm was ninety days away from bankruptcy.

Why would a fierce competitor like Gates climb on the Apple bandwagon—indeed, arguably save the company? Microsoft founder Bill Gates and Apple founder Steve Jobs, the quintessential computer wonderkinds, went way back. Gates had helped design software for Apple's first computers. Then in the 1980s, the collaboration had come to an end. Apple sued Microsoft for patent infringement on the graphical user interface used on the Mac. Microsoft, of course, had countersued. Many times, the rivalry, both corporate and personal, came to bursts of anger and animosity on both sides.

Was the sudden change from enemies to partners just for old times' sake? Or was it a savvy business move by the savviest of business mavens? Not only did Gates settle some lingering patent disputes, but he ensured the use of Microsoft's Internet Explorer as the default browser in Apple's hardware lineup.

Yet in retrospect, the move by Gates seems less than smart, as Apple eventually became the largest company in the world, bypassing Microsoft with innovations such as the iPod, iPhone, iPad, and other box products that do not use Microsoft's software. Indeed, Microsoft felt it necessary to enter the computer "box" market with its Microsoft Surface alternative to the iPad.

The answer to why one of the smartest CEOs in the world would save a competitor lies in the simple, often cited realization that innovation is the driver of profit, not necessarily competition. Apple was a transformative organization right from the beginning. With the first personal computer and the first graphical user interface, the company had developed several niche markets, especially in providing tools for graphic artists around the world. In fact, purchasers of Apple products were almost religious in their belief and commitment.

Founded by Steve Jobs and Steve Wozniak in 1976, Apple Computer (later Apple, Inc.) was determined to be on the forefront of technology. From the Apple II to the Macintosh and on to the new i-products, the company has provided inspiration and innovation to a crowd of customers that live and breathe inspiration and innovation.

Bill Gates was focused on the business market, a segment where Apple had difficulty making gains. Apple focused on the education and graphic arts markets, forming collaborations with Adobe, which made PhotoShop and other products that revolutionized the art world. The company became the largest in the world, however briefly, with innovations in the audio and film industries, music, and graphic design, with a complete suite of tools for all the arts.

The attention of Gates came primarily with the complete differentiation of Apple as the innovator for content. Gates saw the amazing brand loyalty of customers as well as a network of global user groups and knew that there was something about Apple that mesmerized its adherents. Gates was also concerned that the supplier network of software developers, including Adobe's Creative Suite and Macromedia's Flash, which Adobe acquired in 2005, would lose their Apple-induced innovation.

And there was that "old times' sake" thing. While Jobs and his partner, Steve Wozniak, were experimenting with Heathkits electronic projects and Hallicrafter transmitter kits, Gates and Paul Allen were reading a Popular Electronics story on the Altair, the first microcomputer kit. Wozniak put a screen, keyboard, and processor together and invented the personal computer, which Jobs marketed with great success. Gates and Allen started the computer software revolution with a new version of the BASIC computer language. All helped democratize computer technology, becoming billionaires in the effort and crowned as pioneers in the history of innovation.

Today, Apple, Inc. has nearly four hundred retail stores and competes with Exxon Mobile for the largest market capitalization in the world. The fortunes of Apple will rise and fall, not with its ability to destroy the competition, but with its ability to associate and innovate.

Enrich Others and They Will Enrich You:
The Golden Rule as the Moral Drive for Artistry

Does color make a difference? In the 1970s, graphic artists knew the answer. Engineers soon found out, as did the world. Excellent design merged with innovative engineering was soon to make the "insanely great products" that would make Steve Jobs an icon of marketing and commerce.

"Design is the fundamental soul of a man-made creation," said Jobs, "that ends up expressing itself in successive outer layers."[1] The products he conceived during four decades of his rise, fall, and rise again would be an expression of his sense of craftsmanship and artistry as well as his understanding of the technology of silicon, bits, and bytes.

Yet the essential reason that Steve Jobs rose to the top of the Silicon Valley product surge was his attention to a core value in the Golden Rule. Even with his notorious fits of yelling, anger, and childish behavior, he kept his focus on the *other*. The customer was not just king in his language; the customer was deserving of those insanely great products. His mission was to create products that he would wish others would create for him.

How were they made? Jobs was certainly at the right place at the right time. Born near Silicon Valley at the cusp of an era when Moore's Law was to make hardware computer chips cheaper and more powerful, Jobs and Wozniak were men for their time, as were Gates and Allen in the realm of software. Jobs envisioned the future. He was not interested in focus groups that told what people already wanted. He was to develop products that the customers didn't even know they wanted! That was his "reality distortion field" that vexed the practical engineer but drove his various product teams—from the original Apple to the iPad—into realms where the future was malleable and the impossible became possible.

Jobs felt at home with designers such as Vietnam Memorial artist Maya Lin and IBM icon Paul Rand. Jobs heralded the "simplicity is the ultimate sophistication" that appeared on Apple's first brochure. From industrial designer Dieter Rams and the Bauhaus movement to Walter Gropius of the modernist style, Jobs sought sleek and minimalist rather than the bulky industrial style of other computer firms. The evolution of the company's use of color and materials is fascinating.

- Wooden Apple I: The first personal computer, designed by Steve Wozniak by putting a processor, keyboard, and screen together for the first time. "I typed a few keys on the keyboard," Woz later said, "and I was shocked! The letters appeared on the screen."[2]

- Beige Apple II: Jobs saw the sleek, foam-molded Cuisinart food processor and created a foam-molded package in beige. He ran up against Woz when he wanted uniformity inside, which meant a redesign of the circuit board slots. Apple's philosophy of empathy, focus, and imputing established design, as in "people judge a book by its cover," would be core for the company.
- Rainbow logo: Apple was named after Jobs's obsessive fruit diet. The logo was simple and six colors, even though that made it more expensive to print.
- White Macintosh: Resisting the "black, black, black" of current computers, Jobs wanted white, with contours "like a Porche." The Graphical User Interface, essentially "stolen" from Xerox, made artistic expression possible, including bit-mapped fonts. Jobs pushed for expanding its remedial line-and-square capabilities: "Rectangles with rounded corners are everywhere!"[3]
- Colorful manufacturing plant: The factory that produced Macintoshes was repainted with bright colors, as Apple manager Debi Coleman noted, like "an Alexander Calder showcase," which caused production problems. With the iconic product introduction, "Hello. I'm Macintosh," the world was introduced to a truly inspiring machine. "Real artists sign their work,"[4] Jobs said, and the Mac team's signatures are etched on the inside walls of the computer.

During the 1980s, Jobs tried to acknowledge his limited managerial capabilities by bringing in the crack CEO of Pepsi, John Sculley, asking him: "Do you want to spend the rest of your life selling sugar water, or do you want a chance to change the world?"[5] Jobs was soon forced out due to Apple's new direction of pushing profitability over pursuing new dimensions of the customer experience. Jobs left the company and started NeXT, then acquired Pixar before being brought back to the company at its nadir.

- Black matte cube NeXT: a powerful personal mainframe that had the capacity to do lab work such as gene splicing. The corporate logo was designed by seventy-one-year-old IBM designer Paul Rand, who only did one design that the customer could take or leave. The design was a perfect cube at a 28-degree tilt. "In its design, color arrangement, and orientation, the logo is a study in contrasts. Tipped at a jaunty angle, it brims with the informality, friendliness, and spontaneity of a Christmas seal and the authority of a rubber stamp."[6]
- Green NeXT workstation screen: The NeXT computer had a black matte finish that was replicated on the inside where only technicians

would see it. The background color of the screen was a particular green specified by Jobs. "I like that green. Great green, great green."[7] The computer came with the first digital books, including Shakespeare and the Oxford dictionary. "There has not been an advancement in the state of the art of printed book technology since Gutenberg."[8] The NeXT started a revolution in object-oriented programming that would become a boon to designers.

- 3D graphic animated film: Jobs secured the rights to Pixar's innovative animation technology from Lucasfilm as well as the talented John Lasseter, who led the creation of *Luxo Jr.* and *Toy Story*, in which "products have an essence to them, a purpose for which they were made."[9]

When Jobs returned to Apple in 1997 and found the company "90 days away from bankruptcy,"[10] he immediately set out to create a wave of new, creative products. That series of innovations would bring the company back from the dead and take it on to the highest market capitalization in the world.

- Translucent iMac: the plastic case was a translucent, sea-green blue, named bondi blue after the color of the water at a beach in Australia.
- Titanium, then aluminum G4: the PowerBook G4 was the thinnest computer of its time with a sleek titanium, then aluminum case.
- Glittering Apple Stores: with "floating staircases" and glass throughout, the stores allowed customers to touch and play with Apple products. As designer Ron Johnson said, "It glitters like a jewel box."[11] The stores had the highest profitability per square foot and "would impute the ethos of Apple products: playful, easy, creative, and on the bright side of the line between hip and intimidating."

In 1999, Apple began to compete with Adobe and others with a rollout of creative software and digital lifestyle spaces: Final Cut Pro, iMovie, iDVD, iPhoto, and GarageBand. Adobe, which Apple helped raise to the top of the graphics software world, decided not to develop software for the OSX operating system, which caused a rift between the two companies.

- Pure white iPod: Jobs insisted that the white be not just white, but pure white. "Not only the device, but the headphones and the wires and even the power block.... There would be a purity to it."[12] The iPod was the essence of the customer experience, leapfrogging Sony Walkman with the innovative trackwheel and earbuds. The iPod Nano came out in anodized aluminum.
- Glass iPhone: Jobs became aware of Corning's scratch-resistant

"gorilla glass," which he determined would enhance color and usability. A rounded-bottom stainless steel bezel surrounded the glass, which caused problems with the antenna.

- Large screen iPad: Working with the multi-touch sensing technology of FingerWorks, Jobs wanted to move the keyboard from hardware to software, making the screen fluid and flexible. Customers immediately took to the swipe-to-open technology that replaced antiquated buttons and on-off switches.

Part of the brilliance of Steve Jobs was his drive toward perfection, but it was also a source of contention for those he worked with. He was often difficult and childish, pushing the malleable "distortion field" to the limit. He rejected market research for an intuitive sense of what customers wanted even before customers knew what they wanted.

He was comfortable creating end-to-end integrated packages that left little room for customer choice. When a person bought an Apple product, it was easy to use but difficult to modify. When confronted with a decision on whether to work with partners or create the product in-house, Jobs chose the latter. Yet, changing technology necessitated collaboration, as his creation of iTunes would exemplify.

Going where no others had gone before, when Jobs created a legal alternative to Napster, he worked out partnerships and contracts with standalone companies such as Sony, Universal, Motown, and eventually the Beatles, whose Apple Records had sued Apple Computer over the Apple wordmark infringement decades before.

The humanities and art worlds are indebted to Steve Jobs and his understanding of design and engineering. "It's in Apple's DNA that technology alone is not enough," Jobs said. "We believe that it's technology married with the humanities that yields us the results that make our hearts sing."[13]

Aesthetics and the Customer Experience

Art is a broad word that describes many human activities, from painting to sculpture, photography to film. The skilled artist uses a variety of media to express, communicate, and elicit emotions. Creativity is at the heart of artistic endeavors. The branch of philosophy that delves into artistic expression is aesthetics. The artist endeavors toward a sublime expression that is a quality of greatness. It is beyond measure or calculation—some even say beyond criticism and imitation.

As a human species, we endeavor toward artistic expression not only in standard arts such as painting, but also in our day-to-day activities. Whether we work in an office or labor as plumbers and electricians, when we bring creativity to bear on our work, it can become a sublime expression of our individuality.

The philosophy of art—the aesthetics of the sublime—was in the DNA of Apple right from the beginning. Largely due to the leadership of Steve Jobs, Apple had a reputation for clean design and aesthetic appeal. Yet aesthetics meant a great deal more to Jobs than the look of the product.

"Most people make the mistake of thinking design is what it looks like," Jobs said in an interview. "People think it's this veneer—that the designers are handed this box and told, 'Make it look good!' That's not what we think design is. It's not just what it looks like and feels like. Design is how it works."[14]

With the release of the Apple I in 1976, Apple Computer was on the cusp of a revolution in the tools of the artist that would democratize creativity. Soon painting, design, printing, the art of font usage, and color would be available to everyone with a low-cost computer and the desire to create. When Jobs and Wozniak began producing computers with a twenty-dollar chip, the hardware and software design was very elegant for its time.

A natural target market of others who felt the same about technology and art came with the introduction of the Lisa and Macintosh computer lines. The graphical user interface (GUI) gave artists of all capabilities a way to write, draw, paint, and print everything from brochures to paintings. The art world, reticent at first, began to take notice of this tool that might supplement standard tools of the trade such as drafting tables and typesetters, even pencils and erasers.

Jobs and Wozniak introduced a wave of products for others that they would want to have for themselves. Through their innovations, they found purpose and extended the opportunity to find purpose for millions, even billions, of others. Such is the art of the Golden Rule.

"Here's to the crazy ones," trumpeted the 1997 Think Different Apple advertising campaign, "the misfits. The rebels. The troublemakers. The round pegs in the square holes. The ones who see things differently ... Because the people who are crazy enough to think they can change the world are the ones that do."[15]

Chapter 12

Collaborative Distribution

The Golden Rule is not a lonely proposition. To do unto others necessitates a relationship. To have a relationship is to be associated, a form of cooperation with another. With the Golden Rule ethic, simple cooperation can lead to higher levels of collaboration, which entails working jointly with others as equal partners for a common goal. Our cooperative and collaborative associations engage us in greater society for the purpose of satisfying societal demand for goods and services.

As in all relationships, collaborations are expressions of mutual needs. Our economic purpose in life, whether it arises from an innovation or by following our process of creativity for doing the best work we can, is an extension of ourselves into the lives of the *other*. We have the need to show our wares, be recognized for our services, and when appropriate, be compensated and rewarded. To meet these needs, we find help in getting our products and services into as many places and out to as many people as possible. To provide our creative expressions to the widest number of people in need is the implied directive of duty from the Golden Rule: deliver unto others, and, thus, we deliver unto ourselves.

Many times, how much we benefit from our work is directly connected to the distribution of our efforts. One of the four elements of marketing (the others are product, price, and promotion), distribution or placement is an essential measure of success in economic activity. Whether it's an electrician's service or a manufactured table, one's work is sold mainly within the reaches of the local network. We sell to our family and friends, to our neighborhoods and larger communities. If things go well, we move into a wider market.

However, success is not just reaping what we sow; it is also the reciprocal action of sowing what we reap. In all our reciprocations, we need constant cooperation from and with others. We need the professionalism, experience, and reach gained from those individuals and organizations with which we form oral and written contracts. Our partners need us to understand their challenges and opportunities, to empathize and have compassion, and to take actions for mutual gain.

From such examples as participating in local open-air markets and leasing space in enclosed temperature-controlled stores, our partnerships are formalized with contractual agreements both verbal and written. Channels of distribution include a wide range of relationships, from those hosting our websites to the sales networks and media for getting out the word. The extent of our distributions does not necessarily determine the extent of our reward. Collaboration with transportation companies, for instance, is intended to take our shows on the road. However, some things are not efficiently distributed to long distances. The apples grown locally may be ripe and rich in flavor, but apples transported long distances require high transportation costs.

Such inefficient distributions raise the cost of products and, inevitably, cause conflicts by artificially and sometimes violently keeping the price of energy down. Per the Golden Rule, only when the manufacturing/distribution costs are in proportion to the reward is the collaboration successful. This is why intention is a key part of collaboration in a relational economy. Selling is not a one-way exchange but rather an immersion into the other's experience. Intention is the act of determining an intended goal or purpose. We do not exist in a vacuum where we can simply *intend* to make money. There are implications in how we affect others. Our intentions also affect ourselves. Our reputation, sense of accomplishment, self-respect, self-esteem, and personal integrity and dignity are all a part of a successful association.

The guiding principle of the Golden Rule helps us keep our intentions focused on the greatest rewards within the context of a collaborative exchange. It is our duty to form intentional relationships that take into account all of the costs and benefits. We analyze, empathize, act, and transform the way we make our living into a unified service to humanity. As trade is one of humanity's most ancient collaborations, positive and mutually beneficial distribution is where the oneness of humanity is most vividly and practically expressed.

Core Problem

Distribution is primarily considered a mechanical process. Moving products and services into the world is often disconnected from intentional quality and efficiency. Yet the dispersion and allocation of our creations are integral to the Golden Rule ethic. The quality and efficiency with which we provide for others is morally linked to the way we provide for ourselves.

When distribution remains a mechanical process, cost and reward become the highest considerations. Since market share depends on the largest distribution, the urge is to seek business practices that keep prices down regardless of quality. Laws that provide price supports and restrictive barriers are common ways to artificially interfere in the mutuality of the process. Powerful monopolies and lobbyists vie for unfair advantage to the detriment of fair and equitable exchange. The Golden Rule is relegated to an idealistic creed that is of little use in the perceived dog-eat-dog world of economic reality.

Background

Distribution of goods and services has always had an ethical dimension. Hoarding, caching, and discrimination have caused shortages in some sectors of the population. At times, these behaviors have caused unnecessary hunger, health hazards, and violence that come from unequal distribution. Globalization and facilitation of trade has helped to deliver supplies of essential water, food, medicines, housing, and other goods and services to the widest population. However, when the Golden Rule ethic of reciprocity is not applied, problems arise.

For instance, whether it is transporting an apple from Brazil to America, or shipping oil from Saudi Arabia to China, the full value to all parties in a transfer is often more or less than what is reflected in the direct transaction cost. Indirect costs include environmental, social, whole-life, loss of community culture and other hard to determine factors. The result can be a less efficient and sometimes predatory global economy based on self-interested parties with more concern about the bottom line than full value accounting. Movements such as fair trade and sustainable development are addressing the challenges of globalization, and distribution is one of the most obvious parts of the economic process where inefficiencies can arise.

Unless there is a great need or desire to justify the extra cost of transport, shipping goods and services over long distances can be highly inefficient. The end price may be too much for the market to bear. To compete in markets where the cost is too high for natural demand and supply to function requires intervention in the marketplace. The higher price of selling and purchasing can be supplemented by pricing supports and monopolistic practices. Wars and other violent practices are often used to gain access to resources, find less costly labor, increase government contacts or force the market to bear higher prices through tariffs and other fees as well as by embargoes and legal or illegal trade barriers. "The Securing of Iraqi oil fields is a pertinent recent example. Since the beginning of the Iraq war, Halliburton—the Texas energy giant once headed by Vice President Dick Cheney—has seen its stock price more than triple in value. According to Halliburton Watch, Halliburton's contracts under the Bush administration grew by 600 percent."[1]

The true cost of delocalizing the way we produce and distribute products does not include the total cost, including depletion of our base of natural resources and impacts on local culture. In effect, we are borrowing from the earth and from the "other" for current consumption, and when we cannot get something locally we often find inefficient and violent ways to get it from longer distances.

Solution

Intentional collaborations with other individuals and groups can maximize sustainable distribution while maintaining the quality and integrity of the items we produce and the services we offer. These intentional relationships allow us to find the best way to ensure that our products are available for the greatest benefit of others as well as the greatest reward for ourselves.

The contracts involved in the distribution chain start with our talents and innovations as part of our labor. From the beginning of our work career, we fill out paperwork for employment in order to distribute our personal contribution. If we start a business, we build collaborations with others to ensure our products and services are meeting customer needs. As we move along the process of developing a successful business, we promote our wares on the Internet and through marketing practices that include advertising, salesmanship, product positioning, and market research and testing.

Often intermediaries extend our distribution network. Larger collaborations help us with transportation, promotions, and customer service. If our reach is extended, there are more customers and new markets. If the quality and/or innovation of our wares are increased, more people will want to purchase.

In the best case, excellence in products and services design and implementation is needed and highly valued. With the right collaborations, our reach is extended and more money is our reward. Yet distribution can be very inefficient. Sometimes the collaborations we enter into turn out to be good, sometimes bad. At what point does our collaborative distribution become counterproductive? When do we start to lose money? When does our service to humanity become less a duty and more a burden? Attention to the needs of others provides the best way to ensure maximum benefit to the widest population.

Collaborative distribution by the Golden Rule ethic keeps us on the road to productivity and success through its inherent empathy and compassion for others. Whether our channels include informal contracts such as word-of-mouth partnerships or more formal documents such as monetary collaboration for the use of credit cards and bank loans, reciprocal exchange is the dynamic that fine-tunes our efforts. We seek feedback from others and communicate our needs to them. Many times our relationships are simply based on the understanding that we will fulfill our obligations and expect that in return. We often trust others until that trust is abused. The Golden Rule is not a give-or-take exchange but rather a give-and-take reciprocal exchange.

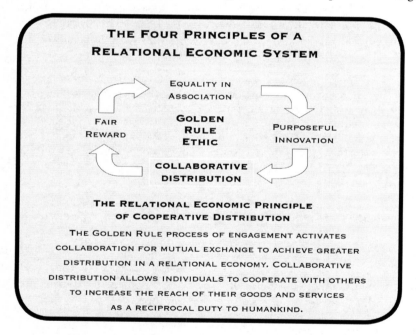

THE FOUR PRINCIPLES OF A
RELATIONAL ECONOMIC SYSTEM

EQUALITY IN ASSOCIATION

FAIR REWARD

GOLDEN RULE ETHIC

PURPOSEFUL INNOVATION

COLLABORATIVE DISTRIBUTION

THE RELATIONAL ECONOMIC PRINCIPLE
OF COOPERATIVE DISTRIBUTION

THE GOLDEN RULE PROCESS OF ENGAGEMENT ACTIVATES
COLLABORATION FOR MUTUAL EXCHANGE TO ACHIEVE GREATER
DISTRIBUTION IN A RELATIONAL ECONOMY. COLLABORATIVE
DISTRIBUTION ALLOWS INDIVIDUALS TO COOPERATE WITH OTHERS
TO INCREASE THE REACH OF THEIR GOODS AND SERVICES
AS A RECIPROCAL DUTY TO HUMANKIND.

Developing a best-practices approach to forming relationships benefits not only the partners in the process but also humankind. Distribution within the Golden Rule ethic is a societal engagement based on individual intentional joint collaborations. The microeconomic relationships build macroeconomies of scale that expand the overall customer/producer base in the most efficient manner.

Diseconomies of scale, of course, result from inefficiencies and increased costs, sometimes due to transportation or logistical limitations. The U.S.

Congress defined local/regional marketing of products as when the total distance of transport is less than 400 miles. With this guideline, the full cost of distribution is factored into the relationship between total cost and reward. Practical distribution and full-cost accounting would protect local jobs and resources without the use of trade barriers, tariffs and other protectionist mechanisms that can escalate into trade and hot wars.

In mathematics, as in economics, the distributive property distributes the weight of a process over simple repetitive addition (ab + ac = a(b + c). The distributive property reduces the number of processes in order to create less work and more opportunity. In other words, efficiencies are rendered when the work is distributed among variables.

This scaling of operations, multiplying one number by another, does not necessarily mean *more*. It can just mean *efficiency*. There is no need to do every process or take care of everything ourselves. The distributive property allows for collaborations that make economic operations more efficient, and therefore more productive. Jeremy Rifkin writes:

> The adversarial relationship between sellers and buyers is replaced by a collaborative relationship between suppliers and users. Self-interest is subsumed by shared interest. Proprietary information is eclipsed by a new emphasis on openness and collective trust. The new focus on transparency over secrecy is based on the premise that adding value to the network doesn't depreciate one's own stock but, rather, appreciates everyone's holdings as equal nodes on a common endeavor.[2]

Prototypes

As in all our economic associations, placement of our products and services has an ethical dimension. There are many examples of collaborations that through mutual consideration provide a path ahead for dutiful engagement with the local and international community.

- Local food movement to foster sustainable and self-reliant local economies and health
- Full-cost accounting to assure social, environmental, and economic cost/benefits
- Local and regional supply-chain databases that provide connections and networking from supplier to customers
- Globalization for integration and collaborations beyond nations
- Sustainable agriculture for preventing depletion of local resources through sustainable farming

- Collective farms as joint enterprises between individual farmers
- Buy-local campaigns to encourage sustainable production
- Triple bottom-line accounting of economic costs
- ISO 26000 and 19011 international standards for environmental practices and auditing
- Plug-in vehicles and other green technologies for sustainable energy
- Distributed electricity smart grids to maximize efficiency of distribution
- Mini-power plants for locally produced power
- 3D print manufacturing to facilitate distribution of products

Result

A collaborative economy provides efficiencies due to the attention paid to both economies of scale and diseconomies of scale. The Golden Rule ethic enables distribution relationships to develop based on their benefit for humanity as well as for the parties involved. Decisions to expand distribution or limit distribution are based on a full-cost accounting. Greater dispersion, or diffusion into the marketplace, can be of greater benefit to those wanting higher quality, lower prices, faster availability, or other factors leading to satisfaction for the greatest number of customers.

A more local distribution system makes those products and services within a geographic area, including farm produce and local crafts, a better buy. Localization, in some cases, energizes local economies and honors local culture, customs, and family life. For instance, reduction of multi-national corporations and centralized economies would reduce the need for immigrant workers, thereby lessening tensions and making local economies work for their historic populations.

The global distribution system will not only remain with us but continue to expand the possibilities of greater prosperity for even remote villages. The reason for the negative effects of globalization is the amoral or immoral intentions of the participants. Globalized strategies for plundering others' resources, doing harm to the environment or other cultures, and extending power in a win/loss competition is completely unaligned with the reciprocal benefits of the Golden Rule. The individual intentions we hold, when considered in a moral context, re-envision globalization as the precursor to reaping the benefits of unity with other people and harmony with the earth.

Challenges for Collaborative Distribution

First, does the desire for collaboration in economic activity always entail cooperation? The Golden Rule, as noted, is not passive. The duty entailed in experiencing the processes of the Golden Rule, from empathy and on toward the compassionate need to fulfill a purpose, requires engagement. Cooperation infuses the collaborative spirit with the capacity to reach farther and deeper into reciprocal needs.

Second, will the economy suffer from the lack of societal cooperation through centralized control? Governments routinely provide price supports and incentives to help some industries and create potential opportunities. These controls have become standard practice and have made the local and global economy a patchwork of economic booms and bubbles that move prosperity toward some at the expense of all. The result is an economy of experiments that often results in the amoral reality of recessions and depressions.

The Golden Rule process of engagement is supported, not by legislated laws that are essentially amoral in nature, but rather in the justness entailed by the previous processes. Empathy and compassion trump greed and ambition. The lack of purpose rampant in society indicates an upside-down economy where amoral processes are imposed by history and fear. The relational economy, on the other hand, is an evolutionary model that replaces survivalist competition with collaborative justice.

Chapter 13

Case Study—
The Environmental Sector

*Hindustan Unilever and
the Freedom to Sustain*

With over 16,000 employees, Mumbai-based Hindustan Unilever is the largest consumer-goods company in India. From foods and beverages to soaps and water purifiers, the company's products provide for the daily needs of one of the largest populations in the world.[1]

Principally owned by Unilever, a Dutch-British company, and the result of a merger with Hindustan Vanaspati Manufacturing in 1933, the company's distribution network includes two million retail outlets across India. Reaching two of every three people in the country with its products and services, the company has embraced its opportunity to affect India's future through its distribution networks. With the Unilever Sustainability Living Plan, Hindustan Unilever has developed a strategy for increasing the sustainability of life for millions.

The Plan endeavors to decouple growth from an expanding environmental footprint while at the same time increasing positive social impacts. "Sustainability is now firmly at the heart of our business model and is driving growth," says chairman Harish Manwani in the company's 2013 Annual Report, "reducing costs and fueling innovations that are good for the planet and for consumers. We see this as a source of competitive advantage for the business now and in the years ahead."[2]

Unilever's Sustainable Living Plan is one part of an overall strategy for putting its vast distribution network to work for the benefit of humanity. In return, the company enjoys customer loyalty throughout India based on respect and appreciation for their actions at the grassroots level. The central objectives of the company's Plan are to provide the following results[3]:

- Help improve the health and well-being of a billion people
- Reduce the environmental footprint of their products by half
- Source one hundred percent of the raw materials used in their products from sustainable agricultural production

One of Hindustan Unilever's product brands is the Puriet® water purification system. Safe drinking water is a human right as well as a global challenge. In Bhopal, India, diarrhea ravages a population where 36.7 percent of the residents have incomes below the poverty line. One in four children suffers from diarrhea, primarily due to the lack of clean water.[4]

To provide effective water treatment at a low cost, Hindustan Unilever provides Puriet water purifier systems free to many Bhopal families. The system provides four liters of safe water for as little as one rupee. In coordination with the global NGO Population Services International, local women are trained as waterworkers. The women identify families most at risk and go into their homes and provide education and demonstrations. The waterworkers check back to ensure that the systems are working properly. The initiative's initial mission is to provide 15,000 of the city's poorest families with this protection against life-threatening disease. In the future, the company hopes that a half-million people will benefit from the system.

Respect Others and They Will Respect You: The Golden Rule as the Moral Driver of Sustainability

Historically, when the ratio of humans to resources was low and there were vast expanses of uncharted land, the way humans viewed nature was based on plentiful resources. Science was a tool of exploitation for the betterment of mankind. The words "environment" and "conservation" were relatively new in our language. Environment was not used in the ecological sense until the 1950s. Conservation meant "preservation of existing conditions," and its tie to the earth was not present until the 1920s.

However, the crucial importance of paying attention to resources goes back to the development of large cities in the fifteenth century. London was already suffering from over-population. Sewage ran from streets to rivers. Forests were depleted. Fish populations were in decline. Bureaucrats reporting to the King's court were put in charge of these challenging situations. There began our collective endeavor to meet the challenges of environmental damaging with laws and public works.

The plight of the salmon in the United States is instructive. Salmon is the common name for an extended family of fish such as sockeye and trout. Salmon live along the coastal river and lake systems. One big difference between Atlantic salmon and trout is that the former migrate and the latter spend their lives in one area. When Louis and Clark were sent by president Thomas Jefferson to explore the new western territories, salmon were plentiful. As human population increased, fisheries exploited the generous populations until a vigorous economy developed and fewer salmon were able to reach their spawning grounds.

"The salmon fisheries of the Columbia River are now but a fraction of what they were twenty-five years ago," said Theodore Roosevelt in his 1908 State of the Union speech. He went on to laud a government solution by taking "complete charge of them."[5] Today, the salmon population along the Columbia River is less than three percent of what it was during Jefferson's era. Clearly the needs of the economy have come into conflict with the needs of nature.

With the passage of clean air legislation beginning in 1963 and the Clean Water Act of 1972, the U.S. government took the lead in environmental strategy. In addition, major corporations soon realized that there is a huge potential public relations opportunity in using company assets to address environmental and health problems. Many companies have put their vast distribution networks to work for global as well as company good.

A great example is the Coca-Cola Company, in partnership with the Global Fund. It created Project Last Mile in 2010 to use company resources to deliver critical medicines to rural Africa and other remote parts of the world. From the company's Atlanta headquarters, the Last Mile project fights AIDS, tuberculosis, and malaria using Coca-Cola's vast supply chain. Beginning in Tanzania, the Project has grown to include Ghana, Mozambique, and other parts of Africa and is contemplating an expanded scope. Over twenty million people have been helped by the program.

In partnership with others including the DEKA R&D, inventor of the "slingshot" vapor distillation system, Coca-Cola has been working to bring clean water to remote communities. The Slingshot units run on little electricity and efficiently boil dirty water, even raw sewage, to deliver a pure product. Each unit distills up to 300,000 liters each year with only 30,000 kilowatts of electricity delivered from solar panels.

The Value of Sustainable Practices

The value placed on practicing sustainability is viewed in various ways. One way is to value an ecosystem based on its natural capital, or its ability to yield value, such as in a commodity market. However, as our understanding of the need for sustainable practices grows, ecological value takes on a more complex meaning. Instead of the value considered only as what it can generate as a commodity, ecological value can be expressed in terms of diverse utilizations:

- Direct utilization
- Indirect contribution to utilization
- Future utilization
- Utilization by its pure existence
- Utilization by others
- Utilization for future generations

This view of our natural world allows for the advent of ethics and deep ecology to be factored into value. With increased awareness of climate change, global warming, and rain forest depletion, inventors and entrepreneurs have begun to meet the challenge of a Golden Rule ecological perspective in earnest.

Green technologies and more sustainable ways to use legacy energy sources have led to the development of major industries. Envirotech or clean-tech entrepreneurs are applying electronic devices and monitoring equipment to determine the negative effects of current processes and develop more sustainable means.

Green chemistry, or sustainable chemistry, is a branch of research and chemical engineering that helps minimize hazardous substances in product and process designs. Focusing at the source of contamination rather than the natural environment, green chemistry engineers have applied their expertise to water oxidation techniques rather than harsh solvents or the use of aqueous hydrogen peroxide for clean oxidation.

Many sustainable energy sources, such as wind turbines, solar panels, and bioreactors, are being developed to reduce carbon emissions. A combination of computer power and electronic devices has added highly efficient monitoring technologies to provide more energy and less waste. Measurements are made and adjustments in the inputs and outputs provide a level of sophistication that lead to efficiencies.

The conflict that arises from the different needs of humans from those of nature has major implications for peace. Control of human resources is a means to power, especially as political factions attempt to gain control of resources. Deep in the throes of political instability and conflict, governments often resort to resource depletion to meet short-term needs. Private companies take advantage of weak and irresolute governments to attain contracts for stockholder gains. Often these agreements give short shrift to the needs of local populations as well as the environment.

Hindustan Unilever and other regional and global companies are taking a more collaborative view of distribution. They are engaged in the communities they serve. Often despite government barriers, their Golden Rule ethic allows managers and employees to immerse themselves in the needs of their customers, thereby enjoying the reciprocal benefit of a more peaceful world.

Chapter 14

Fair Reward

The Golden Rule is about comparison, which is the prerequisite of reciprocity that results in a fair exchange. In the process of selling and buying, extending value and receiving fair value are prerequisites for peace. Fair exchange, necessitated by the unifying values explicit and implicit in the Golden Rule, facilitates the balanced flow that results in societal harmony. Just as good blood circulation ensures a healthy body, a fair and equitable flow of goods and services ensures a sustainable economy.

The word *currency,* indeed, is derived from the Middle English *curraunt,* which meant circulation. In the drive to achieve a healthy economic model, humanity has developed many media for circulation of goods and services. Coins, paper money, banknotes, and other monetary units of nations and confederations have an exchange value determined by fixed as well as fluctuating valuation methods. The U.S. dollar, the British pound, the European Union euro, the Chinese yuan, and other national currencies are measured against each other depending on the conditions of the foreign exchange markets.

Currency values are set primarily by centralized national and international banks as well as by market transactions. With the purchase and sale of currencies in the trillions of dollars a day, valuation is susceptible to speculation and manipulation that contributes to risks as well as huge windfalls. The accumulation of wealth creates powerful blocks that restrict circulation by increasingly sophisticated methods, some of which have led to economic recessions.

Stock markets around the world thrive on uncertainty because there is no windfall when speculative gambling is not central to the economic flow. In effect, there are no unearned jackpots to be made in a stable economy. Powerful influences gain from fluctuation, uncertainty, and unsustainable practices. Unhealthy circulation allows for intervention in the money supply and fiscal policies that fuel inflation and deflation.

Today, vastly more money is transferred by electronic transactions rather than by physical exchange. However, new types of exchange systems are coming into practice as a result of new technologies. These systems use computers to record one exchange done within a network, such as labor done or goods received, so that later that credit can be exchanged for another good or service. "The hallowed nature of property exchange in markets," writes Jeremy Rifkin in *The Third Industrial Revolution*, "has been partially upended by shared access to commercial services in open-source networks."[1]

In August of 2000, the United Nations Millennium Forum addressed a mutual goal for nations to move from old to new and more sustainable economic systems. "To examine their economic models of development for sustainability and strive to restructure away from export-oriented, import-dependent and debt-driven models, if these are unsustainable. To move towards patterns of production and consumption that are sustainable and centered on the health and well-being of people and the environment."[2]

Yet the problem of unequal reward is more easily identified than an effective solution. Manipulation of import/export exchange rates and growth fueled by deficit spending and long-term debt are entrenched national policies. To support this zero-sum strategy of debt-driven competition, barriers to trade and support mechanisms such as tariffs and incentives are standard ways to grow market share. Global boom and bust, or expansions and recessions, are the inevitable result.

New systems of global exchange are slowly being developed. The time-based currency mentioned in United Nations Millennium Declaration C6 to Governments is the United Nations International and Local Employment-Trading System. Started in 1982, UNILETS regulates exchanges among members of the cooperative and provides an option to restructure the global financial architecture. These mutual credit systems are community-based enterprises that allow direct swaps of goods and services. The cooperative facilitates the LETS credits to be exchanged among the members. If a person does carpentry, for instance, their work is recorded and the credits can later be exchanged to purchase other goods and services in the network.

Barter systems, some simple and others more complex such as UNILETS, may be the best example of fair exchange on earth. All of the pricing mechanisms are present: the quality of the offer, the extent of the need, the locality of the transaction, and the integrity of both producer and customer. The competitive focus of our present exchange, complete with complex forms of middlemen speculation and gambling, is opposite to the simplicity and fairness of direct exchange under the reciprocal comparison of Golden Rule values. The mutuality of the Golden Rule ethic does not preclude the use of competition as a motivator, yet the drive toward unity activates cooperation and collaboration as the moral alternatives of a relational economy.

Core Problem

The global monetary system has developed over hundreds of years by a combination of legislated laws and the close association of monied interests both beneficent and malicious. The system is plagued by global speculation, complicated forms of usury, centralized manipulation of monetary supply, and fiscal infusion.

In addition, in order to achieve competitive advantages, nations and trading blocks impose barriers and restrictions to trade, including tariffs, embargoes, licenses, quotas, and devaluation schemes. The result of such interference by powerful interests corrupts the free circulation of goods and services and allows currency speculators to create temporary surpluses and shortages that impact the long-term health of the global economy.

Background

The first way of trading goods and services was "gifting" in small family and tribal units. Evidence of bartering points back at least 100,000 years, and the use of shells and other precious items continues to be discovered in ancient archeological sites. Coinage and currency are relatively modern inventions dating to 10,000 BCE. Value is based on backing by commodities or by government fiat.

Usury, or money lending by use of interest, has also been used as a form of exchange. The term goes back to ancient Judeo-Christian times, but interest was incorporated into law during the 1500s. Today, normal bank lending is linked to the speculative stock market, and government monetary policy is used as an economic stimulus in order to fuel growth as the key indicator of a healthy economy.

The centralization of minting and issuing currency has created lucrative centers of power. State-controlled central banks and Federal Reserve deposit systems legitimize lending as a form of currency, encourage over-consumption, and allow for fiscal and monetary policies that cause uncertainty and manipulation.

In recent years, currency intervention has become a weapon of national interest. When government financial entities purchase or sell their currency on the global exchange market, they can manipulate, or influence, the value of their domestic economy.

Solution

Technology has given us the potential for decentralization of monetary exchange by utilizing computerization of real-time data. Fair exchange rates are now less dependent on centralized exchange rates that can be manipulated. Instantaneous valuation of the product or service can now be based on known variables in the light of real-time data. Mutuality is necessitated by increased transparency, which allows the Golden Rule ethic of fairness to become front and center in a transaction.

With data acquisition and recording, global positioning and free information flow, the value of an offer can be determined through the use of a transaction formula, or *algorithm of exchange*. Millions, even billions of similar exchanges—factored by standardized algorithms that consider quantity, quality, geography, and other variables—will determine worth on both sides of the transaction at the time of each exchange.

With these new technologies, the Golden Rule intention of reciprocity has become a practical consideration. When reciprocity is put into the equa-

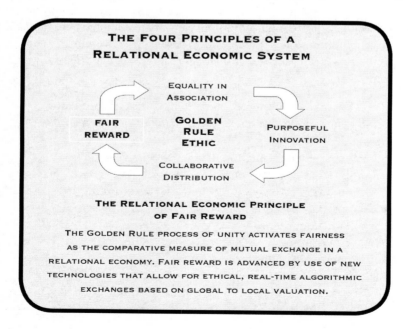

THE FOUR PRINCIPLES OF A
RELATIONAL ECONOMIC SYSTEM

EQUALITY IN ASSOCIATION

FAIR REWARD

GOLDEN RULE ETHIC

PURPOSEFUL INNOVATION

COLLABORATIVE DISTRIBUTION

THE RELATIONAL ECONOMIC PRINCIPLE
OF FAIR REWARD

THE GOLDEN RULE PROCESS OF UNITY ACTIVATES FAIRNESS
AS THE COMPARATIVE MEASURE OF MUTUAL EXCHANGE IN A
RELATIONAL ECONOMY. FAIR REWARD IS ADVANCED BY USE OF NEW
TECHNOLOGIES THAT ALLOW FOR ETHICAL, REAL-TIME ALGORITHMIC
EXCHANGES BASED ON GLOBAL TO LOCAL VALUATION.

tion of exchange, the reward system is based on analysis, comparison, and the expectation of fair return in kind. Orison Swett Marden in *Pushing to the Front* answered his question "What, in your observation, are the chief causes of the failure in life of business or professional men?" with a list of reasons including "disregard of the Golden Rule."[3]

Goods and services exchanged by reciprocal algorithmic currency transactions are based on the effective regional valuation. The commutative property is closely related to the associative property. However, the commutative property allows for changing the order in an expression without changing the value—$(a + b) + c = a + (b + c)$. Multiplication and addition are commutative, but division and subtraction are not. Reciprocal exchange, even though the economic variables are rearranged comparatively, offers the opportunity for a Golden Rule trade.

Prototypes

With cooperatives and monetary innovations leading the way, many examples of the new economy of currency transactions are developing every day. One of the best examples is the recent rise in the use of Bitcoins. This peer-to-peer method of exchange was developed from open-source software as a cryptocurrency below the radar and control of governments and central banks. Through a process called mining, participants can find coins and await market valuation on a real-time basis. Whether Bitcoins will succeed is up for speculation, but its success points to a rising tide of alternative methods of valuation.

- Basket of currency rating methods to limit risk of speculation through a portfolio of currencies to establish valuation
- Bitcoin digital currency
- "Smart" computer pricing that gives real-time valuation
- Community-based microfinance for local lending at lower finance rates
- Credit unions for crowd-source financing and banking
- Checks and money orders that replace hard and soft currencies
- Black market underground economy
- Digital payment methods such as PayPal
- Online transaction sites such as Amazon
- Debit cards that circumvent usury methods
- Global monetary exchanges on the scale of trillions of dollar per day
- Economic indexes such as the Index of Economic Well-Being (IEWB)

and Genuine Progress Indicator (GPI) that measure alternative economic realities
- Timedollar systems such as UNILETS (United Nations International Local Employment-Trading System), a barter exchange for time/skill trading
- Local Employment-Trading System (LETS) as a nonprofit alternative currency exchange
- Community Currency System (CCS) for local, regional and alternative currencies
- *Tauschring* exchange circles
- *Systemes d'Echange Local* (SEL-JEU) barter system
- Optical Character Recognition (OCR) scanning and other techniques for digitizing and expressing information
- Coupon exchanges such as Groupon

Result

The potential for a pervasive microeconomic algorithmic exchange returns currency transactions to their essential function, which is simply to facilitate the circulation of reciprocal trade. Fair price will eventually be based on millions of real-time allocations so that even remote locations will find a fair return on their goods and services.

With an algorithmic goods-based currency exchange, the full cost of products can include many variables not currently considered in the pricing. For instance, transportation costs and resource depletion rates can be included in the formula for how much a barrel of oil costs to take it from the ancient store below Saudi Arabia, transport it across oceans, and refine it in other countries.

Fair exchange, as measured within the moral context of reciprocity, is not the end of the economic transaction between producer and customer but only the beginning. A mutually beneficial transaction increases the economic activity by ensuring mutual benefits to all parties concerned. The unity created by a fair exchange sets the stage for further transactions and increased prosperity. In essence, all boats are lifted by the clear and profitable waters of a Golden Rule exchange.

Challenges for Fair Reward

First, is a sense of unity a precondition for fairness in economic activity? The misconstrued societal version of the Darwinian survival-of-the-fittest theory assumes that individuals are simply concerned with surviving no matter what it takes. However, as the Golden Rule teaches, expanding one's view to the *other* offers unlimited opportunity to ensure not only one's own survival but also a thriving environment of mutual exchange. In essence, unity for long-term sustainability trumps short-term profit.

Second, how can fairness replace reward as the boon of powerful interests for services rendered? Due to the nature of current legislated systems, financial policymakers are necessarily influenced by laws constructed by powerful interests. The centralized structure of economic activity inevitably favors some and not others. New innovative technologies are replacing the need for centralization with fully transparent and equalizing economic processes.

For instance, one of the key functions of governments is to print and distribute bills and coinage. The historical debate on whether money must be backed up by fixed assets is ongoing, but the need for such centralized control is nearly obsolete with digital transactions becoming the norm. Digital exchange rates will be determined by running tabulations of fixed assets rather than the current method of price supports and interference. Subtractions, additions, multiplications, and divisions will, literally, be reflective of comparative worth. The disassociation of currency from assets leaves room for manipulation but also for a more flexible exchange that facilitates fairness and equality within the oversight of transparency.

Chapter 15

Case Study—
The Commerce Sector

Salesforce.com and
the Freedom to Trade

San Francisco-based Salesforce.com admittedly has its head in the clouds—the company was founded fifteen years ago on the simple concept of delivering Customer Relationship Management (CRM) applications via the Internet, or cloud. Nearly gone are the days of fixed office space, rooms with mainframes, and a sales force tethered to corporate headquarters. The proliferation of mobile devices and the use of social media have freed employees from their desks. Today, people can work from anywhere, and the barriers to communication have been removed or drastically reduced.

The relationship between the company and the customer has always been the key to a successful enterprise. The Golden Rule of customer relations, in fact all stakeholder relations, has been standard practice for the most successful organizations in the world. Getting to know your customers is the rule rather than the exception. Understanding leads to empathy, which leads to an action or exchange, which leads to the transformational collaboration that leads to fair value.

Treat your customers as you would like to be treated seems a no-brainer today, but such a moral basis for commerce was not always the case. What a company would do to achieve a competitive advantage was limited only by liability, and the drive to success was centered on winning despite what was best for the customer. Even today, the less enlightened organization will choose short-term momentary gain over long-term success. Look at the derivatives schemes that contributed to the Great Recession.

The *win at any cost* companies are going by the wayside. The customer is now king or queen. Cooperative advantage is the holistic strategy to bring safety, prosperity, and quality of life to all stakeholders. The Golden Rule has triumphed. Today, with social networking and connectivity platforms that accelerate communication, relationships are based on a more realistic comparison of the needs of customers with the products and services that make for a successful exchange. Salesforce.com is at the forefront of Golden Rule technology. The company provides social and mobile cloud technologies—including its flagship sales and CRM applications to help companies connect with customers, partners, and employees in entirely new ways.

The old ways of stovepipe operations for corporations are going the way of the rust belt. Whether it's automation of the sales force, management of partners, or creating and rolling out marketing campaigns, the CRM solution enables companies to connect with their customers in entirely new ways. Leads become potential relationships. Sales channels become partnerships. The world becomes much smaller when technology clarifies the massive data stream into specific chunks of information that can be analyzed and acted upon. Real-time data acquisition results in better calculations to help in making decisions and allocating precious resources.

In little over a decade, Salesforce.com has grown to a market cap of over $20 billion with nearly $4 billion in revenue. It is approaching 10,000 employees. Indeed, the very definition of commerce has become more expansive in recent decades due to innovative companies like Salesforce.com. Commerce is the interchange of goods and services. Companies heed the call of commerce by responding to needs with value. Yet the interchange is now going through a dramatic evolution.

The relationships of commerce have expanded to include all stakeholders in the transaction, including producer and customer, suppliers, and the broader community, employees, and stockholders. "It starts with respect," said writer Doug Smith. "If you respect the customer as a human being, and truly honor their right to be treated fairly and honestly, everything else is much easier." The relationship of commerce now includes not only people but also nature and a broader universe of sustainability that includes efficiency and purpose.

Serve Others and They Will Serve You: The Golden Rule as the Moral Drive of Exchange

Salesforce.com has extended its innovations to the area of corporate philanthropy. From the start, the company experienced the same revenue and profit goals as traditional businesses. Yet even as a new company, they were driven by a transformative vision that was responding to a cooperative environment where all boats rise. "There is a spiritual aspect to our lives—when we give we receive—when a business does something good for somebody," concurs Ben Cohen of Ben & Jerry's, "that somebody feels good about them!"[1]

The folks at Salesforce.com soon found ways to *give back* and contribute to the common good, partly out of altruistic motives, but also because it made good business sense. The Salesforce.com Foundation is based on a simple idea: Leverage Salesforce.com's people, technology, and resources to help improve communities around the world. It created a new social enterprise business model for philanthropic endeavors. The Salesforce.com Foundation offers nonprofit corporations of all sizes the use of their proprietary CRM software for free. As the nonprofit grows, additional licenses and capabilities are deeply discounted.

"With distribution costs coming closer and closer to zero for online media," write Fulton, Kasper, and Kibbe in the Monitor Institute's *What's Next for Philanthropy*, "traditional barriers to sharing information are shrinking. Speeches and conversations can be shared through podcasts and digital video. Data now stored in databases can be turned into public libraries with a simple web interface. And in a more crowded playing field, there is tremendous value in reflecting on your work and conveying your lessons to others. By increasing the amount of information that is available, funders can create an environment where stakeholders can find what they need to make smarter decisions, grounded in the experience and knowledge of others. For mission-driven organizations like foundations, it makes sense to start from a place of sharing everything and then make a few exceptions rather than a place of sharing little where transparency is the exception."[2]

The Salesforce.com Foundation focuses on both nonprofits and higher education customers. Thanks to the Foundation, higher education and other not-for-profit organizations can take advantage of new ways to connect with their customers. The strategy of their Foundation is so innovative that laws and regulations prevented the company from accomplishing its goal. In the United States, 501(c)3 organizations that benefit from tax exemption benefits are limited in their ability to mix profit and philanthropy.

The company decided to go with a 501(c)4 status, which gave them the ability to offer free startup software as well as free and discounted software packages. Today, the Salesforce.com Foundation is a global endeavor. In London, the Salesforce.com Foundation offers the same free software and discounting for global organizations.

The New Business Environment

The concept of stakeholders was developed in the last century as a way to expand the notion of monetary interest to all parties affected by the organization's actions. Stakeholders include not only traditional stockholders but also employees as well as governmental bodies, trade unions, political groups, financiers, suppliers, and the wider community of employees and their families. Any person, group, or community that can be affected by the actions of an organization must be considered in decisions by the Board.

First used in a 1963 memorandum at the Stanford Research Institute, stakeholder relations have revolutionized corporate governance and social responsibility beyond supplier and purchaser. Instrumental in viewing resource acquisition, production, marketing, and all other facets of organizational management, stakeholder theory brings the wider universe into the picture of the health, viability, and impact of organizations.

The concept of stakeholder has continued to evolve. Whereas the stockholder idea of competing interests came from the overall competitive economy school, today stakeholder interests are wholly framed in collaboration. Even competitors are involved in the relationship, which makes sense because the overall market for products and services is a reflection of the health of the entire industry. It's not only "what's good for General Motors is good for the U.S.A." but also what's good for Coke is good for Pepsi. All boats are lifted in a relational economy.

Salesforce.com has laid out many of the principles of putting an organization on the firm foundation of stakeholder relationships. Some of the age-old tenets that offer new opportunities through increased technological options are[3]:

- Get to know your customers
- Connect and collaborate with all stakeholders
- Engage customers in new ways
- Use connectivity to build deeper relationships
- Listen to and learn from your networks
- Clearly define your vision, mission, goals
- Empower employees individually and collectively
- Follow through with purpose
- Treat your customers like trusted partners
- Involve your products in the conversation

Trade as Promoting Peace

Each act of exchanging one item for something of similar value always changes the world. Originally, barter was the method of trade with the direct exchange of goods. Later, a medium of exchange was devised to facilitate transactions. Coins were minted from precious metals and a value applied. Paper money or notes represented precious metals. Today, digital transactions have replaced the physical exchange.

The network in which the exchanges are made is called a market, recalling the central market of ancient times. The act of selling was separated from the act of buying by an unnatural split in the process between supplier and demand. Retail stores sell directly to consumers. Wholesalers sell to retailers. Business-to-business transactions cover industrial and institutional transactions.

Trade benefits both parties when the price is fair. Even more, when the product or service has value beyond the price, the relationship is enhanced as a reciprocal exchange of supplier promise and customer loyalty. The Golden Rule of trade plays out every day in the real world, with many companies flourishing from the strategy of the Salesforce Foundation.

Family Services in San Francisco is one of the beneficiaries of the Foundation's discounted CMS software. In the old days, their paperwork systems were bogging down with over 12,000 clients, over ten languages and thirty programs. Half the time was spent helping the paperwork rather than helping clients.

When they approached Salesforce.com and learned about the philanthropic options for nonprofits, Family Services began implementing a package that is fully HIPAA-compliant (Health/Insurance Portability and Accountability Act). Today the charitable service provider has automated processes, streamlined reporting, developed assessment tools, and integrated fundraising and accounting. Now caseworkers can focus 75 percent of their time on customer and community needs.

"With Salesforce CRM," said Bob Bennett, Family Services Agency CEO, "we have visibility into the effectiveness of our client programs and the ability to set and track metric-based benchmarks for client progress."[4]

Another program that has taken advantage of the Salesforce.com Foundation offer is the Polaris Project. Working to halt human trafficking, Polaris has a network of crisis hotlines, victim services, and legislative lobbying initiatives. Founded by Brown University students Derek Ellerman and Katherine Chon in 2002, the Polaris Project began with their awareness of South Korean women who had been forced to work in brothels.

Salesforce.com's discounted software enabled the organization to improve outreach and victim identification processes as well as identify transitional housing and service provider referrals. "Polaris Project guides victims to freedom with Salesforce CRM and mobile devices,"[5] Sarah Jakiel, deputy director at the Polaris Project, said. Their resource center, with global monitoring and hotline operations, is now more efficient and effective in their main goal of ending human slavery in the U.S. and around the world.

There are numerous global consciousness implications to the idea of fair exchange, yet the Golden Rule does not lose sight of profit. History is littered with failed businesses that did not learn the lesson of reciprocity. Only now has technology enabled a more precise comparison of value in real time, which offers forward-looking companies such as Salesforce.com the edge in the future peace economy. "We have always known that heedless self-interest was bad morals," said U.S. president and New Deal architect Franklin D. Roosevelt, "we now know that it is bad economics."[6]

Judicial Governance

"*What the Court really has refused to recognize is the fundamental interest all individuals have in controlling the nature of their intimate associations.*"[1]—Harry A. Blackmun

Chapter 16

What Is a Judicial Governance System?

Some define peace in a very limited view as the absence of war and violence. Though a subtle difference, war and violence are rather more clearly seen as arising in the absence of peace. This differentiation is more than semantics. Peace is an active rather than a passive or inactive state of being. In large part, peace is the result of our intentions, especially the economic and governing systems we put in place to preserve our safety, prosperity, and quality of life.

History has shown that in times of lawlessness and chaos, those usually hurt are the most vulnerable. The so-called *collateral damage* of war and conflict gives us the most vivid insight into what can happen in the absence of peace. Not only are someone's neighbors and children put at risk, but also the flow of goods and services that enables them to survive and thrive is constricted. The absence of peace inevitably prevents the fulfillment of our individual and collective human potential.

To that end, societies endeavor not only to create economic opportunity but also to develop systems of government to keep the peace in a contentious world full of conflicts and competitive desires. We devise more and more complex systems of government to solve everything from our security fears to how we educate our children. When these systems work successfully, we expand government. When they fail, we cut back and start again.

Central to the need for government is the duty of protection. "Do unto others before they do harm to you" is the fear-based interpretation of imagined reciprocity. This reactive Golden Rule emerges from deep-seated fears of limited resources and concern for safety. Indeed, for those of us who do not have the benefit of being Gandhi, Thich Nhat Hanh, Mother Teresa, Rumi, or any of the great teachers of peace, we have a great deal of trouble, as Jesus commanded, in turning the other cheek.

The original Supreme Court of the United States, established by the Constitution, met in Old City Hall, Philadelphia. At the time, there were only six members, decisions were made by a two-thirds majority, and *justices* were then called judges. Congressional and Executive actions changed the court, increasing it to nine members; judges became justices, and decisions are now made by a simple majority (Independence National Historical Park).

Instead, borders are bolstered, armies are built, restrictions on trade are instituted, imperialistic strategies are pursued, and resources pillaged. Any means to gain a competitive advantage or keep a threat at bay is fair game. Governments, heretofore, have been formed not by the *do unto others as you would have them do unto you* Golden Rule ethic but rather with the mantra *us against the world.*

Yet what would a government look like if conceived on the principles of the Golden Rule? If all governing systems are based on fear and competition, how could humanity possibly conceive of a new politic based on a moral code?

There are, indeed, many historical antecedents for just such a governance system. Many examples exist of nations and peoples working together without violence and war. History is replete with alliances and treaties, trade agreements, the global Olympics, world courts, and efforts to gather for mutual benefit. Most of human activity is spent in trying to develop, and succeeding for the most part, a mutual understanding and respect. War is an aberration rather than the rule. Otherwise, humans would not have survived all these millennia as a species.

Aspects of many governing models have been based on an attempt to incorporate the moral principle of the Golden Rule and the processes it expresses, among them empathy, compassion, engagement, and unity. If it were not for the history of constitutional governments and nations working together for the common good, these processes might seem simply idealistic. Yet justice is an essential element of the documents of freedom. Educational institutions have worked to instill the values of the Golden Rule in children so that they grow into the good people needed to maintain beneficial institutions. Sometimes the institutions put in place work for the good of humanity; sometimes they don't.

Governing systems affect both relations between nations and relations between people. Instead of contention, preserving freedom becomes the essential arbiter between the individual and the collective. Freedom to form associations, to innovate and collaborate, to reap the rewards of personal and group initiatives is good for each of us and good for all. A governing system based on Golden Rule processes, as moral imperatives, would be a government that lets the age-old wisdom and common practice of the virtue of reciprocity lead to freedom.

Still, as history has progressed, so have the challenges of burgeoning population and diversity of race, religion, and culture. There has been intense pressure to build stronger national governments in order to keep the peace between competing cultures. Now an emerging global consciousness, especially with the profound image of the boundary-less earth from space, is weakening the need and desire for national boundaries, cultural prejudices, and economic barriers that circumvent the natural relations among peoples. Technology has leapfrogged nations, connected people of diverse cultures, and informed billions of young people that better ways of governing exist. The future represents an extraordinary opportunity to create a government that is relational rather than confrontational, one that can adapt to positive new realities that offer humanity an opportunity for a more peaceful world.

A Government Based on Justice

What would a governing system as an emanation of the Golden Rule look like in practice?

The best system of governance certainly must be one with justice at its heart. Dictatorships, autocracies, oligarchies, aristocracies, and the like still exist to deliver justice for some and not for others. To counter these antiquated institutions, a new revolutionary spirit has become a part of society for the purpose of toppling a dominant system of governance. Yet wars of revolution have their own dynamic of lawlessness and chaos. They often turn to violence, which begets more violence. As we have seen recent history mimic the past, collateral damage from armed conflict, even in the name of democracy, can be as horrible as wars of aggression.

What government system can actually give people the peace they seek without the constant need for revolution? How can laws and enforcement systems be firm yet flexible enough to allow for new situations without depending on violence to counter the growth of a dominant power?

The chapters prior to this focused on economic prosperity and how the associations we make form the energy of plenty. For a relational economy to flourish, there must be a relational governance system based on justice that encourages the dynamic qualities of economic activity while keeping the peace. Judicial governance, tasked as it is with ensuring equal justice under the law, is essential for a relational economy for, among others, the following reasons:

1. **Associative Organization:** just governance is a necessity in defining contracts and adjudicating disputes.
2. **Purposeful Innovation:** just governance is necessary for clearing away legislative laws and executive implementations that create bureaucratic status quo.
3. **Collaborative Distribution:** just governance can reduce the current competitive international blockage of trade and relations.
4. **Fair Reward:** just governance will allow individuals to engage in fair exchanges with fair incentives and disincentives for behavior.

When Justice Harry A. Blackman wrote in a dissenting opinion for a Supreme Court decision, "What the Court really has refused to recognize is the fundamental interest all individuals have in controlling the nature of their intimate associations," he was considering a case of gay rights. Yet freedom to associate is a right that extends from intimate to non-intimate relationships, from personal to public, from friends to business partners, from individuals to society.

The march toward greater freedom must be free from the aggression and violence that restrict the rights of some for the benefit of others. There must be justice in the decisions that affect all parties in the process. With our societal governing systems we make collective decisions. We define expectations of actions and grant certain powers. As an example of how challenging and necessary a Golden Rule system has become, let's take as an example a woman who endeavors to make a living making clothing for children. The success of this particular business enterprise, common in all cultures and countries, requires unfettered use of her skills and initiative.

> First, in some countries and eras, women have been discouraged or even legally prevented from forming a business. We will assume our female entrepreneur lives in a relatively free society. In most countries, of course, she will need a license. Undoubtedly she will pay sales tax. If she needs an assistant, she might be required to register as an employer and pay unemployment tax and post equal employment posters. Maybe there is a tariff on textiles that raise her costs. Her phone might cost more because it is a business application. For all of the laws and regulations that affect this woman's business, there is a government agency that monitors and ensures compliance.
>
> Each of these extra costs and reporting measures has some justification. Roads need to be paved. Workers' rights need to be upheld. Industries need to be supported or jobs will be lost. Government is applauded on the one hand and disdained on the other.
>
> In addition, for the woman to operate her business she needs to be protected. There are petty criminals who would steal from her coffers. There are con artists who would bilk her out of assets. The policing actions of our governments are charged with ensuring that chaos doesn't disrupt how we make our living.

Current governmental structures often act to the detriment of the individual freedom to make a living, yet laws and enforcement are needed. Bureaucracy, however, is inherently expansive. Each justification for this expansion, whether it is to ensure safety or promote welfare, gives new reasons for more regulations and laws, more bureaucrats to implement. In many countries, government has become the largest enterprise in the economy and threatens its citizens' most basic freedoms. Societies are constantly looking for complexity to solve its problems when simplicity and ancient wisdom are often where to find time-tested truth.

Would a government based on the Golden Rule solve the complexity that arises from a government based on bureaucratic authority?

The culture of a society, of course, has a far greater impact on people's lives than the structure of government. The organization of society governs actions and, in some cases, our intentions. As members of society, we form implicit contracts with friends and family, neighbors and members of our communities. Associations are formed for business purposes and voluntary actions for not-for-profit organizations.

To supplement cultural organization, people submit money to local and national governments to support basic services for communities. They pay taxes to hire those who build roads and bridges. They support schools and pay teachers. They pay fees to ensure vehicles do not pollute and to test for competent drivers. Local governments can be bogged down by petty politics, but the work done is based on a social contract of need that few would contradict.

Laws are the principles and regulations established by a community through either custom or legislation for the purpose of keeping the peace. Natural law is the theory that just laws are inherent in nature. These laws can be understood as arising from nature and cannot be created or designed in the minds of humans. A debate on whether natural laws can, inherently, be unjust gave rise to the positivist interpretation that natural law is not necessarily the end all to a just world. Legal Positivists such as Jeremy Bentham, who lived in the time of kings, spurned natural law but shifted the authority of governments to the *happiness factor,* the greatest good for the greatest number. More modern legal thinkers such as Ronald Sworkin held that natural law is valid but needs to be supplemented by social rules and moral justifications that better guide our actions.

The ancient drive for a society beyond natural law led to codifying human laws. Statutory laws are those written by a legislature or enacted by an executive authority. There are two main areas of statutory law, including criminal law dealing with conduct and civil law dealing with disputes. Civil laws are those that deal with contracts, property, trusts, torts, international situations, constitutional questions, and administrative functions.

A democratic form of government—first experimented with in Greece, fomented during the revolutions of the eighteenth century, and fully expressed in the democratic expansion of our current age—is considered the height of the art and science of governing. As each nation's government has taken a unique form, four basic ideas have provided the basis for increasing *freedom to* and *freedom from.* These ideas could reach their highest form when derived from application of the Golden Rule.

1. **Rule of Law:** The Golden Rule process of empathy activates case law based on precedent as a stabilizing and flexible force for just governance. Case law provides for a stable society while enabling judges to modify the laws for changing conditions.
2. **Separation of Powers:** The Golden Rule process of compassion activates equal access to law as a guarantee of separation of powers required for just governance. Equal access to law with a right to fair trials and appeal ensures that no person is above or below the law.
3. **Democratic Elections:** The Golden Rule process of engagement acti-

vates the self-governing drive toward a democratic judiciary as required for just governance. A democratic judiciary elected by an informed citizenry made possible by new electoral technologies will ensure impartial and competent judges.

4. **Consent of the Governed:** The Golden Rule process of unity activates fair enforcement to assure the mutual consent of citizens required for just governance. Fair enforcement with due process and due penalties in the context of community enables personal transformation within a law-abiding society.

The contention between the individual and society is a subtext of human history. No one likes to be told what to do. Sometimes advice and help are welcome, but the right of individual humans to determine what happens in their lives is basic. The principle of government by law, or rule of law, provides that all people and institutions are accountable to laws that are fairly applied and enforced. Rule of law prevents arbitrary laws and forms the basis for equality under the law. When rule of law is institutionalized in a society, decisions and actions are framed within known legal principles. In theory and sometimes practice, no one is above the law.

The second essential idea of a just government, separation of powers, provides us the theoretical advantage of balance and counterpoise. The intention is to assure that some do not use government to take advantage of others. The evolutionary concept of three branches of government, or *trias politica*—the executive, legislative and judicial—harks back to the Roman Republic. During the French Enlightenment, Baron de Montesquieu formalized the concept in the *Separation of Powers* that became key to the American Constitution and other governments. Though usually considered only in the context of balance of powers between the branches of government, the essential concept of separation of powers is threaded throughout the structure of government. The power of appeal, for instance, provides a separation of the courts so that citizens can find justice when faced with an erroneous ruling. Such separation of powers, currently developing with new judicial technologies, is inherent in the Golden Rule imperative of compassionate government.

The third core idea, democratic elections, is the best way humans have found to ensure competence and accountability in government. Democracy allows the citizens a degree of participation in the process, including voting, debate, and running for office. There is much debate about whether democratic elections are possible to ensure the independence of judges. Yet free elections, or unfettered engagement of citizens in the process, are essential imperatives of the Golden Rule, allowing democracy as a collaborative and relational method of government to flourish.

The last concept is, perhaps, the most important. Contracts are, in most cases, made by the consent of individuals and society as a whole. The broader collective decision-making power of government is in the hands of its citizens. The Social Contract of Jean-Jacques Rousseau gives authority to a society and government based on the general will. This Enlightenment concept has been the basis for legitimate revolutions, such as those in the United States and France during the eighteenth centuries. When the recipient of that authority, especially in national governments, exceeds the general will, revolt and revolution are the inevitable results.

Throughout history, tribes, kingdoms, empires, and democracies have relied on the general will for the perpetuation of their power. Families and business associations are the same. The individuals involved must cooperate and give the collective authority to act as one. Since the general will is difficult to know and determine, a system of laws is necessary to provide guidance and rules. These laws have a profound effect on our daily lives, including our economic activity and relations with each other. Consent is an imperative of the Golden Rule process of finding unity through empathy, compassion, and engagement toward a transformational society where the oneness of humanity is the end result of just governance.

How Would Judicial Governance Support a Relational Economic System?

Just like the economy of freedom it seeks to protect and expand, a judicial governance system also has fundamental principles. The search for justice goes back to the beginnings of human history. The story of Solomon arbitrating a dispute between two women who claimed the same baby is a case in point. Threatening to cut the baby in half, Solomon determined the real mother, in essence the one who loved the child, by her willingness to give up the baby to the other woman in order to save the child's life.

Wouldn't it be wonderful to have the time and wisdom to adjudicate all disputes in such a personal way? Unfortunately, we must rely on systems to do the work of justice. And for that, history has provided many options and innovations from which to choose our future systems. Indeed, the evolutionary path toward ever more just systems of governance has offered many forms of government, from tribal chiefdoms and the Roman Forum to the kingships of Europe and the empires of the East.

A judicial governance system is simply one that allows the natural morality of the Golden Rule to be expressed. Govern others in the way you would have them govern you. However, even the best of our present forms of government, those that have the benefit of democracy, are based on prescriptive laws that find their value in authoritative control rather than the strict reciprocal justice of *an eye for an eye, a tooth for a tooth*. Democratic governments, as instituted today, strive to do the greatest good for the greatest number through codified law, thus reducing the need for individuals to seek retribution and revenge.

However, one-size-fits-all remedies of the Golden Mean in a relational world have become obsolete. True justice is individual in nature. An equal weighing of the needs and desires of the individuals involved, indeed all stakeholders of society, must be taken into account to achieve true justice, as justice is defined by moral rightness. The facts must be weighed and the resulting action firmly fixed in the context of all factors in a dispute or in collaboration of all parties.

One of the historical trends of the last few decades is a fierce debate between those who want less government and those who want more. The argument, in some of the most authoritative nations, has gone to the streets and resulted in the decline of autocracies and dictatorships. Yet the debate also reaches democracies that find polarizing differences in how best to find the benefits of competing economic systems.

Basic to this argument is the question: Are capitalism and socialism the most effective economic models for democratic governments? Both systems are hundreds of years old and are reeling from new dynamics. When governments are allowed to run the economy, as in socialism, more rules, regulations and enforcement are the result. When the market is left to run the economy, as in capitalism, the invisible hand often hands off the spoils to the monied interests. The complexity results in one-size-fits-all legislation.

The modern merger between socialism and capitalism is *state capitalism*. The state capitalist model has not just muddied the debate, it has also answered the question of where societies are headed if we continue on this path of two options. The result is quite a distance from a Golden Rule economy. The woman who wants to make a living from making clothing for children is up against a huge bureaucracy that is incapable of the flexibility and justice required to allow her to reach her potential.

Indeed, the impact of rule of law on economic development for individuals is profound. A stable government and legal framework should enable people to make good decisions. Future plans, investments, and checkbook decisions require the freedom that a clear understanding of the legal environment provides. Arbitrary laws and chaotic changes are the nemesis of prosperity. Stability leaves the day-to-day decisions firmly in the hands of the individuals. Laws should become instruments in the hands of people pursuing their dreams.

A judicial governance system would be one in which people make a living based on what gives them purpose and quality of life, which requires freedom. Yet freedom can only be realized if there are systems in place to allow for people to safely venture into occupations that bring them prosperity. The importance of local, national, and global justice systems is becoming more evident in every person's life. From local jurisdictional courts to the World Trade Organization, the decisions of these seats of judgment determine in many ways the food we eat, our access to water, the safety of our neighborhoods, and the righteousness of our laws. Judges, magistrates, mediators, arbitrators, committees of experts, law enforcement officials, clerks of courts, and the entire system of justice affects each one of us.

The reasons for the expanding influence by government in our lives are complex. However, the essential purpose of our governments is simple: to keep the peace. For thousands of years, societies have built systems to take the place of arguments, disputes, and outright warfare. Systems of government have been devised on the Golden Staff or the Golden Mean, where separations and divides were at the core of societal control and direction. The connectivity and complexity of our current era requires more attention to considering all of the stakeholders in a dispute—all of the relationships that are affected by any legal decision.

The world's current governing systems are institutional rather than relational, amoral rather than moral. The legislative and executive bodies of nation-states generate and often dictate laws that reflect the interests of the most powerful institutional sectors in each society. In a relational economy, two key components are essential:

1. Prevention of accumulated power
2. The ability to adapt to rapid change from innovation

Currently and in large measure the bureaucratic, institutional nature of government prevents both of these from happening. The main reason for inflexibility and inequality of power and wealth is found in the very nature of the legislative and executive branches of government. Legislators and executives are subject to powerful influences, and they are empowered with the ability to change society arbitrarily through legislation and executive rules. In most cases, laws and administrative rules may be reasonable, yet there is no assurance that a sense of morality was used as the basis for their construction. Consideration of morality is often banished from institutional set-tings.

In the developing relational economy, society is becoming more depend-ent on a judicial system that provides the possibility for relational rather than institutional justice. The judiciary is able to weigh the facts and respond with

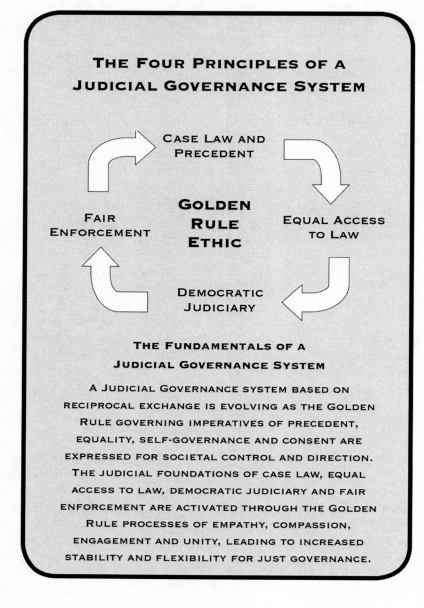

THE FOUR PRINCIPLES OF A JUDICIAL GOVERNANCE SYSTEM

CASE LAW AND PRECEDENT

FAIR ENFORCEMENT

GOLDEN RULE ETHIC

EQUAL ACCESS TO LAW

DEMOCRATIC JUDICIARY

THE FUNDAMENTALS OF A JUDICIAL GOVERNANCE SYSTEM

A JUDICIAL GOVERNANCE SYSTEM BASED ON RECIPROCAL EXCHANGE IS EVOLVING AS THE GOLDEN RULE GOVERNING IMPERATIVES OF PRECEDENT, EQUALITY, SELF-GOVERNANCE AND CONSENT ARE EXPRESSED FOR SOCIETAL CONTROL AND DIRECTION. THE JUDICIAL FOUNDATIONS OF CASE LAW, EQUAL ACCESS TO LAW, DEMOCRATIC JUDICIARY AND FAIR ENFORCEMENT ARE ACTIVATED THROUGH THE GOLDEN RULE PROCESSES OF EMPATHY, COMPASSION, ENGAGEMENT AND UNITY, LEADING TO INCREASED STABILITY AND FLEXIBILITY FOR JUST GOVERNANCE.

a measure of justice for individual cases. The system of blind justice developed in Greco-Roman times established the judiciary as the main arbiter in society, focused on finding justice in laws despite the powers that be.

The success of blind justice is debatable, yet throughout history citizens have depended on the courts for moral rightness. Today, due to the obvious polarization between the legislative and executive branches, the judicial branch of government has come to the fore. The judiciary is currently handling most situations where laws need to be changed to adapt to innovation or where the accumulation of too much power is causing inequity. Indeed, the question of whether the courts are more just is also debatable, yet an assessment of progress, from civil rights to protection of the environment, will show how society is relying on the courts for ultimate justice.

The thought of a slow transition from three branches of government to one, of course, causes great trepidation. Indeed, the term *kritarchy,* which is derived from *kritikós,* the Greek word for skilled in judging, is the term for rule by judges. The concept, however, has a negative connotation due to its misuse by authoritarian regimes, from Iran to Somalia. Yet the problems of the executive and legislative branches must be addressed. Where there is an executive branch, there will always be executive rules that wield arbitrary power. Where there is a legislative branch, there will always be laws that protect constituents regardless of equal justice.

Though the judicial process is far from perfect, the judiciary is conceived as a means of weighing conditions and rendering decisions that are just. As society moves toward a government where the judiciary is primary, the courts will adapt, create their own balances of power and evolve in ways we currently can only imagine.

Expert theorists on the evolution of the judiciary are sorely needed, yet the clarion call for a judicial governance system will begin with the people. To begin a discussion of what constitutes a government based on justice, a few terms need to be refreshed in memory:

Judiciary: the court system tasked with ensuring equal justice.
Common Law Jurisdictions: courts interpret and apply statutory laws of legislatures and/or make new law by establishing equitable principles where statutory laws are unclear or do not exist.
Civil Law Jurisdictions: courts interpret and apply legislative statutes.
Statutory Law: written laws (statutes) enacted by legislatures.
Administrative Law: courts interpret and apply a body of common law (previous court decisions).
Case Law: decisions of courts, which can be cited as precedent.

Precedent: a previous court decision that is binding in subsequent similar cases.

Collaborative Law: a private holistic approach to conflict resolution, which empowers the parties to a conflict to resolve the dispute themselves with the assistance of those trained in collaborative law and the utilization of resources designed to heal the core causes of the conflict and facilitate a resolution.

Private Law: laws pertaining to relationships between private individuals; to be distinguished from public law, which pertains to relationships between the general population (individuals and organizations, such as corporations) and the state.

The powers and jurisdictions of judiciary systems around the world are complex and not easily generalized. In most countries, disputes are resolved by court rulings based on case law or statutes. Laws already on the books regarding all aspects of civil and criminal law are constantly updated through the adjudication of cases brought before the courts or new bills and rules generated by legislatures and executives.

In many countries, including the United States, courts are limited in their ability to make law. The judiciary under the Constitution's separation of powers is not tasked primarily with making laws but rather with interpreting and applying laws. A Supreme Court, as established in the Constitution, serves as a powerful check on the executive and legislative branches and can change laws through the process of judicial review. Laws are deemed constitutional or unconstitutional based on the judicial interpretation within a certain jurisdiction.

The judiciary branch, as noted, is tasked with pursuing equal justice. The judiciary's core function is, therefore, *justice-based*, as courts rule on disputes by weighing circumstance and evidence, then rendering decisions that form case law and, sometimes, new precedent. On the contrary, the core function of the legislative and executive branches are necessarily *agenda-based* to control and direct society through statutory laws and administrative rules.

With its limited ability to change or create new laws through discrete court cases, the judiciary has expanded its power and jurisdiction to new areas of law. The judiciary is better able to respond objectively to conditions required by a relational economy based on innovative change. General codified laws by legislative and executive actions restrict the ability of the economy to adapt quickly and are subject to powerful influences that seek external control.

The ability of the judiciary to create law is reserved mainly for common law jurisdictions where it can apply equitable principles in cases where statutes fall short. In a judicial governance system, the court's ability to apply equitable principles would allow for the evolution of historically legislated and administrated laws that are bogged down in bureaucracy and agendas.

With an evolving ability to adapt statutory laws and provide enforcement under the domain of a democratically elected judiciary, the need for legislative and executive bodies would be drastically reduced. A judicial governance system does not entail a revolution but simply an evolution of governance based on relational justice and the institutional use of the Golden Rule reciprocal ethic. New theories and expansion of the standard and appellate court systems, as well as alternative methods such as collaborative law and private law, are needed to handle the increase in case load and responsibilities that will come from changing economic activity and the demand for governance to reflect justice.

The Golden Rule as the Moral Imperative for Just Governance

A global judiciary governing system, reflective of the current federal and state model, is now emerging as a progressively just and equalizing means to settle contract and other disputes. The international nature of modern challenges has, necessarily, created a judicial system that goes beyond national boundaries. The historical desire for maintaining cultural and national sovereignty is weakening under the strains of globalization, but strong limits are still in place.

In a full judicial governance system, explicit and implicit contractual cases would be brought before the correct jurisdiction within a system of local and global courts. These cases would force interpretation and modification of old law and the creation of equitable principles, or new interpretation and applications, based upon the merits of the arguments used by the plaintiff and defendant. The use of collaborative and integrative law, which have as their basis relational processes, would support the evolving judicial system with evolutionary means of resolving and transforming disputes. In addition, a developing system of judicial appeals, disciplinary commissions, and judicial complaint mechanisms is ensuring the essential benefits of separation of power far beyond the appellate court processes of today.

More and more, the world is using the hierarchical system of local, regional, and global courts, staffed by judges and mediators, to provide dispute resolution for all aspects of human relations. As a result, the rising back-log of cases has necessitated alternative forms of dispute resolution. Methods of nonviolent conflict analysis and resolution include mediation, negotiation, diplomacy, counseling, conflict transformation, and other processes. Judges and mediators invoke methods of conflict resolution or apply relevant case rulings based on precedent to render rulings that are, in many cases, binding on all parties. Variously termed collaborative law, private courts, mediation, and integrative law, these evolving legal institutions are rising to the call for a more relational legal system less focused on the conflict at hand but rather on the long-term resolution and transformational aspects of justice.

As the judicial system takes advantage of new legal technologies as well as communication and educational advances, judges might eventually be elected in a one-person, one-vote democratic process. The solution will necessarily come when computerized polling and objective election monitoring are matched by an informed electorate that rejects negative campaigning and money politics.

For a judicial governance system to be practical, a global/local policing organization would need to be administered by the judiciary. Currently, the courts are limited to *proceedings supplementals,* whereby the court orders such actions as freezing of assets to pay fines. Enforcement is then handled by the police or other federal or state administrative bodies. In a judicial governance system, judgments of the bench would be secured by a networked police force, exemplified by such entities as Interpol; however, local jurisdictions would report to and be managed by local, democratically elected magistrates. This type of system is very controversial, but not unlike today's enforcement networks managed by mayors, governors, presidents, and their staffs.

The hallowed structures for this evolving relational system of justice are case law based on precedent, equal access to law, democratic elections, and fair enforcement. Without the guiding light of the Golden Rule imperatives of empathy, compassion, engagement, and unity, these structures of the judiciary remain amoral institutions. However, with the rising global consciousness and recognition of the mutuality of the human family, the Golden Rule can infuse these flat institutions with the moral roundness of justice.

Chapter 17

Case Study—
The Recreational Sector

The Olympic Spirit and
the Freedom to Celebrate

The point of our economic and governing systems is to allow us to have the best life we can while on this earth. The celebration of life through sports, music, games, and other recreations gives us time away from the workday to relax, be with friends and family, and keep physically and mentally fit. Indeed, recreations provide a way to reduce the stress of everyday life and refresh the spirit.

However, our recreations are sometimes reflective of life's stresses and can be cultural manifestations of the anxieties and disquiet of our collective journey. For instance, music lyrics sometimes exacerbate the racial and cultural divide. Some contend that ultra-violent video games have a measurable effect on our children. Intense competition in sports often leads to fights and angry mobs. Opposing players or teams can become the enemy, a false Darwinian selection of survival trumped up to make the games more interesting and challenging, pushing the competitors to their very best and, sometimes, worst.

The Golden Rule may seem out of place on the playing field, yet camaraderie and teamwork are evident. The reciprocity of goodwill and concerted action is a big part of why we play sports. Cooperation, individual and collective accomplishment, and simply being a part of the action are fundamental to the spirit of the games.

Indeed, sports and physical education are "fundamental human rights for all," as defined in 1978 by UNESCO. In 2003, the United Nations Inter-Agency Task Force on Sport for Development and Peace defined sport as "all forms of physical activity that contribute to physical fitness, mental well-being and social interaction, such as play, recreation, organized or competitive sport, and indigenous sports and games."[1]

From refugee camps to war zones, sports have contributed to reducing stress, building community, and preventing more violence due to inhumane conditions. In communities around the world, sports have succeeded in teaching basic skills and discipline, raising confidence and self-respect, and providing leadership through cooperation and respect for others.

According to the U.N. Office of Sports for Development and Peace (UNOSDP), "By its very nature, sport is about participation. It is about inclusion and citizenship. It stands for human values such as respect for the opponent, acceptance of binding rules, teamwork and fairness, all of which are principles which are also contained in the Charter of the United Nations."[2] Sports can be a low-cost, high-impact way to help achieve the United Nations' eight global Millennium Development Goals (MDG):

1. Eradicate poverty and hunger by providing jobs and skills development, preventing diseases, and increasing self-esteem, self-confidence, and social skills.
2. Achieve universal primary education by motivating children to enroll in and attend school.
3. Promote gender equality and empower women by improving female physical and mental health as well as leadership opportunities.
4. Reduce child mortality by delivering health information to young mothers, providing sports-based vaccination and increasing physical fitness to improve children's resistance to diseases.
5. Improve maternal health through programs that offer girls and women greater access to reproductive health information and services.
6. Combat HIV/AIDS, malaria, and other diseases through prevention and healthy lifestyle promotion.
7. Ensure environmental sustainability by increasing participation in community actions to improve the local environment.
8. Develop a global partnership for development by catalyzing collaboration and increasing networking among governments, donors, NGOs, and sport organizations worldwide.

Nowhere are the Golden Rule and reciprocity more evident than in the expression of the Olympic Spirit. Every two years, Olympians from around the world gather with a sense of universal humanity for the summer or winter Olympics. Organized to reflect the original competitions in Greece over two thousand years ago, the Olympic games were revived by French Baron Pierre de Coubertin in 1894 to foster international communication and peace.

Today, the Olympics echo the first contests held in Athens during the eighth century BCE. In order to adapt to seasonal sports, the summer and winter games were organized as distinct events and hosted by separate venues. The Fundamental Principles of the Olympic Movement are[3]:

- Olympism is a philosophy of life, exalting and combining in a balanced whole the qualities of body, will, and mind.
- Blending sport with culture and education, Olympism seeks to create a way of life based on the joy found in effort, the educational value of good example, and respect for universal fundamental ethical principles.
- The goal of Olympism is to place everywhere sport at the service of the harmonious development of man, with a view to encouraging the establishment of a peaceful society concerned with the preservation of human dignity.
- The practice of sport is a human right. Every individual must have the possibility of practicing sport, without discrimination of any kind and in the Olympic spirit, which requires mutual understanding with a spirit of friendship, solidarity, and fair play.
- Any form of discrimination with regard to a country or person on grounds of race, religion, politics, gender, or otherwise is incompatible with belonging to the Olympic Movement.

Olympian missions have included such wide-ranging Golden Rule objectives such as encouraging women's sports, opposing commercial abuse of athletes, encouraging sustainable operation of the Games, blending sports with culture and education, and preventing exploitation of the Olympic Spirit by political and social agendas. The Olympic Spirit is the most cherished of the Games' considerable assets. "The important thing is not to win, but to take part,"[4] said Pierre de Coubertin. The competition allows for winners and losers, but the Olympian Spirit also honors the Olympians who may finish last but do their best and show a love for the sport. The struggles and challenges are what bring the world together, and the Golden Rule is central to the Olympian Spirit, where competitors show respect and love for each other and boundaries of culture and nation fall away into a unity that binds.

As the news continues to uncover ever more complex and bloody human experiences within and without national boundaries, the Olympic Spirit is akin to the global quest for democracy and human rights. As noted, the absence of peace prevents the fulfillment of our individual and collective potential. The success of the Olympics in doing just that is a harbinger of hope that the world can apply the Golden Rule toward a new model of just governance.

Celebrate Others and They Will Celebrate You:
The Golden Rule as the Moral Drive of Recreation

The entertainment quality of recreational sports is a social occupation that diverts the mind from volatile issues such as politics to more manageable competition of games. The pleasure and camaraderie of team sports such as football and soccer or individual sports such as gymnastics and downhill skiing afford participants and spectators a moment of pleasant diversion. Players are heralded and encouraged. There is emotional attachment for favorite teams.

The celebration of the game is a reciprocal rite that is part of every society and culture. Evidence of games has been found in Egypt from over five centuries ago. A game board from the Royal Game of Ur, played in Iraq around 2600 BCE, still provides the basis for those playing it today. Some games are purely for fun and relaxation and others provide an educational aspect, but all games contribute to our culture.

Games are structured with rules and goals that provide a means of challenge and interaction with other game players. The typical game pits all the players against each other where only one can win. Sometimes games provide an extra complexity where all the players can lose. Still others include all-against-one and traitor games, where a hidden conspirator provides an impediment to cooperative play.

Partnership games establish rules for alliances and teamwork. Players can be penalized or lose the game if they do not respect partner opportunities and work as a team. Many corporations use partnership games for team-building. Role-playing games are particularly useful in getting team members to put themselves in others' places.

The video industry has tapped into cooperative gameplay to increase profits. Co-op games encourage players to work together as teammates. Simultaneous play allows providing assistance to other teammates and receiving help in the form of healing, tools, or information. Cooperation usually increases the chances of winning, and the level of difficulty is increased as more players are added to the game.

A new industry of peace games has nonviolence at its core. The role-playing aspect of Peacegames, for instance, puts players in conflict situations. One player is put in the role of mediator and helps the parties find their way to agreement without the use of violence. The World Consensus Game is another game based in nonviolence. Players use maps of viewpoints and learn of different philosophies used to approach a conflict. Expressing agreement or disagreement, players then put their comments on the table and try to find consensus.

These cooperative games have little or no competition between the players. By finding agreement and reaching their mutual objectives, the players win the game. With no agreement, no teamwork, or no consensus, the players lose.

The Mathematics of Recreational Nonviolence

Cooperative behavior, according to game theory, can be taught, even subliminally enforced, by cooperative gaming. When players use a consensus building process, the coordination and teamwork involved may be translated to real-life situations. Mathematics has been used to express cooperative gaming, yet the same mathematics is applicable to everyday life.

In the simplest form of cooperative gaming, a value is given for a grand coalition or team (N). Within the rules, the team has a function, which the team must perform in order to receive a payoff (R). The mathematic formula for a cooperative game is as follows. V represents the value of the process or the benefit from working in a coalition.

$$v : 2^N \longrightarrow R$$

The players form a grand coalition from all possible coalitions. The amount of the payoff is based on how the coalition matches the criteria of the challenge. This is often called a profit game, or value game.

Another form of cooperative game is defined as a cost function. In this type of game, where players begin with a set value, the play is represented as a cost of constructing a useful coalition in order to win the game. In some games, the cost of not forming a coalition is larger than the cost of forming a team to achieve the goal.

The mathematics of nonviolent recreational gaming is an apt metaphor for how we can create a just society. Cooperation and teamwork are evident when we achieve our greatest accomplishments. The Olympic Spirit and the U.N. Office of Sports for Development and Peace exemplify the opportunity that fair play and participation offer to the human drive for justice. Around the world, sports and other recreations represents the celebratory teamwork required to create the playing field of freedom necessary for a healthy economy and just governance.

Chapter 18

Case Law and Precedent

Precedent grounds us. It provides the content and history of stabilized society. Through hundreds, even thousands of years of judicial rulings, precedent gives authority to current law and provides the basis for governments built on rule of law. The body of precedent provides insight into the difficulties of human relations and the resolution of human disputes. From legal precedent flows the positive evolution of human history in the context of how peace was and is being created.

The Golden Mean and Golden Rule ethic are both at the core of legal precedent. Whether a law *on the books* is upheld, modified, or overturned depends on the sustainability of the justness in its ruling. According to the Golden Mean ethic, does it achieve balance? Is it too harsh or too lenient?

In this new era of the rising Golden Rule ethic, precedent provides a comparison. Does the law meet the standards of fairness developed over time? Does it meet the criteria of empathic justice, "There, but for the grace of God, go I?"

Common law is the body of precedent based on case law established by decisions of the courts. The other type of law, statutory law, is composed of the codified laws established by legislatures or parliaments. Together common law and statutory law have provided the firm foundation for a society based on rule of law. Common law and statutory law provide the means for us to live in relative calm as well as establishing guidelines for our future actions. When a law is just, society benefits. When laws are unjust, our judicial systems work to modify the law. Laws are changed based on new information or changing conditions.

Rulings relating to contracts, both implicit and explicit, or unwritten and written, provide precedent for how judges will consider new cases. As defined by *Black's Law Dictionary,* precedent is a "rule of law established for the first time by a court for a particular type of case and thereafter referred to in deciding similar cases."[1] The principle of *stare decisis* is "to stand by decisions and not disturb the undisturbed."

A court is obliged to generally keep precedent in place unless new information or circumstances require a change. Legal rulings established in past cases are binding on citizens until they are modified.

Case law can be cited as precedent by judges making new interpretations of law. Statutory laws or administrative rules, as the body of written laws established by a legislature or executive, do not create precedent. Yet the courts have flexibility in considering how statutory and administrative laws are to be interpreted during new cases, which allows for flexibility in rulings. There is great wisdom in this. With statutory and administrative laws, the law can change arbitrarily depending on who has the power to make the law.

To keep up with a future economy based on increasing innovation as the driver of prosperity, the legal system must have increasing flexibility. In a relational economy, current laws will need to evolve to reflect changing circumstances. Explicit and implicit contractual cases brought before the global/local courts system will increasingly necessitate interpretation and modification of the old laws as well as the creation of new laws to free the economy from constrictions.

The Golden Rule process of empathy provides the first step toward the reciprocity required to achieve justice. For justice to reign in society, it is imperative that judges approach each case with an understanding of how the outcome will affect the disputants. That entails experiencing their feelings, thoughts, and attitudes, which is usually considered anathema in courts of blind justice. Yet global consciousness is in a sense looking at the world as a mirror of one's self. Until what is good for the other is considered just as important as what is good for ourselves, the laws of society will continue to be rife with inequality and inequity. Empathy activates case law as the stabilizing and flexible foundation for just governance.

Core Problem

Anyone who has been caught in today's justice system understands that the power of those who make the laws can quickly impact our lives in very positive or negative ways. In our current legal system, statutory and administrative laws are mired in politics and are difficult to change. Our statutory legal system is institutional rather than relational. The legislative and executive bodies of nation-states generate and often dictate laws reflecting the interests of the most powerful institutional sectors in each society.

In most nations, the judiciary, under the tenet of strict separation of powers, is not tasked with making laws but rather interpreting and applying law to the facts and circumstances of the case before it makes a ruling. Laws are deemed constitutional or unconstitutional based on the judicial inter- pretation. Under articles of federal and state constitutions, the judiciary sim- ply serves as a check on the executive and legislative branches and can change laws only by negation, through the process of judicial review.

Without the ability to make rulings and create new laws on a case-by- case basis, the judicial system has little authority to change statutory laws. This inflexibility and restraint is little prepared to ensure a dynamic economic system that can thrive under natural innovation.

Background

A common law court system currently has three levels of courts: trial courts, appeals courts, and a supreme court. Precedent is binding for the lower, or inferior, courts when rulings are made by a higher court. Case law made by other courts of the same level, such as trial court to trial court, is binding only on the basis of respect.

The principle of *stare decisis* is the principle that courts are to respect and apply the law but endeavor to "not disturb" single rulings of previous courts. The principle of *jurisprudence constante,* which is similar to *stare deci- sis,* recognizes past practice and gives strong credence to any series of deci- sions where consistent application of precedent applies to current cases before the court. These two principles establish precedent as the firm basis for case law.

In systems where civil law does not consider *stare decisis* as a fixture, such as in France, judges may only reference precedent. Courts are then only interpreting the laws made by the legislature. Therefore *how* the law is written takes primary concern rather than the *what* of prior rulings of the court.

The advantage of binding precedent puts a degree of certainty in the system by saving time and allowing the courts to understand the laws they can change and those they cannot. Another advantage of binding precedent is that it provides society with certainty, consistency and continuity in the conduct of its affairs, thus providing stability and order to society at large. Disadvantages of the binding system of precedent are rigidity and complexity. It is difficult to change or modify laws. Reform of laws is expensive and time- consuming.

The word *jurisprudence* is based on the Latin roots for *law* and *prudence.*

As the study and theory of law, jurisprudence has a long history that involves scholars and legal theorists who have grappled with understanding the nature and reasoning of law as well as societal systems and institutions. In the Vedic tradition of ancient India, writings on law took the form of poems, or *Manu Smrti*. Called Dharma in Hindi, these laws were social norms and outlined the obligations and rituals of good personal and societal behavior. Around the same time, Aristotle wrote in the *Nicomachean Ethics* and other books of a natural law, which for him was a moral view rather than a system of law. His ideas on natural justice involved the Golden Mean, which was a description of moral virtue. Justice became a balance between opposing vices.

To answer the question of what a just act would be, the consideration of justice took two forms. *General justice* involved a completely virtuous act. *Particular justice* involved treating others ethically, in essence the beginning of the Golden Rule ethic applied to legal cases. Laws, as such, were grounded in morality until Roman jurisprudence began to distinguish civil law from natural law. Whereas traditional law as given "father to son" through oral teachings of customs, the new civil law was based on *edicts,* or annual pronouncements of punishable offenses. An *iudex,* Latin for law or judge, would provide a remedy based on specific facts in the case.

As legal systems and interpretation became an academic study, schools of thought developed. Judges aligned with the Sabinian school, named after consul Caelius Sabinus, tended toward strict interpretation of Roman law. The Proculians, named after the jurist Proculus, preferred greater latitude in their rulings. The culmination of Roman legal history came with the Justinian *Corpus Juris Civilis*, and the codification of law became the cornerstone for jurisprudence. In Roman times, the sentences of judicial authorities became the subjects of wide debate. The pronouncements, once codified and documented, could be interpreted and considered in view of changing conditions. The idea of *Evolutive Institutionea,* or legal concepts, enabled law to escape the realm of habit and enter the dynamic and more equitable age of interpretation.

In more modern times, schools of thought regarding law focused on basic questions. First was the practical question: What is law? Second was the moral question: What should law be? Analytic jurisprudence holds that the clarification of laws is a continuing process. Within the analytics of legal theory, the Positivist view contends that a law is *posited*, or made valid, by social rules made by society in any one time and place. Laws enforce our sensibilities of justice and morality. Whether they succeed in providing a just society is a separate question from validity. Yet analysis, according to the positivists, is not for the average citizen. Laws are duly enacted by authorities and must be obeyed.

Constructivist theory, especially in the writings of Ronald Dworkin, holds a middle path between natural law and positivist theory. The Scottish philosopher David Hume in *A Treatise of Human Nature* held that pure logic prevents us from determining that what *is* actually is what should be. Therefore we need to analyze and clarify rather than assume there is a norm. As jurisprudence evolved, laws began to be differentiated by the way they were enacted. While civil law hails back to the Roman legal system, common law is primarily based on English judicial history. Sometimes referred to as unwritten law, common law is composed of rules by custom or by court decisions, which became case law. New case law has the same force as the current legislative statutes or executive actions. In history, some judicial systems have been restrained by legislative or executive actions. For instance, in the Napoleonic code, the judiciary was prevented from pronouncing general laws.

Today, with change happening so quickly, society is struggling to be relieved of constraints in the antiquated systems of government. The historical limit on the court's ability to modify case law, within the reality of the legislative and executive branches' inability to resist powerful influences, is causing much of the pressure.

Solution

To ensure a dynamic economic system, the judicial system must have the authority to modify laws so that innovation can be released from unnecessary legacy restraints. Statutory laws, or those made by the executive or legislative bodies, are difficult to change and mired in the politics of the Golden Mean. For a relational economy to thrive, the judicial system must be able to change laws as needed without the delay and power politics of changing statutes. The judiciary, with its task of ensuring equal justice, is best suited for grappling with the evolution of law in the coming relational economy.

The evolution from the Golden Mean to the Golden Rule entails institutionalizing the principle of reciprocity as expressed in the processes of empathy, compassion, engagement, and unity. Empathy provides the foundational basis for changing the case law of our blind justice era into the equal justice needed for the next expression of our legal history. "Do as you would be done by," wrote Bishop William in his 1679 book, *The Comprehensive Rule of Righteousness*. "The Royal Law [ed. later called the Golden Rule], lastly, say others," William wrote, "because of its latitude and extent, upon which all other Laws depend, which takes in and comprehends all other Laws itself."[2]

The overarching judicial maxim of the Golden Rule has always been fundamental to just laws. A judicial governance system, with the stability of the extensive body of historical case law, would be enabled to hear cases and modify, if needed, any law to reflect changing circumstances. "All human laws are, properly speaking," said Edmund Burke, "only declaratory; they have no power over the substance of original justice."[3]

A global judiciary system of governance reflective of the current federal and state/provincial model would create a progressively just and equalizing means to settle contract and other disputes. Case law, along with the statutory law already on the books, provides the basis for court actions in both criminal and civil disputes. With evolving authority in a judicial governance system, the courts could not only consider the *balance of justice* approach but also the essential basis of justice as the quality of being just—as in righteousness, equitableness, or moral rightness—to uphold the justice of a cause.

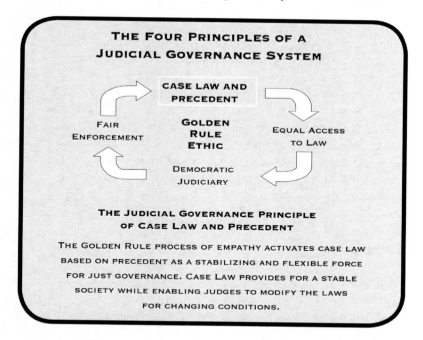

THE FOUR PRINCIPLES OF A
JUDICIAL GOVERNANCE SYSTEM

CASE LAW AND PRECEDENT

FAIR ENFORCEMENT

GOLDEN RULE ETHIC

EQUAL ACCESS TO LAW

DEMOCRATIC JUDICIARY

THE JUDICIAL GOVERNANCE PRINCIPLE
OF CASE LAW AND PRECEDENT

THE GOLDEN RULE PROCESS OF EMPATHY ACTIVATES CASE LAW BASED ON PRECEDENT AS A STABILIZING AND FLEXIBLE FORCE FOR JUST GOVERNANCE. CASE LAW PROVIDES FOR A STABLE SOCIETY WHILE ENABLING JUDGES TO MODIFY THE LAWS FOR CHANGING CONDITIONS.

For a judicial governance system to function, courts would be given more latitude in making rulings based on precedent and changing circumstance. Some statutory barriers to the court's authority would be modified over time. As consensus grows in recognition of the practicality of judicial governance in relation to a thriving economic system, the courts' ability to establish equitable principles in cases of obsolete statutes would be expanded.

To assure consensus of citizens, a more democratic election process would be implemented to maintain the integrity of the court.

A hierarchical system of local, regional, and global courts, staffed by judges and persons trained in alternative conflict resolution, would provide paths toward solutions in all aspects of disputed human relations. With a system of separation of power, as expressed in courts of appeals and various private and public commissions, additional options for redress would provide for reaching transformational resolution or the striking down of unjust rulings.

A governing system based on precedent also allows the legal principle of equity law, which enables judges to "mitigate the rigors of common law." Equipped with this flexibility, those in a position to judge are given flexibility to consider the equities of each situation, thus liberating them from the application of strict laws that otherwise compel an unjust or harsh result. Such is the nature of Golden Rule justice in that self-correction allows for changing circumstance.

The slow transfer of practical authority from the executive and legislative bodies to the judiciary is already happening. Necessity is causing most of the change, but additional methods to facilitate the transition are contributing factors. A school of legal philosophy called Legal Realism has challenged the assumption that the current legal system is sacrosanct. With increased transparency, not only the failures of the judicial system have become more apparent, but also the inherent agenda-driven nature of the amoral legislative and executive branches. A judicial governance system is adapting to this reality, and the Golden Rule is in waiting to elevate equal justice beyond the fair and blind justice limitations of historical jurisprudence.

Prototypes

The evolution to a judicial governance system can be seen in many global institutions as well as individual rulings of courts with local or regional jurisdiction. History also provides many precedents where nations have understood that the needs and interests of localities must be protected by the consensus values and rules of international justice.

- International Trade Laws for rules and customs of trade between countries
- World Trade Organization (WTO) providing a framework for negotiating trade agreements

- World Court, or International Court of Justice, the judicial branch of the United Nations
- International Copyright Laws, or intellectual property laws for intangible property such as music and literary works
- General Agreements on Tariffs and Trade regulating international trade established in 1947 and updated in 1994
- Doah Development Round with an agenda for lowering trade barriers through the WTO
- Group of Twenty (G20+) meetings of global finance ministers and central bank governors
- Admiralty law for marine commerce, navigation, and salvaging
- Aviation law for flight and air travel
- Labor law for regulation of issues between workers, employers, and trade unions
- Commercial law, or business law, for issues of commerce
- Private Law involving interactions between citizens
- Collaborative Law as a legal process to resolve conflict without the need for trial
- Integrative Law as holistic processes of transformation conflict resolution

Result

In a judicial governance system based on evolving case law, societal laws will be able to meet new circumstances based on continuous rulings of the judiciary. Instead of fixed coded laws and decrees by legislatures and executives, case law provides the judiciary with a stable yet flexible body of laws to achieve the society goal of justice for all. By considering the guidelines of precedent as well as new facts, judges would create new case law to facilitate economic and social activity as well as limit the accumulation of power.

As communication and interdependence increase, the need for a global judiciary will become more important. The inherent nature of the judiciary as a self-evolving structure of justice will continue to transform the mechanisms of global institutions. The Golden Rule as the ethic of jurisprudence is uniquely capable of providing guidance for a just global governance system. Judges must endeavor to understand their own emotions in experiencing what the parties in the case are experiencing in order to rule based on an empathic code. The legal system has evolved from the Draconian law of the seventh century BCE to the *Codex Justinianus* of balanced justice during the reign of the Caesars. Now the court system can fully embrace the insight provided by Golden Rule jurisprudence to achieve the dream of equal justice for all.

Challenges

Why should judges use empathy to achieve justice? Fundamental to justice is equality and fairness. To determine what is fair for individuals is difficult when the courts are not free to consider moral implications in a case. Rather, the current system simply strives for a balance between the parties in order to achieve blind justice. Historically, decisions that took into account the feelings and thoughts of the parties were considered arbitrary. As the global consciousness emerges, there is a rising demand for the morality of equal justice. When case law is relieved from undue restrictions, judges will be able to redefine just rulings as an imperative of the Golden Rule process of empathy on the moral foundation of mutual exchange.

Another challenge would arise when the lawmaking power of the executive and legislative branches become less important. Can the judiciary handle the rise in caseload? Currently the number of cases coming before justices all over the world is rising due, among other circumstances, to the advent of a relational economy based on innovation. Courts are finding alternative forms of dispute resolution to handle the workload, including professional conflict analysis and resolution support structures. Methods of collaborative law include mediation, arbitration, negotiation, diplomacy, counseling, and other dispute resolution and transformation processes.

Chapter 19

Case Study—
The Civic Sector

*The High Line and
the Freedom to Share*

How would a judicial governance system revitalize our communities? Just as in honoring the body of laws we call precedent, we weigh what our communities already have. We consider the blessings of the past and ponder our common heritage. With that deeper understanding, we find ways to leverage the glories of our heritage as well as current realities for the benefit of the future. In the process of creating a Golden Rule society, all stakeholders in a community must be considered. Only by making a better community for all can we ensure a better community for ourselves.

The old High Line elevated rail track on the West Side of New York is a case in point. Today, New Yorkers and tourists walk high above the street, surrounded by a beautiful natural environment, a panorama of the city within eyes' reach. People go for walks and runs, meet friends, and look over the railings at signs of neighborhood improvement. The blight of the past has been turned into a model civic project that is being emulated the world over.

It is an extraordinary story of how community activism, combined with a collaborative spirit and the legal rights of the commons, turned adversity into civic pride. Little more than a decade ago, houses and businesses shriveled under an eyesore of rusted steel beams and unkempt weeds. Mile after mile of the commons of New York's skyline had become a spindly girder-barred prison holding for ransom the potential beauty of urban living.

The High Line railroad line began as an amazing testament to technology in the 1930s. Much as the contemporary version, it was a harbinger of a way to improve New York's increasingly crowded and decaying neighborhoods.

Since 1847, the railroads had been at street level. A proposal to erect steel structures to elevate railroad freight cars into the air above the businesses and neighborhoods along 10th Avenue resulted in the High Line.

In 1929, the New York Central Railroad, with funding from the city and state, opened the elevated line, which removed 105 street crossings. All was well until the 1950s, when railroad traffic decreased. The rail line was finally shut down, the last train running in 1980. Left over was a rusty, blighted, thirteen-mile steel scaffolding, an eyesore and liability for the neighborhoods to try to ignore.

Or was the abandoned High Line actually a community asset? Should residents rally forces to demolish the remnants of another time, or should they preserve their heritage? Enter the Friends of the High Line, a grassroots effort founded by residents Joshua David and Robert Hammond to repurpose the railway.

The idea of a public access park hails back to the common land, or *the commons,* where villagers had the right to share pastures for grazing sheep or simply enjoying the view. The interest in New York's West Side's common railway began to gain momentum with a study that determined the potential tax revenue generated by the increases in commercial and residential value would more than offset the cost of creating the public park.

In 2002, the city offered the High Line plan its support by brokering the donation of the elevated structure by the CSX Transportation Company. A consortium of landscape artists, community activists, lawyers, and city officials created one of the most beautiful urban parks in the world. The first section opened in 2009, the second in 2011, and the third and final section— High Line at the Rail Yards—is set to open by the end of 2014. New Yorkers have reaped the benefits ever since.

Support Others and They Will Support You: The Golden Rule as the Moral Drive of Society

The civic sector of a peace economy is about building strong communities. It is people working with people. The peace we create in our neighborhoods and towns is an expression of how we handle the close-quarter associations with our neighbors. Violence comes from not considering all parties; peace comes from collaboration and consensus.

Citizenship comprises all the duties required in our association with others. It entails respecting rights due the individual and group, as well as the privileges gained from actions in support of the community. Civic duty

The High Line is a beautiful example of grassroots and civic collaboration, which reenvisioned a section of the former New York Central Railroad as a community park (Friends of the High Line).

was a part of life from the beginning of civilization. The tribal system of pre-history is sketchy, but the fact that *homo sapiens* survived as a species when others did not attests to our ability to work together.

Innovation by our ancestors brought us through darkness into light and through fear into courage. Huddling family units turned into tribal organizations. Tribes soon began to merge into more sophisticated models, the apogee, according to our current history books, being the kingdom. With centralization came power and with power came manipulation. History moved from the story of innovation to the story of consolidation of power and the wars that resulted from competition for power.

In return for power, chiefs and kings were burdened with a social contract. The masses would pay homage; the leaders would keep them safe and prosperous. The courts of kings became centers of pomp and circumstance. As more sophisticated models of tribal organization developed, the need for court functionaries became greater. A new class of people designated to solve the problems of community organized into organs of state, or bureaus. These bureaucrats rose to positions that became hereditary. Aristocrats and oligarchies developed. Land was accumulated, wealth entrenched.

The rise of the civil bodies of government was a leveling of the aristocratic urge by the advent of democracy. The fall of divine right of kings let power fall into the hands of the nobles, who lost a majority of that power to the rise of the common people. Instead of serving kings and nobles, those who chose a life of service gave fealty to the community. They felt a calling to civic duty.

However, working for today's democratic governments does not necessarily bring a sense of accomplishment or great respect. Bureaucracy, for many, is out of touch with the needs of those it serves. In some quarters, government is seen as part of the problem. Balancing the main responsibility of government—that of keeping order—with the drive to achieve prosperity has given rise to many government programs that benefit only a few. The drive toward a military-industrial complex, which U.S. president Dwight D. Eisenhower warned about in his final speech to the American nation, can militarize a nation, lead to war, and create a boon to arms suppliers.

Some grand government programs lead to sustained economic prosperity that benefit the many. Under common law and, in some cases, statutory law, the state can take the land for common purpose but has the obligation to compensate the rightful owner. The legal concept of eminent domain, or appropriation of private land for use by the commons, goes back thousands of years. The term was first used in 1625 in a treatise by the Dutch jurist Hugo Grotius. Property, he maintained, can be appropriated by the state for use "in the case of extreme necessity" because there is a public right that supersedes individual rights.

The Golden Rule, of course, would ensure that justice is done. "I would have no one touch my property," said Plato in *Laws*, "if I can help it, or disturb it in the slightest way without some kind of consent on my part; if I am a man of reason, I must treat the property of others in the same way."[1]

The balance between societal rights and individual rights has always been in contention. While Eisenhower, for instance, cautioned about the rising military-industrial complex, he promoted a grand scheme through appropriation of land for the common good. At a cost of $425 billion, Eisenhower threw the weight of the presidency behind the U.S. Federal Highway System. It ranks as one of the most expensive civic projects in history.

The extensive network of freeways, highways, and expressways creates an efficient grid across the United States for two main purposes: commercial traffic and national defense. The seed of the idea for a national highway system goes back to the 1920s, when the U.S. Bureau of Public Roads created the Persing Map. A list of roads that were considered important for national defense, this map became the skeleton structure for the state highway system. In the late 1930s, President Roosevelt delivered a hand-drawn map of a national highway grid to the Bureau of Public Roads. This vision of eight superhighway corridors became know as the interstate highway system.

The National Highway System is one of the major legacies of the Eisenhower presidency. It was important to General Eisenhower not only in terms of enabling troop transport, but also in response to changing economic factors in post-war America. In the 1950s, the post-war economy in the United States was expanding. Manufacturing and consumption had increased, and the need for easier methods of distribution was rising.

When General Eisenhower became President Eisenhower, the quandary of an expanding economy gave an opportunity not only to set the U.S. on a future of prosperity but also to address the need for domestic security in transporting military troops and supplies in an emergency. Eisenhower was an adherent since he had driven the Lincoln Highway across America in a 1919 army convoy. He had also seen the German Autobahn after the Allies defeated the Nazis and understood the necessity for national defense.

Given a major boost and help in planning by General Motors chief Charles Erwin Wilson, the Federal-Aid Highway Act became law in 1956. The huge public works program was not complete for thirty-five years. Beyond the original plan, today the highway system now reaches nearly 50,000 miles.

The Civility of Peace

These examples of how people have changed the world through innovative approaches to the commons gives us great pride in humanity. Yet as our population, weapons, and impact on the environment create the potential for great destruction, we are moving toward a more flexible approach to government, economics, and community.

The commons is being revived as a thoughtful and rational approach to mutual problems. Our current focus on sustainability needs to be broadened toward resiliency. As our environment changes at breakneck speed, as the stresses on our families and cities increase, we need to respond with greater prescience for what the future brings.

Resilience thinking is becoming an integral part of urban and rural planners. Our reactionary response to natural disasters is, in itself, becoming a disaster. We build higher walls after the storm. We update our electric grid after the blackout. To get ahead of such challenges is now, more than ever, critical to preserving the peace. We are developing new infrastructures to combat potential disasters. We are borrowing from NASA's technology, the military's logistics, and Silicon Valley's ability to create open systems and achieve the exponential improvements of Moore's Law.

Resilience planning "doesn't propose a single, fixed future," wrote Andrew Zolli in the *New York Times*. "It assumes we don't know exactly how things will unfold, that we'll be surprised, that we'll make mistakes along the way."[2]

Communities are coming together in response to current and potential challenges. This commonality has brought the Golden Rule to the forefront of how we approach the world. Schools, security forces, and infrastructure professionals are beginning to see that resiliency, even beyond sustainability, is a human characteristic that can be the savior of our cities and rural communities.

"Unfortunately, the sustainability movement's politics," said Zolli, "not to mention its marketing, have led to a popular misunderstanding: that a perfect, stasis-under-glass equilibrium is achievable. But the world doesn't work that way: it exists in a constant disequilibrium—trying, failing, adapting, learning and evolving in endless cycles."[3]

The communities that have been devastated by disasters have come together and are now preparing for an unknown future. We are developing a Golden Rule civic pride that goes beyond accomplishment toward unity in the commons. Pride may be one of the notorious seven deadly sins, but it harks back to a deep connection to place. We are of the ground where we are born. To be disconnected from our birthplaces results in feelings of dismemberment. We need these connections and the precedent they create to feel peace. Our deep-seated civic duty, our responsibility, is to keep connected with our neighbors, our environment, and our communities in addition to the love we feel for our family and friends. The more distant we become from our roots, the more our primitive fears come to control our decisions. Our duty to civility arises out of the deep desire to ensure our spaces for peace.

Chapter 20

Equal Access to the Law

The Golden Rule's inherent human right for equal access to the law is both subtle and profound. Most accept the concept that no one is above the law. It has been the societal justification for deposing kings and bringing down notorious criminals and corrupt politicians. Yet little attention is paid to the idea that no one is below the law, either. Justice, according to exquisite beauty of reciprocal exchange, must be achieved for the least powerful among us.

The Golden Rule processes of empathy and compassion activate our desire and need to allow our fellow humans equal access to justice. The comparative process used to achieve empathy causes each of our actions to be subject to review. We realize our actions have repercussions, positive and negative, for one's self and the whole of society. According to physics, two waves on the same wavelength combine to increase energy. When two waves of counter frequencies combine, they can destroy themselves. As all the great religions of the world tell us—whether as a karmic experience or as the humble rewards of faith—the consequences of our actions come full-circle.

The Golden Rule also teaches us that laws, as far as humanly possible, should be flexible enough to allow for compassionate implementation. Compassion follows empathy with a strong desire to help the misfortunes of the other. Compassion activates the desire to achieve justice. When laws are just, they stand the test of compassion. When they are unjust or obsolete, there must be more flexible processes to invalidate or change laws based on consideration of the *other* within changing circumstances. The great challenge of humankind is devising a legal system that works for everyone, the poor and rich, man and woman, people of different faiths and persuasions: Everyone must have equal access to the law.

To be the recipient of just actions is the human moral right at the base of Golden Rule justice, as defined by the concept of *moral rightness*. In most societies, laws created by the legislative and executive branches are in some measure subject to review by the third branch of government. It is the duty of the judiciary to annul acts of legislators and executives when a law conflicts with a higher authority, such as a constitution.

This powerful authority of the judiciary hails back to the ancient concept of branches of government. Separation of powers—with its modern expression of executive, legislative, and judicial—was an ancient concept honed by the French Enlightenment philosopher Baron de Montesquieu. Since then, most modern constitutions have provided for distinct branches of government, each with distinct powers that can be used to equalize their power and authority.

Over time and in different societies, the power has shifted from one branch to the other and back again. The concept of branch supremacy holds that no branch should have more power than the others and that they each perform checks and balance on the other two branches. Legislative supremacy is when the legislative branch is the most powerful. Supremacy of the executive branch is when the chief executive holds most of the cards.

When a power shift results in a circumstance where the judicial branch is the most powerful, it incites great emotions in both the left and the right political ideologies. When a supreme court has the last word on important issues such as abortion, election results, or political contributions, the judicial nomination process becomes mired in politics.

The debate on which branch has the most power is not new in any society. In the United States, it goes back to the first decades under the Constitution, in particular to the 1790s, when two American icons, both believing in democracy, clashed against the allocation of power. The New Yorker Alexander Hamilton is considered the father of the Federalist Party, which wanted more centralization and power in the hands of the central government. Washington and Adams, the first two presidents, were more or less of the Federalist persuasion.

When news of the chaotic French Revolution came across the Atlantic Ocean, Hamilton and his allies became concerned that the power of the people in the United States could result in revolution and dissolution of the national government. Congress, at the Federalists' urging, passed the Sedition Act of 1798, which made criticism of the government a crime.

Virginian Thomas Jefferson, who had formed the alternate party, the Democratic-Republican Party, was committed to limiting the power of government. Jefferson and his allies won the presidency in 1800. They strongly opposed the Sedition Act on constitutional grounds and, soon, the lower courts began annulling the sedition statutes.

The Hamiltonians contended that only the Supreme Court could consider constitutional issues, and the debate was elevated to the highest court. In 1803, Chief Justice John Marshall wrote the decision on Marbury v. Madison, which settled the issue. The Sedition Act was ruled unconstitutional. In that landmark decision, Marshall specifically referenced the Constitution. Establishing the right of the court to judicial review of statutory laws elevated the judiciary to equal status with the legislative and executive. Courts could and should reference the Constitution in their decisions, Marshall maintained. In doing so, the Constitution, with the Bill of Rights, in effect the people's power, became the highest authority and the final arbiter of laws.

As Jefferson wrote, all branches of government are "equally independent in the sphere assigned to them" by the Constitution. The debate has gone on ever since as one branch gains temporary power over the other. Yet the system of checks and balances and "rule by exception" has kept the people in relative control of government. To elevate the law from exception to active compassion by way of equal access would require less control of people as consent confirms the social contract of Rousseau.

Core Problem

On a macro level, the ability of democratic governments to adapt to economic innovation is plagued by antiquated laws and institutions that are difficult to change. Montesquieu's concept of separation of powers at the foundation of contemporary democracies has ensured a reasonable balance. Yet that same separation has now become a polarizing influence that slows, even stops progress.

On a micro, societal level, when someone believes he suffers under an obsolete law, he has few avenues for relief. "Law and order exist for the purpose of establishing justice," said Martin Luther King, Jr. "and when they fail in this purpose they become the dangerously structured dams that block the flow of social progress."[1]

To change an obsolete law through the legislative branch is bureaucratic in nature, requiring great deliberation and the influence of political contributions. Executive orders have little accountability, and those who would object are routinely routed to ombudsman and suggestion boxes. The institutional reliance on the legislative and executive branches makes the legal environment static and limits the ability of the economy to adapt to innovations.

Indeed, the two branches generally considered to be the law-making branches are subject to political manipulation and limited in their power to view rules and regulations in the pure context of changing circumstances. However, the third branch of government, the judiciary, is the one institution of government where laws can be adapted relatively quickly and with reasoned deliberation. Though the judiciary is flawed in practice and by structural problems, such as inconsistency of election procedures and potential for corruption, its very nature provides the basis for equal access to justice by all citizens.

Background

The court systems of the nations of the world vary widely, yet at the core of their existence is the human endeavor toward justice. When the United States Constitution was written, separation of powers became a cornerstone of democracy with its emphasis on balance of power. Separating the executive, legislative, and judicial branches of government prevents, in theory, any one branch from dominating another. The checks and balances defined by the Constitution were instituted to prevent tyranny by any one branch.

Whereas the legislative branch is mainly concerned with passing bills, and the executive branch with carrying out the law, the judiciary has the responsibility for reviewing the constitutionality and just application of laws. The court system is mainly tasked with interpreting laws and making rulings in search of justice. In some circumstances the courts have the ability to make laws but are limited in their responsibilities to specific situations and types of law.

The powers of the judiciary to review legislative and executive actions are based on constitutional provisions, precedent, and tradition. Under the strong leadership of Marshall in the early 1800s, the court firmly established the principle that if laws violated the Constitution, they could be disregarded. The Marshall court established precedent that federal law trumped state law. When a case is brought to the court, the judges must rule on the legitimacy of the law in terms of higher authority and can rule a law unconstitutional.

The doctrine of judicial review is based on several basic tenets of democracy, in one form or another. One aspect, as we have considered, is separation of powers. Another aspect is the differences between the systems of civil and common law in terms of review powers. An appeal is the process that citizens use to challenge a decision of the judiciary. The court addresses an appeal by reviewing the cases on the record to determine if the law has been correctly applied.

Civil law is the body of legislated written statutes that apply to private rights and disputes between individuals, businesses, and other organizations. Common law is the body of law consisting of previous court decisions, which judges are obliged to use as a guide to rulings on new cases. Both systems, with a few exceptions, use the same appellate courts, or appeals courts, which review previous cases based on an appeal of a court ruling by the parties concerned.

The purpose of the appeals court system in general, of course, is to correct decisions made in error by a lower court. In a court of appeal, judges review findings of the facts for sufficiency in a case as well as the conclusions of law for correct legal interpretation and application. A change in a lower court ruling can be made in the event that the law was misapplied, a jurisdiction was abridged, there was bias, judicial powers were abused, or additional evidence is found that rendered an incorrect ruling.

In most nations, there are three different levels of courts. The district court hears evidence in the case and renders a decision. If that decision is contested, an intermediate appellate court hears the case. If the contest continues, a final decision can be made by the Supreme Court, or court of last resort. Rules in these matters can vary by nation and state or province.

The intermediate appellate system comprises appeals courts, or circuit courts, within a federal court system. Lawyers write arguments, called briefs, and in many cases are allowed to present oral arguments before the judges. The district courts try cases within their districts, and citizens can appeal decisions to the higher federal court for that district. In the United States, there are also state appellate systems.

Due to the fact that there is only one Supreme Court for the federal government as well as the states, the caseload requires a determination by the justices of the cases the court will hear each year. Issues of public importance and impact are considered. In the United States, fewer than one hundred cases out of thousands appealed are actually heard at the federal level. Currently in the U.S., there are thirteen federal courts of appeal, including eleven geographical "numbered" courts, the Washington D.C. appeals court, and an appeals court with national jurisdiction. In addition to the structure of the three-tiered federal court system, there are specialized courts and tribunals such as those dealing with military court-martial cases, special trial cases, and trade disputes.

Decisions by the courts of appeals establish binding precedent. Each lower court in the district where a decision was made is bound and guided by their rulings. When a case comes before a court, the decision can be:

- affirmed where the reviewing court agrees with the lower court's ruling,
- reversed where the reviewing court disagrees and overturns the result of the lower court's ruling, or
- remanded where the case is sent back to the lower court.

Providing the structure and hierarchy of the appeals process, jurisdiction is the authority granted to a geographical area or to a court. Jurisdictional separation prevents the concentration of judicial responsibilities and separates the power between courts. It also allows for the establishment of courts with specialized expertise. The decisions of courts with limited jurisdiction are subject to oversight by courts with higher jurisdictions. If unsatisfied with the outcome in a lower appeals court, a citizen may take the case to higher courts of appeal until the highest court of appeal, or the Supreme Court.

Appeals are time-intensive, and citizens are usually allowed only one appeal in a particular level of court. In addition, the cost of trials has made access to justice virtually the domain of the wealthy. Though the right to a public defender and *pro bono* attorney options have helped mitigate the situation, inequities remain. There is a limited docket in each jurisdiction, and the paperwork involved, as well as the legal knowledge to navigate the courts, limits the ability of the average citizen to successfully mount a suit.

Solution

Justice based on application of the Golden Rule ethic is the moral right of everyone. If people are to be invested in their system of government, they need to know they have the same right to justice as others. Equal access to legal recourse is essential. The right to a fair trial and due process are cornerstones of ethical democracy. Without the basis of judicial morality, even alternative forms of dispute resolution such as arbitration and mediation, if reserved for the wealthy, are at best amoral, at worst immoral.

Application of the fundamental imperative of equality in the Golden Rule is paramount if the law is to benefit more than just the powerful and privileged. The Sixth Amendment to the U.S. Constitution ensures that citizens have particular rights during criminal prosecutions:

> In all criminal prosecutions, the accused shall enjoy the right to a speedy and public trial, by an impartial jury of the State and district wherein the crime shall have been committed, which district shall have been previously ascertained by law, and to be informed of the nature and cause of the accusation; to be confronted with the witnesses against him; to have compulsory process for obtaining witnesses in his favor, and to have the Assistance of Counsel for his defence.

The Fourteenth Amendment to the U.S. Constitution ensures due process and equal protection:

> No State shall make or enforce any law which shall abridge the privileges or immunities of citizens of the United States; nor shall any State deprive any person of life, liberty, or property, without due process of law; nor deny to any person within its jurisdiction the equal protection of the laws.

These rights and protections are just the beginning of the equality under the law necessary in a judicial governance system. Equal access to the law entails but is not limited to the following:

- Right to a fair, speedy, and transparent trial
- Right to impartial juries, judges, and mediators
- Right to counsel or self-representation
- Right to appeal
- Right to have laws that are fair
- Right to have laws equally applied

A relational economy requires a highly efficient judiciary with an appellate system designed for fast review of cases. For a relational economy to be healthy, a free flow of information and debate as well as adaptation to changing circumstances is essential. Debate on contemporary issues, with increasing frequency, is occurring in courts of law where naturally arising conflicts are considered rhetorically as well in the context of the issue at hand in order to find a creative and practical solution. Rulings provide the way forward by defining the processes and logistical realities that will ensure the evolution of law toward higher relevancy.

In a judicial governance system, much like today, justices at the lower levels would continue to agree to take cases and hear arguments from litigants as well as their representative attorneys. To relieve case load, the judges invoke methods of conflict resolution such as mediation and arbitration, which may be used before a dispute reaches trial. When it becomes necessary to involve the courts, relevant case rulings based on precedent would be duly considered in order to render a ruling in light of new circumstances.

In addition to standard court cases involving precedent as applied to disputes under civil and criminal law, justices in a judicial governance system would have the power to make new rulings, or laws, to facilitate, clarify, and arbitrate evolving economic and social conditions. The ability of the judiciary to create law, or provide equitable principles in a case, is currently reserved mainly for common law jurisdictions. This ability would also be extended to cases of civil jurisdictions involving statutory construction in order to allow for the evolution of historically legislated and administrated laws.

THE FOUR PRINCIPLES OF A
JUDICIAL GOVERNANCE SYSTEM

CASE LAW AND
PRECEDENT

GOLDEN
RULE
ETHIC

FAIR
ENFORCEMENT

EQUAL ACCESS
TO LAW

DEMOCRATIC
JUDICIARY

THE JUDICIAL GOVERNANCE PRINCIPLE
OF EQUAL ACCESS TO LAW

THE GOLDEN RULE PROCESS OF COMPASSION ACTIVATES EQUAL
ACCESS TO LAW AS A GUARANTEE OF THE SEPARATION OF POWER
REQUIRED FOR JUST GOVERNANCE. EQUAL ACCESS TO LAW WITH
A RIGHT TO FAIR TRIALS AND APPEAL ENSURES THAT NO PERSON
IS ABOVE OR BELOW THE LAW.

The right to appeal is institutionalized with historical precedent as an essential human right. The current system of judicial appeal elevates rulings to higher courts until the highest court makes a final ruling. New judicial theories for the structure of the courts will need to address overload and practical function of a judicial governance court system. Perhaps parallel supreme courts would institute another right of appeal or alternative dispute services would achieve greater legitimacy, with their agreements rising to the level of authority now reserved for trial courts. Only the future will tell of these necessary innovations. Yet new views and implementations of separation of powers are certainly needed as the court systems adapt to the rising call for equal access.

Indeed, with societies increasingly depending on their judiciaries for fast and definitive action, the court system has begun to burst at the seams. Instead of looking at the situation as a negative, we must see it as pointing to a future expansion of historical proportions. The rising interest in collaborative law is indicative of society's response to the increasing dependence on the judiciary as well as a trend toward greater understanding of the global consciousness. Collaborative law is a relational process whereby the parties in a dispute engage in a voluntary effort to address concerns, find common ground, and agree to a path forward.

Most familiar in divorce cases, the parties involved in a collaborative process work with lawyers or mediation specialists to find an agreement as a way to avoid the uncertainties of a trial. In most cases, a "participatory agreement" contract is signed by the parties to bind them to the collaborative process. Working together and with lawyers and other legal professionals, the parties endeavor to understand the concerns and rights of all stakeholders in the case and find creative and practical ways to reach compromise. Collaborative law is a formal process in many states, regulated under the 2009 Uniform Collaborative Law Rules/Act, which standardized its use as an alternative dispute resolution method approved by the courts.

In addition, the legal system of private trials has become important in some jurisdictions where the parties to a disagreement agree to have a *judge pro tempore,* usually a retired judge, listen and rule in a case. The trial is held in private. The briefings and deliberations are in confidence. An agreement to use a private trial is sometimes called a *stipulation* that is filed with the court. Verdicts in private trials can be appealed and be brought to trial in the case of a verdict considered unjust. Private trials, collaborative law, and other methods are part of the options available to citizens in a relational governance system that is overburdened because of the very success the judiciary has had in furthering its focus on equal justice.

Prototypes

Today's judicial systems vary from country to country, yet many of the basic rights of citizens to fair trials and appeals are expressed in current constitutions and practice. As the case load increases, global judicial systems will begin to rely on alternative ways to settle disputes.

- Sixth Amendment for rights related to criminal prosecutions
- Fourteenth Amendment for citizenship rights and equal protection under the law
- Judicial review by which executive and legislative actions are under review by the judiciary
- Appellate courts empowered to hear appeals of a trial or other court
- Criminal Cases Review Commissions in England, Wales, and Ireland for review of miscarriage of justice
- Alternative Dispute Resolution (ADR) processes and techniques for agreements short of litigation
- Settlement conferences as meetings between disputing parties to find agreement before trial

- Mediation typically with third party mediators as an ADR option
- Arbitration both binding and non-binding where parties defer to or are required by the court to have a third party settle the dispute
- Collaborative or cooperative law where couples in divorce situations avoid the uncertainties of court rulings
- Early neutral evaluation as a mediation technique to assess the strengths and weaknesses of the parties to a case and recommend resolution
- Family and group conferencing as a psychotherapy alternative that emphasizes relationships
- Mini-trials as an informal dispute resolution technique used by businesses and government
- Private trial judges and summary jury trials as time- and cost-saving alternatives
- Peer mediation, with the mediator having similar characteristics to the parties in dispute, such as age or environment
- Workplace mediation through human resources departments
- Mediator codes of conduct such as neutrality and avoiding conflicts of interest

Result

The evolution to a judicial governance system will affirm the right of equal access to the law, the right to a fair trial, and the right of appeal. The free flow of debate resulting from increased transparency and the ability of citizens to get their disputes reviewed will result in a continuous evolution of case law.

The justice system in a relational economic system would not only provide the judgment functions based on precedent but also review a law's pertinence to changing conditions and create new law in harmony with a thriving society. All of the tools of the court process, including attorney preparation of briefs and the use of discovery and evidence, would be used as they are today in determining a just ruling.

As the judiciary begins to use necessary powers to modify and create new laws based on specific court cases, a healthy economy will result. Equality in association, collaborative distribution, and fair rewards would be released from the constrictions of legislative and executive laws, which have intentions other than basic and practical compassion for individuals at risk and for society at large.

Challenges

Laws are complex. For there to be equal access to justice, the average person needs to have a basic understanding of laws and their rights under those laws. In addition, judges need to be current on changes in law.

As advances in the technology of search make information on laws and cases more accessible, the ability of citizens to understand and take action on legal matters will increase in quantity and quality. An essential part of the justice process is the free flow of information on cases and rulings. Without documentation, legal precedent would not be possible.

Currently, much like the *Congressional Record,* opinions and decisions of the judiciary are published in written and online databases. In the U.S., a private company, West Publishing, publishes decisions of the courts of appeals. In addition, online databases such as LexisNexis® or Westlaw® provide access to many case histories and studies. The courts also have websites with varying degrees of information.

More transparency and education will make the reasoning behind rulings available not only to judges and lawyers but also to concerned citizens. With better tools and information, access to justice will be increased, unnecessary lawsuits will be reduced, and the backload of cases will be reduced over time.

Chapter 21

Case Study—
The Wellness Sector

Intuitive Surgical Inc. and
the Freedom to Heal

Technological innovations in the medical field have far outpaced our ability to leverage their highest potential for the bulk of humanity. Even as lifespan increases in wealthy countries, large segments of the population still suffer from obesity, diabetes, depression, and the rising health issues of violence and abuse. People in developing countries suffer in the backwater of health technology, with malnutrition, hunger, and diseases such as HIV/AIDS taking a huge toll.

However, as the Golden Rule rises with global consciousness, the drive to extend quality health care to all people on earth has come to the forefront of the debate on national and international priorities. The needs are vast, the suffering bottomless. Providing medicines, potable water, and nutritious food has always been the objectives of foreign aid and nongovernmental groups. Yet organizations are now using technology and logistical innovations to target areas of greatest need. With more consideration for how medical care affects the wellness of human beings, many innovations now consider a matrix-of-life approach that connects the dots between one system and another.

A case in point is Intuitive Surgical of Sunnyvale, California. The company has rolled out several innovative robotic-assisted surgery systems that offer advanced 3D visualization and what it calls wristed instrumentation for a host of surgical procedures. With minimally invasive surgical techniques, patient hospital stays are shorter and blood transfusions and post-operative infections are reduced. While available globally, access to these innovations is still limited, though the vision is to have these lifesaving technologies eventually reach every human on earth.

Intuitive Surgical's products enable procedures that are unlike traditional open surgery, which is a more invasive approach. Post-surgery trauma, the effects on family, and the cost of extensive hospital stays all create complications that tip the balance of the Hippocratic Oath to one of caution and privilege.

The minimally invasive surgery technique of Intuitive Surgical and other innovative companies allows surgeons to perform complex procedures with a few tiny incisions. The precision these techniques enable reduces complications and provides benefits through improved operational efficiencies.

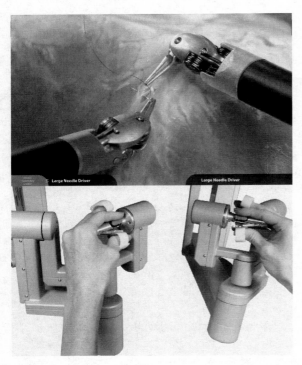

Innovations such as minimally invasive surgery are expressions of Golden Rule, patient-focused health care prescribed by the Hippocratic Oath: "I will prescribe regimens for the good of my patients according to my ability and my judgment and never do harm to anyone" (photograph of surgeon console and operative screen showing hands on the master controls courtesy of Intuitive Surgical).

The company's da Vinci Surgical System was rolled out in 1999, four years after the company was founded. Prior to that, the technology was developed in the 1980s from an association between researchers at the Stanford Research Institute and the U.S. Army. Battlefield operating was the initial driver of the technology, but commercial applications became immediately obvious.

In 2000, the da Vinci system was approved by the Food and Drug Administration for general laparoscopic surgery procedures. Advances in 3D high definition visualization and dexterity enabled more precise operation as well as ergonomic comfort. Along with the da Vinci Surgical System, the company designed the EndoWrist® Instrument line which allows for natural dexterity and even greater range of motion than the human hand. Using this technology, even heart valve and certain cancer surgeries can be accomplished with a few one- to two-centimeter incisions. Successful applications of the da Vinci System include minimally invasive hysterectomies as well as prostatectomies.

During the procedure, there is less blood loss. This approach also enables shortened hospital stays and minimizes the need for pain medication. Such minimally invasive surgeries lower the risk of complications as well as minimize scarring. With faster recovery, patients can be back at home and office more quickly and with less need for drugs and continuing care.

Competition in the minimally invasive market soon rose, and in 2003 Intuitive Surgical acquired Computer Motion. Associations have formed between the company and other industry leaders, including Erbe Elektromedizin GMBH, Johnson & Johnson, Olympus/Gyrus, Novadaq Technologies, Inc., and Mimic Technologies, Inc.

Clearing new procedures through the U.S. FDA as well as global organizations is a constant process. The company continues to apply for U.S. and foreign patents with, to date, more than 1,400 applications pending.

Heal Others and They Will Heal You: The Golden Rule as the Moral Drive of Health Care

The term wellness harks back to the 1950s when Halbert Dunn wrote the book *In High Level Wellness for Man and Society*. The medical doctor forwarded the concept of a healthy life being "an integrated method of functioning which is oriented toward maximizing the potential of which the individual is capable."[1]

Wellness has given people the ability to see their health beyond attention to illness. In addition to the basic essentials such as food, water, and shelter, the individual needs love and belonging, as well as self-esteem and self-actualization. Global wellness addresses the entire matrix of life for all of humanity. Beyond Maslow's original hierarchy of needs, global wellness is the drive toward providing safety, prosperity, and quality of life for society as a whole. From literacy and life expectancy to standard of living and sustainable development, global wellness considers every animate and inanimate entity on earth, indeed the earth itself, to be within a web of life that is interrelated and integrated into a Gaia field of existence.

The concept of wellness also involves recreation and creative expression. Freedom, human rights, and happiness are indicators of quality of life. Beyond standard of living, which is bounded by issues of income, wellness is an entirely holistic concept that has its root in the Golden Rule.

The debate between adherents of socialized medicine as opposed to the free-market system has often overshadowed advances in providing health care. The term socialized medicine appeared over one hundred years ago and was considered a positive term that meant better care for the masses of people. When president Harry S. Truman proposed a medical system in 1947, the term had taken on the implication of a government takeover of personalized health care. The American Medical Association considered it to be a pejorative term. Yet socialized medicine is simply a system that provides healthcare to all citizens through government regulation and services provided by taxation.

Today the reviews are mixed, with some saying government in health care creates bureaucratic and inefficient care. Others say the free-market health care system provides excellent health care for the rich but hinders ancient and alternative methods that have been the mainstays of people throughout time. Most health care systems are a mix of the two, allowing private companies to charge individuals and groups for health care with regulation and basic services provided by the government.

For hundreds of years, as the debate between government and private health care went on, the overall trend in medicine has been to treat the disease rather than the cause. Holistic medicine has a much larger mission. Health is a matter of all aspects of one's life. Taking into consideration the whole of people's needs, from physical to psychological, social and spiritual, emphasizes preventing illness and prolonging life.

Also called alternative medicine, holistic health practices include nutritional supplements, natural diets, herbal remedies, exercise, and relaxation techniques. In addition, meditation techniques, psycho-spiritual counseling, and breathing exercises approach the spiritual traditions. Ancient techniques of acupuncture, homeopathy, and massage have been updated with modern science and innovative instrumentation.

Many of these techniques are shunned by institutionalized medical organizations such as the American Medical Association. The pharmaceutical lobby also puts an emphasis on drugs that treat disease rather than supplements that support the immune system. The result is that the holistic medicine industry is driven by individuals and alternative practitioners rather than government programs and legislation. Often legal action is required to open doors to alternative medicines and pave the way for funding to achieve further innovations.

Collaborating for Global Health

As population rises, the world struggles to keep up not only with basic health issues, but also famine, hunger, and pandemics that arise from the globalization of travel. To combat these huge public health issues, a new level of association is rising to the challenge. World organizations like UNESCO and thousands of nongovernmental organizations are venturing to the edges of the earth to combat disease and malnutrition.

"The lessons of the nation's past tell us that liberty and justice cannot be secured for ourselves and kept from others without turning sour," said Art Simon, founder of Bread for the World. "Because we have cherished liberty for others, this country has sacrificed enormously (if not always wisely) in lives and material resources. We have not cherished justice as much. But justice and equality are no less a part of the nation's ideals, and we build on them by exercising them in our relationship with others. When we are rich and others are hungry or impoverished beyond description, justice calls for ending this imbalance."[2]

Many of these donor-based organizations apply innovation to their techniques of providing health services. The Gates Foundation, for instance, which gives millions of dollars each year for the treatment of a wide variety of global health challenges, has held four principles as its guiding spirit, each firmly fixed in the Golden Rule and peace.

- Optimism: taking on the world's most intractable challenges, such as AIDS and malaria
- Collaboration: building consensus and sharing resources
- Rigor: a disciplined approach from thoughtful analysis
- Innovation: challenging convention, assumptions, and stereotypes to take risks in pursuit of solutions

Many global foundations are guided by similar principles. The Carter Center, for instance, began after former U.S. president Jimmy Carter and his wife Rosalynn began working outside the government on humanitarian efforts. The center has had great success in eradicating Guinea worm, an unthinkable achievement in many parts of the world. The female nemotodes, *Dracunculus medinensis,* migrate from wounds below the knee to form painful blisters. Sometimes they emerge from the head or buttocks or genitalia. The longest worm recorded was thirty-one inches.

The World Health Organization, with support from the Carter Center, has delivered great progress. In 1985 there were 3.5 million cases reported each year. By 2008, the number of incidents was less than 5,000.[3]

The matrix of life is, indeed, being addressed at the individual as well as the planetary level by organizations both nonprofit and for-profit. From personal trauma to collective threats from disease and poverty, the Golden Rule motive of reciprocal equality drives our efforts toward a more just and healthy society. "The day that hunger is eradicated from the earth," said Spanish poet Federico García Lorca, "there will be the greatest spiritual explosion the world has ever known. Humanity cannot imagine the joy that will burst into the world."[4]

Chapter 22

Democratic Judiciary

Direct democracy is one of the highest forms of collaboration. With one person, one vote, the result of the voting process becomes the resolution of an issue by the will of the majority. Though far better than immoral autocratic methods, direct democracy has a flaw. By the very nature of "majority rules," direct democracy can be an amoral system, i.e. without a moral base that considers the needs of all parties. Minority rights, indeed, are not assured. Even in the days of Athens, democracy was reserved for those who had power, which was held by the males in the population who owned land.

For direct democracy to become a moral method of just governance, citizens must engage in the process and consider each of their votes in the context of the Golden Rule. In effect, there is a necessity to consider others in your vote as you would want others to consider you in their vote. Hundreds of glowing examples of Golden Rule voting have resulted in great progress, including civil rights, health care, environment, women's equality, child labor, on and on through the pantheon of progressive legislation.

Direct democracy under the aegis of the Golden Rule requires the free flow of information about the long-term consequences of an issue. As conflict analysis methods teach, a resolution can never be found unless the needs of all parties are considered. The empathy, compassion, engagement, and unity inherent in the Golden Rule provide people with the processes to self-govern, which is the vision of contemporary government. Citizens vote with their consciences and especially with their actions. Each person is responsible for what he does. Each person votes by way of his decisions each moment of the day for what he wants the world to be. It is how people vote that will determine the reciprocating actions of those treated justly.

With large populations, the hope established in Greece more than 2,000 years ago for direct democracy voiced acclamation has gone by the wayside. Yet today, even with populations in the billions, there is potential that our technology can revive the idea that each of our votes will go directly toward the resolution of questions and conflicts. One verified click, one legitimate vote.

In the meantime, representative democracy is our alternative to direct democracy. Globally, our constitutions provide for a medium between the masses of citizens and the actual voting on issues. Whether it is an electoral college that provides the final representative vote for the U.S. president, or the members of Congress that represent geographical districts, there is a space between voters' views and the eventual outcome.

Unfortunately, representative democracy is corrupted by powerful forces that "do unto others" what is best for personal gain. These private interests use intimidation, money, and other means to unduly influence the process. This has made our right to vote for the executive and legislative branches far less useful for peace than it is to be hoped that democracy would be.

The legacy of democratic election of the judiciary has also been, at best, spotty. Graft and corruption, the influence of money in political parties, negative campaigning, and lack of information about important decisions all contribute to the election of unqualified judges. The judiciary suffers also from additional weaknesses in some democratic societies. Judges in many locations are simply appointed by the president, governors, or other entrenched representatives in the government. In and of itself, the appointment of judges does not denote weakness. Yet wealthy interests funnel millions into the coffers of those in political positions as well as judges hoping to stay in office. Consequently, there are back-room deals and litmus tests. In the current judicial system, politics and polarization often rule.

As a result, the independence of the judiciary, an essential tenet of democracy and an essential part of an expanded view of separation of powers, has been weakened and nearly abandoned. Most of the public discussion has been to pull back from the tradition of voting for judges and simply institute appointing methods.

This begs the question: Isn't this trend of turning away from electing judges admitting that democracy does not work?

We know the political process of electing legislators and executives is corrupted by influences. Abandonment of democratic election of judges is tantamount to giving in to the notion that people are not capable of democracy. Why not abandon the election of the executive and legislative branches, if that is the sad state of our affairs? By this logic, would not a super-cloister of brilliant congresspersons and senators, appointed by the most successful and powerful of society, be better than the ragtag representatives of the masses? Autocratic efficiency has been used as the justification for reserving power for the few by the opponents of democracy for millennia.

Three women currently serve on the U.S. Supreme Court: Sonia Sotomayer, Ruth Bader Ginsburg, and Elena Kagan. The first woman nominated was Sandra Day O'Connor in 1981, indicating the evolution of the Court to reflect a more democratic institution.

For the judicial bench to be of the people and by the people, for the institution to be strengthened and trusted, democratic institutions must not be abandoned but rather expanded in scope. Qualified and moral justices can be found only if society has free flow of information and direct voting for justices by taking advantage of new technologies. The amoral compass of historical democracy must be set on the moral true north of the Golden Rule, and there are structural, technological, and educational actions that can do just that.

Core Problem

Thomas Jefferson declared, "The exemption of the judges from [elections] is quite dangerous enough. I know no safe depository of the ultimate powers of the society but the people themselves."[1] In an attempt to keep the judiciary both professional and independent of influences, society has tried alternatives to direct democracy. It is as if the sacrosanct nature of justice deems judges above the inefficient democratic process as well as the ignorance and/or influence of the masses. Consequently, judges have avoided accountability except to the powerful few.

In addition, legislated laws, the influence of mass media and an amoral educational system have given short shrift to the requirements of democracy. The proprietary nature of our legal system has made judicial processes and decisions a mystery beyond the scope of most citizens, thereby casting doubt on the ability of people to fathom understandable issues and rulings of judges.

Background

The associated system of judges and magistrates forms the judiciary, which is called the *bench*. Judges are public officials who hear and decide cases and administer justice. The powers designated, the appointment or election processes, and the daily functions of judges vary widely from jurisdiction to jurisdiction.

In addition to the judges and magistrates who make rulings, the bench has a staff, professional support, and government workers to ensure the system runs smoothly and does not burden the justices. These include bailiffs and office personnel, jailers and probation officers, local and national police, and mediation and arbitration personnel.

Another important part of the judicial system are attorneys, who are legally empowered to act on behalf of clients. Also called lawyers or solicitors, attorneys must be admitted to the bar in order to have the authority to practice law in a certain jurisdiction. Attorneys review the cases and precedents, then represent their clients' interests, whether it be in civil or criminal cases.

Some judges are elected; others are appointed by an executive or legislative body. The history of democracy goes back at least 2,500 years and perhaps longer. "Man's capacity for justice makes democracy possible," said Reinhold Niebuhr, "but man's inclination to injustice makes democracy necessary."[2] During the fifth century BCE in Athens, Greece, a form of direct democracy was created where those eligible to vote met in the center of the city. Though many were prevented from voting, such as women, slaves, and people without land, Athenian democracy remains one of the few pure, direct voting democracies in history.

A few centuries later in the Roman Republic, "citizen lawmaking" allowed those eligible to pass laws and veto legislation. This form of direct democracy lasted until Julius Caesar declared himself emperor, thus ending the Republic.

Currently, most nations have representative democracy, where people vote for representatives to vote on issues for them. One of the keys to an effective democracy is the secret ballot. Called the Australian ballot because it was developed in that country, the secret ballot ensures that people's votes are anonymous, thereby helping to thwart intimidation by abuse or money.

Election of judges has always been controversial due to its perceived effect on an impartial and independent judiciary. In most countries, judges are appointed. However, in the United States, Switzerland, and Japan, elections of judges take many forms. The debate surrounds a particular question: Will elected judges be free from special interests that bias their decisions due to the influence of campaign contributions?

Even without elections, judges are subject to many corrupting factors. If appointed, will they be influenced by those who appoint them? In addition, will they be biased by previous contacts with parties in a case? The tradition of *recusal* allows judges to withdraw from a case where a conflict of interest is involved.

The question of whether voters are able to elect competent and independent judges is valid. Yet, as noted, the same question could be asked about legislators, presidents, and prime ministers. Competent election of all three bodies of government surely depends on the free flow of information in order for the electorate to do its duty.

In 1934, the California state legislature established a new system to ensure that appointed judges were competent and moral. After appointment, judges were subject to a retention election, whereby the voters could decide whether the appointee stayed or went. The judge's name would appear on the ballot without an alternative. That way voters could give a straight yes or no.

In Missouri during the 1940s, the state legislature devised a new system called the Missouri Nonpartisan Court Plan, or merit plan. A nonpartisan commission would send the governor a list of potential judges. If the governor did not make a decision in sixty days, the commission would make the appointments. Drawing from the California plan, Missouri voters had the chance to retain or reject the appointments in a general retention, or referendum election.

All systems, of course, are subject to corruption and inefficiency, yet the California and Missouri plans have attempted to elevate judicial morality to new standards. In the original U.S. Constitution, the framers sought to "bridle" the power of the judiciary. As expressed in the Federalist Papers, "the Judiciary is beyond comparison the weakest of the three departments of power ... the general liberty of the people can never be endangered from that quarter."[3]

To ensure that weakness, federal judges were appointed and could easily be removed by impeachment. The grounds for impeachment were broad and included not only gross neglect of duty and usurpation of power but also personal misconduct and general "disregard of the public interest." Though the grounds for impeachment are less broad today, the power of the judiciary is still, within the inefficiencies of politics, bridled to ensure a remedy for gross negligence of duty.

Recently, a campaign to stop the democratic election of judges has gained strength due to the backing of the respected former Supreme Court Justice Sandra Day O'Connor. "I believe that campaigns for judicial office and elections and the increasing flood of money that that system of selection entails," she said, "is in fundamental conflict with the promise that a judge's only constituency is the law."[4]

When Sandra Day O'Connor was a state legislator in Arizona, she wrote a merit selection system for justices that is still in effect. That initiative stopped what she termed "politicians in robes" from turning the public's mind from respecting the judiciary to considering judges as mired in the same tawdry politics as members of Congress and the president.

To ensure competent judges, the integrity of the merit system is maintained, proponents of the initiative say, by regular retention elections. Citizens can put forward a referendum by gathering enough signatures to require a judge to be subjected to a retention election. Voters can decide whether or not to keep the particular judge on the bench by reviewing the recommendation of judicial performance panels, if available, and going to the polls to remove or retain.

However, would this not entail the same influence of money and political favor?

Solution

In cases where individuals or groups have grievances that cannot be addressed by democracy, the judiciary provides the ability to find solutions to conflicts short of violence. If a ruling adds to the injustice and reignites conflict, citizens must also have the ability to appeal and redress those grievances. For justice to take place, judges must be independent of powerful influences. They must be accountable. There must be a system to place competent and honest justices and remove those who are incompetent or corrupt. The judiciary must be subject to the highest form of governance available to us in our evolutionary state. Direct democracy may not be the only way to stop corruption and incompetence, but through informed engagement, citizens can endeavor toward a system that is closer to the Golden Rule imperative of self-governance.

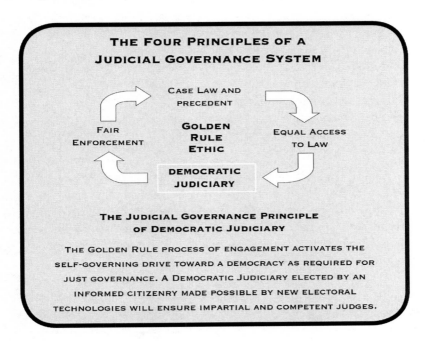

The gift of democracy is providing society with the ability to make better decisions than those decided by a select few. Democracy is relational, unifying, and collaborative, as opposed to autocratic, isolating, and secretive. In many cases, true democratic elections can prevent violence from being the solution to conflict. In cases where individuals or groups have grievances that cannot be addressed by a general election, the judiciary provides the most direct and efficient process to find solutions.

To further the practicality of a relational democracy, new technologies are providing the means of fine-tuning our democratic processes. For instance, the digital revolution has given us the means to offer voting to the greatest number of people, collect that data, and deliver the result. More efficient and transparent methods for the election of justices will soon be available for a one-person, one-vote process through computerized polling, increased communication, and education, as well as objective election monitoring.

However, the actual voting is in some ways less important than attention to the overall process. To ensure that democratic elections are fair and efficient, the following need to be in place:

- An informed electorate
- Open political debate
- Freedom of the press
- Objectivity in the press
- Freedom of speech
- Limited influence of money
- Limited control by entrenched power
- No gerrymandering
- No interference or harassment
- No tampering with the vote

An informed electorate entails access to the facts and figures about the records of judges. It also entails a thorough understanding about practical application of the process of the Golden Rule. Were the concerns of minority rights considered in the judgments? Is the judge paying attention to the long-term health and peace of the populace? Does the court fully embody the Golden Rule in its application of justice?

In a relational economic system, the Golden Rule provides the self-governing principle to achieve just governance. To be ruled by another without consent is against the moral nature of the Golden Rule. Democracy is the relational and collaborative system that can best gain consent of the voters. When an informed electorate casts a vote using the processes of empathy for others as for themselves, the compassionate engagement in the process of democracy results in a firm commitment to follow the laws. With increased transparency and information for voters on judicial nominees, democracy will inevitably assure citizens that the end result of a qualified judiciary is in their hands.

Prototypes

Election of the judiciary is currently the least democratic process in the election of representatives for the three branches of government. However, there are positive developments, including the following:

- Public financing of elections, especially in South America and Europe, funds campaigns from the government budget.
- Direct election of justices in some states and provinces enables the

citizens of those jurisdictions to vote on higher and lower court judges.

- Judicial independence derived from constitutional separation of powers.
- Judicial impartiality, so that judges are not biased or partial to one side or the other in a case.
- Justice of the Peace is a *puisne* or inferior justice appointed or elected in some countries to keep the peace.
- Political contribution laws, some of which require transparency, assign limits, and regulate expenditures.
- Judicial voter guide to provide information on judicial candidates for election.
- Judicial nominee commissions as a stakeholder collaborative process for appointment recommendations.
- Judicial qualifications for education and years practicing law.
- Term limits for defining the term a judge can serve on a particular court.
- Missouri plan, or Missouri Nonpartisan Court Plan, for commission selection of judges on merit.
- Judicial retention election, or retention election, first used in California in 1947, where judges are subject to a voter referendum.
- Judicial disqualification or recusal, where judges are excused from a case due to a potential conflict of interest.
- Impeachment, or removal of a judge by a vote in the House and Senate, for such reasons as malfeasance, high crimes, or gross misconduct.

Result

There has never been a better time to hope that the promise inherent in the principles and processes of direct democracy can be reached. In an economy of peace, the free flow of information will help achieve transparency and an educated electorate. The withering away of the legislature and executive branches of government will remove the threat of laws and orders that subvert democracy. Judges accountable to the electorate will begin to open the mystery of the justice system to those whom they are tasked to serve: the people in their jurisdictions. When trust returns to a judiciary firmly fixed in Golden Rule morality, a sustainable process for peace will be the result.

"We have fought for social justice," said U.S. Senator Barbara Boxer. "We have fought for economic justice. We have fought for environmental justice. We have fought for criminal justice. Now we must add a new fight—the fight for electoral justice."[5]

Challenges

How does society find competent justices? Will campaign contributions and graft entrench the most corrupt judges? Democratic election of judges is a controversial concept. As we have noted, if the democratic process will not work in the judiciary, how can we assume that democracy is working to elect competent legislators and executives? The debate is interesting, yet without democratic election of the judiciary, power blocks will continue to have unbridled rule.

Democratic elections for judges are much the same as for other elected officials. The need for voter information is crucial. With education and communications technology rapidly evolving, the potential for an informed electorate has never been greater. In addition, technological progress on digital voting is beginning to increase the sophistication of election monitoring. The principle of equal access to law provides adequate precedent on limiting the influence of money on elections. Justification for huge influxes of money into politics is based on constitutional rights, which in some ways protect the rights of wealth and power. Those fixed legislated justifications would be removed by the evolution of legislated law to that of case law.

Another challenge might be that without separation of powers between the other two branches, there are no judicial institutions that would serve to check and balance power. Currently, the judiciary has an appellate court system that offers redress to those suffering from unfair rulings. Whether it be an expansion of these separate powers within the judiciary or an entirely new idea for creating a parallel or bicameral court system to provide checks and balances will remain for the future. Yet within the judiciary are the seeds of power separation that will need to be nourished in order to provide adequate guarantees for equal access.

Chapter 23

Case Study—
The Academic Sector

*The Khan Academy and
the Freedom to Learn*

When you're thirteen years old and the homework becomes too intense, it's nice to have a cousin who is destined to revolutionize the way people learn. That's what happened in 2004 when American teenager Nadia Khan needed help with her math.

Salman Khan, Nadia's older cousin and son of a Bangladeshi immigrant to America, is a verifiable practitioner of the Golden Rule. "My basic philosophy of teaching" he said, "was straightforward and deeply personal. I wanted to teach the way I wished that I myself had been taught."[1]

In effect, Khan's philosophy of education was a restatement of the Golden Rule. With his connection to Nadia, he saw an opening to put his ideas into practice and responded with some familial support that eventually became a breakthrough in global education.

Nadia was a "serious-minded twelve-year-old," Salman Khan remembers in his book, *The One World Schoolhouse: Reinventing Education,* "who had just had the first academic setback of her life. She'd done poorly on a math placement exam given at the end of sixth grade. She was a straight-A student, highly motivated, always prepared. Her subpar performance baffled her. It wounded her pride, her confidence, and her self-esteem."[2]

The intrepid uncle used the Yahoo!® Doodle Notepad to illustrate to Nadia in a clear, concise way the mathematical principles that seem so complex to many people. His graphic method was colorful and methodical. His voice was calm and empowering. It helped, of course, that he held degrees in mathematics, electrical engineering, and computer science, as well as an MBA from Harvard.

As Nadia progressed in math, family and friends began to notice. Many requested Sal's help. To meet the demand, he took advantage of the new YouTube® Internet site and began uploading his lectures. Soon it was not just acquaintances, but people from around the digital globe viewing his Doodle videos—tens of thousands of hits.

Sal began to realize the potential. With a burgeoning fan base and exploding requests for his practical video method, he soon quit his job as a hedge fund analyst. In 2009 with friend Josh Gefner, Khan founded the Khan Academy, an online education platform with the vision of "delivering a free education to anyone, everywhere."[3]

Sal and Gefner ran the Academy out of Sal's home, but that wouldn't last for long. He was given a $100,000 donation from philanthropist Ann Doerr, wife of American venture capitalist John Doerr. In addition, one of the users of Sal's educational service just happened to be Bill Gates of Microsoft fame, who was using it to help his own children. Gates took notice and invited him to speak at a TED conference (ideas worth spreading in Technology, Entertainment, and Design). Later Gates provided $1.5 million to expand the innovative startup.

The "free education" Khan Academy soon had hundreds of thousands of subscribers, young and old, men and women, from every sector of the globally diverse human family. The mission of the Khan Academy was simple: to accelerate learning for students of all ages.

"It's my belief," Sal wrote, "that each of us has a stake in the education of all of us. Who knows where genius will crop up? There may be a young girl in an African village with the potential to find a cancer cue. A fisherman's son in New Guinea might have incredible insight into the health of the oceans. Why would we allow their talents to be wasted? How can we justify not offering those children a world-class education, given that the technology and resources to do so are available—if only we can muster the vision and the boldness to make it happen?"[4]

With interactive diagrams, pie charts, color-coded circuit diagrams, flow charts, and kinematic graphs, the Khan Academy team produced thousands of videos. In addition to mathematics, there was help for physics and chemistry, history and literature, biology and astronomy, economics and finance, and most other disciplines.

Users ran the gambit from students and tutors to home-schoolers and teachers. "With so little effort on my part," Sal said, "I can empower an unlimited amount of people for all time. I can't imagine a better use of my time."[5]

The success of the Khan Academy has not only exceeded Sal's expectations but also those of the education community. In 2012, Khan was selected as one of the most influential people in the world by *Time* magazine. Videos from the Khan Academy soon far outpaced alternatives from such innovators as MIT's OpenCourseWork and other hallowed institutions such as Yale, Harvard, and Stanford.

The online course movement started at Germany's University of Tübingen, when it published videos of lectures. When MIT began a program in earnest, the online opportunities proliferated. Yet it took Salman Khan to bring his exceptional talent for communicating to the movement before the excitement of online courses began to change the way people look at the digital education revolution.

"There's an old saying that life is school," Sal wrote. "If that's true, then it's also true that as our world grows smaller and the people in it more inextricably connected, the world itself comes to resemble one vast, inclusive schoolhouse.... I like to think of Khan Academy as a virtual extension of this One World Schoolhouse."[6]

Teach Others and They Will Teach You: The Golden Rule as the Moral Drive to Lifelong Learning

The creation of a global schoolhouse and the democratization of education have wide implications for individuals, society, and a relation-based economy. Education and free flow of information are essential not only to voting but also to how we make our livings and the positive associations we form to fulfill the archetypal motive of the Golden Rule. Our first thoughts may be survival, but it is soon after that we think of the *other*. The other, like us, deserves to be treated with kindness and benefit. Goodwill among our associations is the standard until the natural flow of reciprocity is obstructed, and that is a moral understanding that is often left out of primitive, amoral education models.

Salman Khan, of course, already had a close association with his niece, but he extrapolated his goodwill toward her to the wider world. Sal went on to develop an associative business that went against the grain of the educational establishment and people's preconceived notions. In effect, he had come up with an innovation that would benefit not only Nadia but also the entire educational community, however reluctant.

The time it took for the academic world to fully embrace online learning was partly due to its insistence on ensuring a measurable, quality education. Partly, it had to do with the collegiate community's reticence to change, as with any bureaucratic institution tasked with setting standards. "We are faced with the paradoxical fact," said philosopher Bertrand Russell, "that education has become one of the chief obstacles to intelligence and freedom of thought."[7]

The history of education is ancient, and its institutionalization began during the age of Aristotle and the first academy. In ancient Roman times, the *collegium* was a club or society where people lived together by a common set of rules. The modern word *college* is a fourteenth-century term that originally denoted an association of colleagues as a scholarly body. Today, colleges and universities find the associated "collegiate bodies" joined by additional contractual obligations to teach vocational and technical skills, such as medicine or law, veterinary medicine, and other professions.

"The orthodoxies that we take for granted," Sal notes, "and are now in thrall to—the length of the school day and the school year; the division of the day into periods; the slicing of disciplines into 'subjects'—where did these things come from? For that matter, who decided that education should be tax-supported and compulsory, that it should begin at a certain age and end after a certain number of 'grades,' and that it should be the business of the state to decide what should be taught and who could be a teacher?"[8]

The standardized classroom experience is rooted in the Enlightenment Age's Prussian model. In the 1800s, the model came to America and benefited from the innovative educational theories of John Dewey. In *My Pedagogic Creed,* published in 1897, Dewey contended that education was a social and interactive process. Through "democratic" education, social reform could be accelerated for the betterment of society. As George Washington Carver said, "Education is the key to unlock the golden door of freedom."[9]

In this view, students not only should be encouraged to take part in their own education, but they also could use the opportunity to learn how to live a productive life. The educational experience should be interactive and not contained in a prescribed set of skills. Realization of individual potential should replace the emphasis on inactive and sedentary rote learning.

This holistic approach to learning has expanded by way of technology and opportunity to a lifelong learning environment. Today there is great optimism within the academic community to overcome an antiquated Prussian system of standardized learning. "Technology has the power to free us from those limitations," wrote Salman Khan, "to make education far more portable, flexible, and personal; to foster initiative and individual responsibility; to restore the treasure-hunt excitement to the process of learning."[10]

The Sublime Interaction Between Student and Teacher

New technology-accessed free education is revolutionizing the way we learn and educate, yet there are many challenges. One is the limited role of human interaction. "For the majority who find mathematics extremely difficult, instructional videos have known problems," says educator Dr. Keith Devlin, "and we currently know of no approach that comes close to regular group interactions with a good, inspiring, human teacher. Changing the way a human mind works, which is what teaching amounts to, is a difficult task. Moreover, it involves emotional, psychological, and social factors. It would be impossibly hard, were it nor for the fact that teachers are themselves emotional, psychological, and social creatures, at heart very much like their students. The key is for the teacher and the student to establish human contact."[11]

Great teachers will never be out of the picture. Teachers are adept at understanding that learning is a highly personal skill and that people learn at different rates and manners. "Moreover, a student who is slow at learning arithmetic," Sal notes, "may be off the charts when it comes to the abstract creativity needed in higher mathematics."[12]

Motivation, interaction, and inspiration are the domain of the great teacher. The mentoring of teachers leads to a level of mastery where students are introduced to the next level: creativity. "The higher goal of our school," Sal says, "would be deep, conceptual understanding rather than mere test prep; students would be given the time and latitude to follow their curiosity as far as it would carry them. Thus my belief that creativity would emerge because it would be allowed to emerge."[13]

Creative teachers are not few and far between, but they are in some sense undervalued in society. They take the current technology of education, at whatever evolutionary stage they find it, and put their particular genius to work for teaching students in need of inspiration. It is a useful exercise to imagine what today's technology could do for the greatest teachers of all time—Confucius, Socrates, Aristotle, St. Thomas Aquinas, Roger Bacon, Will Duran, and Allan Bloom.

The late theoretical physicist Richard Feynman, for instance, is known for many accomplishments, not the least being his Nobel Prize-winning development of the space-time view of quantum electrodynamics (with Sin-Itiro Tomonaga and Julian Schwinger). His dramatic Sherlockian solution to why an O-ring caused the horrific explosion of the space shuttle *Challenger* in 1986 amazed millions. Feynman simply dropped the rubber ring into a glass of ice water to show how it would break under the strain of low temperatures.

The ingenious and dramatic Caltech professor is also remembered for mixing humor and brilliance in his lectures on physics. Many grad students tell of his creativity and innovation, his ability to blend his great mind with an intense questioning of his students that led to insights and epiphanies. He was a beloved teacher who participated in the college's drama club and student life.

Feynman's credentials for bringing the quantum world to a larger audience came from a series of videos of his lectures and the *New York Times* bestseller *Surely You're Joking, Mr. Feynman.* In 1993, the Richard P. Feynman Prize for Excellence in Teaching was established to laud the work of classroom and laboratory teachers, especially in the sciences.

Great teaching is a collaboration between teachers and students. "The truth is that anything significant that happens in math, science, or engineering," Sal notes, "is the result of heightened intuition and creativity. This is art by another name, and it's something that tests are not very good at identifying or measuring. The skills and knowledge that tests can measure are merely warm-up exercises."[14]

The role of the teacher in this mysterious knowledge should always be valued. "It's not enough to put a bunch of computers and smartboards into classrooms," Sal notes. "The idea is to integrate the technology into how we teach and learn; without meaningful and imaginative integrations, technology in the classroom could turn out to be just one more very expensive gimmick."[15]

The guidelines for the Richard P. Feynman Prize for Excellence in Teaching support this idea. The Prize is to be awarded annually to a professor "who demonstrates, in the broadest sense, unusual ability, creativity, and innovation in undergraduate and graduate classroom or laboratory teaching."[16]

George Steiner in *Lessons of the Master* wrote of a teacher's Golden Rule calling: "There is no craft more privileged. To awaken in another human being powers, dreams beyond one's own; to induce in others a love for that which one loves; to make of one's inward present their future; that is a three-fold adventure like no other."[17]

A Contract of Human Rights

Education is a consensus value for all rational human beings and essential for democracy. The First Protocol to the European Convention on Human Rights established education as a human right. Signatories of the 1952 convention were to guarantee an education to all citizens. The 1966 U.N. International Covenant on Economics, Social and Cultural Rights further established this right as "higher education shall be made equally accessible to all."[18]

With the breakdown of centralized, state-controlled, legislated learning environments, mentoring has become the defining characteristic of superior education. In the early 1900s, Maria Montessori began to develop the theories that led to Montessouri Schools, which emphasize independence and freedom for a child's natural instincts.

In the 1990s, a movement in the United States resulted in charter schools that emphasize choice and responsibility. The first was organized in Philadelphia when educator Ray Budde suggested that the school system give contracts to teachers to create innovative schools.

Free association and application of the Golden Rule will continue to revolutionize the educational contract between teacher mentors and students of all ages. The new ideas are simply new incarnations of well-proven principles, Salman Khan believes. "Still, what really matters is whether the world will have an empowered, productive, fulfilled population in the generations to come, one that fully taps into its potential and can meaningfully uphold the responsibilities of real democracy."[19]

Chapter 24

Fair Enforcement

Police, cop, copper, bobby, constable, marshal, flatfoot, patrolman, heat, troopers, law, long arm of justice, bluecoats, fuzz, *carabinieri, Bundespolizei, gendarmerie,* the People's Armed Police, Interpol: the many names and nicknames for security forces around the world elicit respect and sometimes fear. The most exact title for the job might be peace officer. After all, it's their purpose, their responsibility, and duty to keep the peace.

The Golden Rule is essentially about mutual exchange and the sense and practicality of fairness inherent it its expression. What is fair for you, more than likely, is fair for others. Fundamental to fairness is mutual responsibility. We take responsibility for our actions, so we want others to take responsibility for theirs. Yet we are not isolated. In a world that is dangerous, we must unify, join together for better or worse, gather our wagons in a circle to ensure the safety of our family and homes.

Indeed, as individuals we are indebted to our tribes, our cultures, our nations, and our species. Since the beginning of humanity, we have been our brother's keeper. The Golden Rule, with its transformative progression from empathy and compassion to engagement and unity, has given us an evolutionary sense of responsibility and duty, which has enabled humanity to survive and thrive amid mortal dangers from without and within.

In order to keep the unifying consciousness required for a stable society, individuals need to give their consent to be governed by that society's guidelines and rules. Consent is not given through fear and constraint, which carry an inherent resentment that abridges the freedom required for voluntary consent. Instead, consent is given through agreement, which depends to a large degree on developing relationships that result in fair enforcement of the law.

A process for determining what is fair for one's self as well as others provides the practical reasoning for consensual government. We certainly have empathy and compassion for self when it comes to laws. The Golden Rule ethic gives us the imperative to use those processes when it comes to others. As society, we attempt to institutionalize and fine-tune that determination. When laws are just based on the reasoning of the Golden Rule, we make a commitment to society to follow those laws. The commitments we make to others in our communal as well as in our personal lives can come from a sense of duty or an expression of love. Both are expressions of the Golden Rule and its moral expression of fairness.

When someone's actions are not fair, then fairness in return becomes only one of the options. When someone does not take responsibility, he must be answerable for his actions. When one person benefits and the other does not, there is abuse of the mutual exchange of the Golden Rule. The system of consent, whether in personal relations or societal governance, will eventually break down.

The scope of the human rights we enjoy in our homes and in wider society depends on our attention to the obligations we have to others. When people shirk their responsibilities, the two-way street of the Golden Rule is abridged. If the infraction does harm to the other, there must be accountability even in the midst of forgiveness. Accountability means some type and measure of sanction. From the mild disapproval of ignoring someone to locking someone in prison, the measure brought upon the villain should be proportional to the infraction.

To ensure that responsibilities are taken seriously by every individual, societies have developed complex systems of enforcement and correction. Enforcement can come in many ways, but it usually entails a form of punishment or penalty. In addition to personal enforcement methods such as spite, revenge, and other negative reactions, there is enforcement from an authority, either legal or social. Punishment involves a specific loss to the person committing the crime or rule infraction. Examples are loss of freedom, property, or reputation.

As humanity evolves, societies are developing much more humane and realistic methods of enforcement. From the penal colonies and torture mainly of the past, methods of societal control have moved into a relational mode, which entails consideration of other factors such as mental health and environment. New enforcement technologies have responded to this transitional awareness with advanced legal prescriptions that incorporate all stakeholders in the process with integrative and collaborative techniques intended to stop the cycles of violence often exacerbated by one-dimensional and harsh punitive approaches.

Core Problem

Today, policing involves not only local police forces but also a vast network of national and international security and military organizations. Enforcement costs untold billions in expenditures and fuels a continually expansive arms industry, which from small arms to weapons of mass destruction makes the world a tinderbox.

Police forces have, many times, been used by those in authority, especially authoritarian governments, for protecting their institution's power as well as those who wield that power. Even in democracies, policing entails ensuring that legislated and executive laws, no matter how just or reasonable, are enforced. Consequently, respect for the police depends on the justness of society. Police are simply the *long arm of the law.*

In addition, the penal system in many societies is overextended. In America alone there are millions held in prisons—by some accounts one out of every thirty-two citizens. As society evolves, so do extensive and costly contemporary rehabilitation methods. However, the Golden Rule processes

Activity around the FBI's Jacksonville Division is monitored from the operations center. The division is an example of the jurisdictional structure of law enforcement, with the Division handling more than 40 of Florida's 67 counties (FBI photograph).

of empathy, compassion, engagement, and unity toward transformational love have for the most part been left out of the penology equation. "There is a higher court than courts of justice and that is the court of conscience," said Mahatma Gandhi. "It supersedes all other courts."[1]

Background

The police are extensions of nation-state power. They are organized to enforce the laws, which means protecting property and person as well as reducing civil disorder. Whether they are called police officers, constables, sheriffs, *garda*, or *gendarmerie,* each unit is organized in a territory and have expressed limitations to its power.

In addition, the policing function has always been fundamental to the military and security forces of nation-states. With jurisdictions intended for securing borders, the armed forces often go beyond the nation-state and can include preemptive and imperialistic aggression. The use of the army for domestic policing is a debate that continues in all countries.

Jurisdictional inefficiencies in the new era of international commerce, travel, and crime have required policing to be more collaborative. The International Criminal Police Organization (Interpol) was established in 1923 as a transnational, neutral policing force. As crime became increasingly global, Interpol focused on terrorism, organized crime, drug trafficking, weapons smuggling, and other crimes that eclipse national boundaries.

Increasingly, all forms of violence are seen as aberrations. Even violent self-defense can be seen as a lost opportunity to deal with a situation in a nonviolent manner through conflict resolution. Whether by a person, group, or nation-state, the use of violence must be seen as criminality and be resolved by nonviolent means or stopped by a professional police force with limitations on its ability to gain extraordinary power.

The law enforcement system is vast, from patrols on the beat to prisons that hold those accused or convicted. Individual titles include police, peace officers, state troopers, sheriffs, deputies, marshals, special agents, customs officers, prison officials, court bailiffs, probation officers, investigators, detectives, and many others.

Security guards and neighborhood watch patrols can be an important part of law enforcement if particular powers are granted in a particular jurisdiction. There are many other categories. In fact, in the United States the New York Criminal Procedure Law 2.10 lists over eighty different categories of persons designated as peace officers, from park rangers to tax department employees.

The purpose of these authorities is to encourage or force adherence to the law. The powers of a law enforcement agency within a jurisdiction include the right to give direction as well as search, seizure, and interception. Police can use force and constrain suspects. Expanded powers provide exemption from the law to use legal deception and override certain jurisdictional restraints in order to provide for the public safety. Lethal force can be used in certain situations, but most occasions require non-lethal weapons or non-lethal force such as restraint.

Limits on these powers are accomplished by the need to provide grounds for using extraordinary invasions of privacy and property rights. For instance, in order to search a house or tap into communications, the officer must usually go to a judge to get a warrant.

Leading-edge technologies and communications advances have increased the need for morality to be infused into societal enforcement systems. As recent history shows, unbridled security efforts, made apparent by the latest spying revelations, necessitate that a moral dimension to investigations and enforcement must be considered for consent of the citizens to be given. The Golden Rule, with its processes of mutual exchange, is the only practical guideline for understanding the difference between abusive enforcement and just enforcement.

Solution

Whether in a national jurisdiction or state or local, the enforcement arms of governments are usually under the executive branches within the boundaries. This top-down structure, in the context of the evolution of consciousness of our tribal Golden Staff and amoral Golden Mean societies, has been the most efficient structure for execution of our laws. There is decision-making at the top and enforcement at the street level, though there are many relational programs and initiatives that are supplementing this dynamic with a multilevel flow of information and engagement.

As the benefits of a global consciousness expressed in the relational economy put more reliance for solving natural disputes on the judiciary, enforcement of laws is still a street-level procedure. The focus on contract law in a relational system puts the onus on legally enforceable promises, either explicit or implicit, made between parties to the contract. Disputes brought before the courts are to be resolved with a ruling, which is binding upon the parties, at least until a successful appeal.

Laws are increasingly enforced by professional organizations that are trained in policing with established processes and facilities. Judicial, or just, governance does not mean doing away with the institutions of enforcement or resorting to vigilante justice. Governance by the judiciary would put justice front and center. Fair enforcement would be based on the court's ability to weigh the facts in a case and make rulings and determine sanctions within the context of the Golden Rule ethic.

Just as the saying *all politics are local* expresses the community nature of governance, criminality is also mostly local and requires neighborhood and community policing. Yet as the world becomes more accessible, enforcement is adapting to a global necessity. Organizations such as Interpol are essential in the cross-border and increasingly digital profiles of crime.

Sometimes, of course, violence needs to be stopped by the use of violence at a level that can be considered necessary and justified. At this point in our history, nonviolent approaches have been relegated to supplemental enforcement methods by our reliance on weapons and war. On a multinational level, as the rattling of sabers and the inefficient unleashing of military war are being assessed through their human expense, methods of nonviolent resolution are coming to the fore. Instead of calling for a cultural war, a national war, a religious extremism war, or a war on the evil forces of terror, the dynamics of tribal and national aggression or *acts of terror* are now being identified as simple criminality. Nationalist wars will become obsolete and terrorism a matter for police. The Golden Rule is the basis for nonviolent enforcement, and the judiciary is the governmental institution best suited for mutual exchange and consent through fair enforcement of laws.

Humanity is moving quickly toward global policing organizations functioning as a collaborative network of street-level local jurisdictions. The enforcement of global standards in the context of local needs will continue to be implemented by criminal and civil rulings of the judiciary. A distributed police organization resident in every locality with global connectivity and coordination is already replacing today's isolated national policing organizations as well as nation-state military institutions. Everything from breach of contract to robbery, from murder to war crimes, is considered criminal activity to be dealt with through professional investigation, apprehension, and incarceration structures based on judicial control and reporting.

Relational Model for Just Enforcement
1. Judiciary command and reporting
2. Global/local jurisdictional structure
3. Best practices investigation and apprehension
4. Transparent trials with fair penalties (fees, incarcerations, probations)

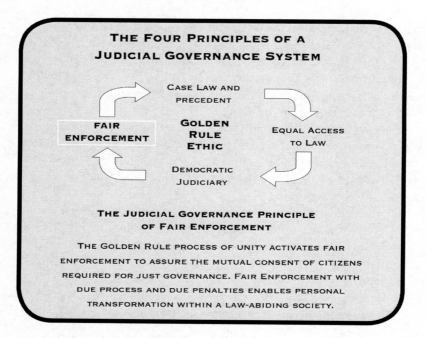

THE FOUR PRINCIPLES OF A JUDICIAL GOVERNANCE SYSTEM

CASE LAW AND PRECEDENT

FAIR ENFORCEMENT

GOLDEN RULE ETHIC

EQUAL ACCESS TO LAW

DEMOCRATIC JUDICIARY

THE JUDICIAL GOVERNANCE PRINCIPLE OF FAIR ENFORCEMENT

THE GOLDEN RULE PROCESS OF UNITY ACTIVATES FAIR ENFORCEMENT TO ASSURE THE MUTUAL CONSENT OF CITIZENS REQUIRED FOR JUST GOVERNANCE. FAIR ENFORCEMENT WITH DUE PROCESS AND DUE PENALTIES ENABLES PERSONAL TRANSFORMATION WITHIN A LAW-ABIDING SOCIETY.

A judicial enforcement system would be very much like today's executive policing organizations. The personnel, reach, function, and follow-through would only differ in the reporting structure. The organization would be an arm of the judiciary, not very different from today's structure, where there is executive branch control of enforcement.

Local police would be structured much as they are currently, in precincts and specialty units. With increasing networking technology, tools available for communicating and coordinating standard police activities will see rapid advances. Daily beats and immediate response would generate trust and respect from populations due to the local nature of community policing as well as the overarching mission of preserving the peace.

The investigative and apprehension process would continue to evolve in best-practices technique and implementation. Once a person is brought before the justice system and determined to be guilty, pretrial and trial processes would be transparent and lead to fair penalties ranging from fees to imprisonment.

An emphasis on equity law would provide, especially under a Golden Rule moral structure, for judgments based on justice. In the complex cases that are sure to be on court dockets of the future, judges will need great leeway in applying the law. The principle of equity keeps the "rigors of common law" from demanding strict punishments or harsh rulings. With discretion and flexibility within the context of transparency and democracy, judges will have the latitude to consider judgments in the context of natural law and case-by-case circumstance.

Methods of enforcement are, in the final result, intended to prevent further negative actions and allow for the transformation of convicted individuals as well as those in greater society. Integrative law is one leading-edge advancement in the technology of enforcement that seeks this transformation to a stakeholder emphasis. The integrative approach is highly relational and collaborative, with its roots in a holistic level that combines all aspects of the social and personal realm.

"'Integrative Law' is an integration of the practices and methods of the adversarial system with newly emerging more humanistic and relational approaches to law," according to proponents. "The term is relatively recent, and is mainly promoted by proponents of alternative legal models. It includes some forms of alternative dispute resolution plus some new models of problem-solving courts, such as drug courts. Some law schools have courses in integrative law topics, including therapeutic jurisprudence, comprehensive law, restorative justice, collaborative law."[2]

Such relational expressions of a more humanistic approach to law are a positive reaction to past failures of the adversarial system. Enforcement is key to the shift toward thinking of criminality and peace as an interrelated system. The punishment focus is replaced by a restorative approach. For instance, drug courts have developed over the last few decades as an acknowledgment that criminality does not occur in a vacuum. The intention of drug courts is to actually stop the cycle of violence by engaging the drug user in a participatory environment where all stakeholders in a community are considered and programs are geared toward resolution rather than simply punishment.

Some of the evolving ideas of relational legal practices such as integrative law include:

- Restorative justice and mediation
- Reentry programs
- Transformative conflict analysis and resolution
- Mediation focused on the relationship rather than evaluative settlement negotiations
- Law as a healing profession
- Lawyers as counselors
- Conflict coaching
- Preventive law

- Problem-solving and collaborative courts
- Therapeutic jurisprudence
- Integrating spiritual aspects law and enforcement
- Dialogue and civic engagement

We are all in this world together, and harm to one, even in the context of punishment for infractions, breaks the transformative nature of evolutionary society. Empathy becomes accusation, compassion becomes anger, engagement becomes retribution, and unity is abandoned for isolation. There is a reason why enforcement with a Golden Rule understanding of our duty as brother's keeper is the only way to achieve fair enforcement and encourage better behavior. Golden Rule justice and governance ensure the unity and consent of the governed.

Prototypes

The globalization of enforcement has many expressions in the current reality of cross-border disputes and implications of rulings on global citizenry. The institutions developed to handle international cases are fledgling in their sophistication and, often, transparency is lost in the complexity of the briefings and rulings. Yet the future will build on these prototypes as the Judicial Governance system evolves by necessity.

- International Criminal Police Organization (Interpol) for intergovernmental, nonpolitical cooperation on public safety and investigations of terrorism, corruption, crimes, and trafficking
- U.N. peacekeepers to monitor and observe peace processes and implement peace agreements
- Bailiffs as legal officers to assist judges, juries, and maintain decorum in the courtroom
- Court costs usually paid by the loser in a court case for administrative handling
- Local police jurisdictions with responsibilities and funding at the local level
- International police for transnational cooperation
- Prison systems and jails on the local and federal levels for incarceration as a form of punishment
- Rehabilitation methods to restore through therapy and education a prisoner's ability to function in society
- Criminal codes define crimes and penalties

- Alternative prison time such as home detention, confinement, and electronic monitoring
- GPS tracking devices that determine the precise location of people, vehicles, and other materials
- Reconnaissance satellites for intelligence applications
- Truth and reconciliation commissions for revealing wrongdoings and finding resolutions, forgiveness, and justice
- Integrative and collaborative law for including all stakeholders and humanitarian practices in the judicial process

Result

A distributed network of local, regional, and global policing organizations will report to the judiciary within specific jurisdictions and be subject to scrutiny under the wisdom of case law. These networks can be provided with the tools, training, and authority to ensure that judgments on contracts, criminal activity, and disturbances between individuals are kept from escalating into further illegality and violence. The focus on local police forces with only jurisdictional authority will also ensure that the enforcement networks do not burgeon into blocks of militaristic and oppressive power. Court cases can be brought against law enforcement organizations and resolved for the benefit of a peaceful society.

Fair enforcement—the reciprocity of responsibility and duty—builds integrity and respect for the law. With the Golden Rule as the essential moral base of policing, innovations such as proactive policing encourage police action to engage criminals before they commit a crime. Incarceration, fees, and community service for both criminal and civil law would match the measure of an infraction.

With empathy and engagement built into the judicial system, the Golden Rule provides a path beyond enforcement through reconciliation, education, distributive justice, and other methods of engaged rehabilitation and conflict resolution. The Golden Rule also provides for the transformative nature of forgiveness and practical love for fellow humans. "Justice that love gives is a surrender," said Mahatma Gandhi in reference to the highest form of transformative enforcement, "Justice that law gives is a punishment."[3]

Dwight D. Eisenhower bridged the divide between amoral enforcement and the higher goals of moral society with his statement, "Though force can protect in emergency, only justice, fairness, consideration and cooperation can finally lead men to the dawn of eternal peace."[4]

Challenges

Who would police the police? Internal affairs departments currently keep tabs on criminal actions by police. External judicial commissions and appointments, such as today's independent prosecutors, contribute to maintaining an honest police force as well as investigate public corruption. An evolution of these institutions would continue to enforce the credibility and efficiency of public institutions.

How do we pay the judiciary and its structure of enforcement? Options for payment of members of the judiciary include, among others, a tax on transactions. With current technology, banks can add a small percentage in order to raise billions of dollars each year.

Chapter 25

Case Study—
The Security Sector

*iRobot and the
Freedom from Fear*

The basic survival mechanism of humankind is fear. Whether the danger is an open flame or a threat of physical harm, fear of a potential outcome gives us reason to act. Many of our emotions, such as anger and hate or sadness and nervousness, are expressions of rational or irrational fears. If the perceived danger is great enough, we can freeze up, even experience paralysis.

Prior to that extreme, we depend on biological response mechanisms that were developed in the early days of humanity. Fight-or-flight is a point of decision. We are free to either stand our ground or take measures to avoid the problem. The Golden Rule provides a rational touchstone for how we make our fight-or-flight decisions. To choose violence, of course, is adverse to the very purpose of the Golden Rule: to survive and flourish as a unified humanity. Through Golden Rule thinking, we have many options in standing our ground or avoiding the problem. The decision point is not black and white, but rather a spectrum of responses at our disposal. We can reconcile, alleviate, manage, or transform our fears. We can think ahead and increase the security in our lives. The objective of our societal security systems is to address current and potential violence before it happens, thereby reducing fear and generating a feeling of calm and comfort.

The anxiety fueled by our fears has been the creative source of many nightmares as well as great works of art. Such was the narrative of fear at the core of science fiction guru Isaac Asimov's short stories and over 500 books. The antagonist in Asimov's tales could be the natural world, or technology, or the dark side of human nature, but most presented a fearful challenge to humanity.

In the short story *Runaround*, which was made into the popular movie, *I, Robot*, Asimov kindled our fears with out-of-control robots that had super-human powers to do good as well as evil. How did fictional humanity solve the challenge of living safely in the age of robotics? The "Three Laws of Robot-ics" are essentially a rewrite of the Golden Rule applied to the relationship between humans and thinking machines[1]:

1. A robot may not injure a human being or, through inaction, allow a human being to come to harm.
2. A robot must obey the orders given to it by human beings, except where such orders would conflict with the first law.
3. A robot must protect its own existence as long as such protection does not conflict with the first or second law.

Other than that, robots in Asimov's futuristic world were to be used to make life for human beings better and more secure.

At least that was the plan. The movie *I, Robot* was a science fiction block-buster based on Asimov's story. Released in 2004, it brought Asimov's fears and solutions to the general public just as robots were proliferating.

Enter iRobot Corporation. With headquarters in Massachusetts, iRobot was having success after success. It was turning the knowledge and expertise of roboticists into a series of products that increased quality of life and safety around the world. Co-founded in 1990 by robotics engineers Colin Angle, Helen Greiner, and Rodney Brooks, the company soon developed several models of robot intelligence. This included the Genghis robot for space explo-ration, which had legs for mobility. Following Genghis was Ariel, a robot that screened for mines in ocean environments. The robot not only could detect mines in hard-to-reach areas but also set explosives for safe detona-tion.

Once the viability of the company and the competence of the roboticists were established, a DARPA contract came from the military for security appli-cations such as bomb disposal and reconnaissance. With the tactical mobile PackBot®, iRobot entered a collaboration for responding to terrorist attacks and battlefield threats. After the 9/11 attack, for instance, PackBot surveyed buildings at the World Trade Center site for structural integrity. The company has gone on to produce several robots that keep troops and first responders safe. They were used after the earthquake and tsunami in Japan to investigate and help with cleanup efforts at Fukushima in 2011.

iRobot's PackBot is used to investigate potentially dangerous environments and objects without putting the operator at risk (iRobot).

Protect Others and They Will Protect You: The Golden Rule as the Moral Drive for Safety

For millennia, our societies have constructed security apparatus and networks to prevent our sources of fear from affecting our lives. Security entails having adequate food, water, shelter, and the rest of Maslow's basic hierarchy of needs. Today, with population increases and globalization, the needs of energy and technology, as well as health care, human rights, and environmental sustainability enter the scope of security.

The United Nations Human Development Report puts the need in perspective with its definition of security as *freedom from want* and *freedom from fear*. The intention was to link much of human security to the underlying causes, in effect conjuring the ancient wisdom of the Golden Rule.

Yet security is not only a global concern but also a local need. Neighborhood watches in America are volunteer associations that keep a keen eye on houses, streets, and communities. In the 1960s, an incident in Queens, New York, where Kitty Genovese was raped and murdered within hearing distance of a dozen bystanders caused a rise in calls for citizen action. Since then, neighborhood watches have proliferated. These security activists are not necessarily trained, so they are encouraged to call the police and avoid direct intervention.

Many first-line responders are volunteers who have been important to community safety and security throughout time. Fire departments hail back to ancient Rome, when the wealthy used their slaves to man the bucket lines. In the 1700s, Ben Franklin imported the British fire insurance model to the American colonies to create the Philadelphia Contributionship and its Union Volunteer Fire Company.

First responders have always been important to communities, yet their recent hallowed place in society came in the aftermath of the 9/11 terrorist attacks on the Twin Towers in New York City. Brave men and women came to the call, many climbing toward the flames only to die when the towers collapsed. Their valor will ever be recalled when we think of first responders.

The fire and police departments are just a part of the vast network of safety and security defenses against both natural and manmade disasters. Emergency medical technicians, hospitals, and volunteer paramedics are the first to the scene. Training for each of these responders has increased the chances of thousands to survive.

When security is looked at as a national challenge, the result is often that the priority of the national budget becomes military. Tax money is directed toward industries that contribute to the national security. The military-industrial complex, a term coined in the farewell address of President Dwight D. Eisenhower, is a symbiotic relationship between the private and public sectors. The defense industry lobbies legislatures, which approve more funding, which is given to the legislators in the form of political contributions and support.

In its extreme, as in the case of fascist countries such as Italy in World War II, or in more modern countries such as Egypt, the military eclipses its central security objective and becomes part of the industrial sector. Businesses are owned by military committees or commanders; therefore the economy becomes indistinguishable from government and, inevitably, makes democratic elections virtually nonexistent.

The military-industrial complex is not a recent phenomenon. Since the beginning of human history, trade created the drive for interaction between societies. Greed provided one or both trading partners with the urge to dominate. Armies were created to make war or protect borders. At the root of security is justice. Security entails not only protection in the present from those who would do us harm, but also the reasons for potential violence to the satisfaction of both parties concerned. Otherwise, there is no security for the future.

Non-lethal Weapons

Sharp sticks under foot, caltrops to stop enemy advances, rubber bullets, tear gas, water cannons, and police dogs—non-lethal weapons have been developed and used to solve conflicts. Weapons devised to incapacitate the enemy without causing death, these pain-inducing, non-lethal technologies can be used in combat situations and prevent escalation of the conflict. Strategists envision their use in riot and crowd control, containing a conflict, or in self-defense situations where killing needs to be avoided.

Today, a new industry is responding to the need with a wide range of non-lethal weapons. From electroshock tasers to paintball guns that explode on impact with a release of capsaicin or pepper spray, these weapons are used by police forces as well as the military. Acoustic weapons using very low-frequency sound can penetrate buildings and vehicles. The effects on humans can be nausea and vomiting as well as damage to internal organs.

Now there are sophisticated microwave technologies that use focused high-frequency blasts to heat all matter in their path. The Active Denial System can raise a person's body temperature to 130 degrees in two seconds. The penetration is only a few millimeters, so once the beam is turned off, there seems to be no lasting effect.

With the proliferation of drone technologies, essentially unmanned robotic airplanes, the era of non-lethal weaponry is here. Yet as with any weapon class, once Unmanned Aerial Vehicles (UAVs), microwave weapons, and other technologies are available, they can be used by anyone with the drive to use them. Political and religious terrorists, unbalanced individuals, the angry dispossessed, even precocious kids with immature intent are all potential users who could render with the touch of a trigger even the U.S. military's technological force impotent.

Perhaps humanity needs to take the three tenets of Asimov's rules for robots as a touchstone of Golden Rule use of robotic technologies.

For robotics companies such as iRobot, non-lethal weapons and surveillance tools are only the start of huge opportunities for both commercial and military applications. Early products from iRobot were hailed as safe alternatives for data acquisition as well as convenience. In cooperation with the National Geographic Society, for instance, iRobot developed a robot to search the Great Pyramid. In 2002, with the Roomba vacuum cleaning robot, iRobot rolled out the first of their robots to increase home quality of life.

Following the development of the Scooba® floor washing robot, shares of iRobot began trading on the New York Stock Exchange. In 2010, iRobot deployed the Seaglider to help monitor the oil spill in the Gulf of Mexico. A line of programmable robots for every application from pool cleaning to telepresence, or being present through cameras, have added to the output of the company. iRobot also helped create National Robotics Week and launched a STEM education initiative to inspire schoolchildren.

Today, millions of robots have been sold for hundreds of applications. In the field of safety and security, thousands of small unmanned ground and air vehicles (SUGVs and SUVs) are deployed for domestic use as well as conflict zones worldwide. Robotics has become a major source of innovation to monitor and communicate potential trouble zones. In our endeavor to find more humane and practical ways to alleviate our fears, robotics has upsides in terms of transparency and downsides in terms of privacy. Yet the advent of robotic and non-lethal alternatives to violent responses is expanding our options for allowing Golden Rule ethics to work even in dire circumstances.

The Case for Transition

The nature of innovation is that it will arise at a fringe where it can afford to become prevalent enough to establish its usefulness without being overwhelmed by the inertia of the orthodox system.[1]—Kevin Kelly, cofounder of *WIRED Magazine*

Chapter 26

How Do We Transition
to a Just Economy?

The seeds of the relational economy and judicial governance systems are already in place and growing rapidly. With proliferation of the associative environment, innovative products are being developed at an astounding pace. New technologies are being tapped for full-cost accounting and fair pricing. The dockets of local and global courts are bursting with issues from local discrimination suits to national trade and patent disputes. Terrorism and wars are being adjudicated as criminal and understood in the context of *freedom from* and *freedom to.*

Attention to the *other* is resulting in more food for the hungry, better health-care systems for the sick, an accessible global classroom, new scientific discoveries we can barely grasp, and open technologies that bode well for transparent democracies. The human race is experiencing the astounding benefits of a rising global consciousness, yet, as with any innovative or revolutionary time, the positive benefits from rapid change can be easily exploited.

How can we ensure that our evolving twenty-first-century economic and governing systems are not co-opted by the avarice and ambition of the few?

At first glance, the vision of a relational economy with a judicial governance system looks like a rose-colored-glasses view of the future. Indeed, it is difficult to fully grasp the opportunities without tempering our excitement with lingering trepidation and suspicion. The only approach more costly than imagining a false utopia is not to imagine the future at all. Without the power of intention, we will end up with a society that is *not* based on the Golden Rule. The amoral, sometimes immoral structures of institutional capitalism and socialism will continue. Democracy will plod along with well-meaning but power-influenced legislators and executives passing and enforcing laws that guarantee freedom for some. The Golden Mean will split the pie with a few gaining miraculous favor, the many still struggling to subsist.

Indeed, the large macroeconomic and macro-political innovations of tomorrow can be co-opted by avarice and ambition if humanity remains pessimistic and passive. The same dangers of corruption and apathy remain. If there is a persistent lack of foresight by today's citizens of the world, the potential of the coming relational economy and judicial governance systems will be lost. In essence, what we do today is setting the wave of change in motion, for better or worse.

The evolutionary path of human thought and consciousness has the power to determine our future systems. As more responsive and equitable economic and governing models continue to develop naturally and seamlessly, how we as individuals choose to make our livings and govern society needs to keep pace with technological and social advances. If our minds do not embrace and understand the opportunity, the full potential of this opportunity to finally achieve the full scope of freedom will be lost.

There will certainly be an urge, for instance, to implement a free and just system before world opinion and technology are in place, before we fully understand its requirements. We are an impatient species. If there is a benefit, we want it now. We want to have our cake and eat it too. However, there is great danger in demanding that the future arrive before its time. History has shown us repeatedly that to foment a violent revolution or form an international body to implement a relational economy and just governance system is folly. Any group of people in charge will inevitably entrench power for themselves and their constituents. Power corrupts, as the oft-quoted maxim tells us, and absolute power corrupts absolutely.

The relational economic and just governance systems are evolutionary rather than revolutionary, to be unfolded from the emerging layers rather than engineered from scratch. These new models for economy and governance will become institutionalized by necessity and efficiency rather than by idealism or strategic modeling. The Golden Rule will be the driver of our new models because our global consciousness is now powerful enough to understand its ancient wisdom and contemporary relevance.

"Only with the institutionalization of new form," said the New York journalist Henry Demarest Lloyd, "thus eliminating the old apparatus, could the political economy of the golden rule be made operative."[1] Nineteenth-century Christian reformist philosophers such as the Russian Leo Tolstoy, the Ohio Quaker William Dean Howells, and others knew that it would take not only the emotional inspiration but also attention to the evolution of the forms of the economic and governance system to institute a just society.

There is an interesting precedent for institutionalizing political and social structures based on the Golden Rule. In 1894, an oil industrialist in the U.S. state of Ohio was elected mayor of the city of Toledo. "Golden Rule" Jones "resolved to make an effort to apply the Golden Rule as a code of conduct."[2] In 1897, he said, "After nearly three years of a test I am pleased to say that the Golden Rule works."[3]

According to poet Ernest Crosby, Jones was "sowing the seeds of a new harvest" and "as a sort of visitor from some other planet where brotherhood and harmony have been realized in the common life, dropped down here in a semi-barbarous world and calmly took his place in the midst of its crude and cruel institutions."[4]

The progressive policies of "Golden Rule" Jones resulted in many societal and political innovations such as his Golden Rule Dinner, where people could get a hot meal for fifteen cents, though each one would actually cost twenty-one cents. Toledo's Golden Rule Park and Golden Rule Hall were places where regular folk could enjoy the bounty of the city. As Jones said in his book, *The New Right: A Plea for Fair Play Through a More Just Social Order,* "Every tramp is a good citizen spoiled ... Release men from this iniquitous profit-system, and tramps will be as rare as lepers."[5]

Yet even then bumps in the road to Golden Rule progressivism were apparent. The party of Lincoln, the Republican Party that had elevated him to power, was alarmed at Jones's reforms and refused to endorse him for reelection. Jones decided to run as an independent and won 70 percent of the vote. Unfortunately for the common folk of Toledo, he died in office in 1904, but his legacy in history was firmly established.

The benefits of top-down revolutions such as that tried by Jones are difficult to sustain. The forces against egalitarian policies and justice for all are strong and determined, fueled as they are by the legislative cover for human natures of avarice and ambition. The dichotomy of individual and societal consciousness will always be a hindrance to utopian efforts, no matter how pure their intent. "I don't want to rule anybody," said Jones. "Nobody has a right to rule anybody else."[6]

To legislate against the status quo of history may sound ideal, but it is not practical. Rather than commanded or legislated, the relational economy must come incrementally as technology and human thought abandon the inefficiencies of the old legislated and authoritarian economy. A relational economy does not require a top-down strategy but a bottom-up realization and leveraging of positive changes in our modes of production.

Only by way of the Golden Rule ethic and attention to the *other* can society be released from the fears and strategies that have dominated its past.

A relational economy is about the associations we form not only with the future in mind but also with the present opportunities that will enable us to prosper. A just governing system is about seeking justice for all under our equal status as humans within our species.

With our educational and faith-based systems acknowledging its essential wisdom, the Golden Rule can be the fundamental and universal principle for how we teach our children. We can show them the way to behave during times of conflict, how we transform from human isolation to human relations. Only through the timeless secular and spiritual ethic of the Golden Rule can we find our purpose as individuals and as humanity. Peace is the spirit of our times, and all we must do is let the Golden Rule manifest in our lives.

Evolving to a Relational Economy

The intention of this treatise is not to propose a political platform. Rather, it is conceived to extrapolate on present evolutions and, thereby, to project one hundred years into the future when the inevitable implementation of a more just and practical economic and political society will be realized. To succeed, we must allow ourselves to collectively embrace a global consciousness and the essential processes of the Golden Rule: to teach and live the principles of empathy with others and compassionate engagement toward unity and transformational love.

In essence, a relational economy and judicial governance system must come not by violent revolution or by legislated laws, but through nonviolent evolution and reasonable adaptation to change by an economy based on innovation and a judiciary steeped in the process of justice.

Yet there are particular ideas that might encourage that evolution. Innovative and professional economic and judicial theorists are needed to provide ideas on how to relieve history of the current systems and nonviolently clear the way for the economic and judicial frameworks of the future. Here are some ideas for consideration:

- Pass an amendment to global constitutions requiring democratic election of justices, just as the U.S. Constitution's Seventeenth Amendment cleared the way for direct election of senators.
- Dismantle legislated laws in favor of contractual law in the formation, control, and incentives provided to corporate entities.
- Increase the funding and legitimacy of collaborative and integrative law practices in supplementing current trial system that focuses on punishment rather than transformation.

- Remove tax supports and other laws that create unfair advantage for large corporations and other sectors of society.
- Legalize and provide transactional legitimacy for the underground market, including the black, grey, white, and other sectors that operate outside the formal economy.
- Legalize alternative forms of currency transactions that contribute to a decentralized exchange.
- Move tax policy toward a progressive sales tax that would be handled through automatic payments at the point of purchase.
- Implement new electoral and election financing technologies that enable direct, fair elections.
- Reduce global stockpiles of weapons of mass destruction and lesser weapons and abandon laws that create incentives for the global arms trade.
- Reduce tariffs and other barriers to international trade while limiting the effect of their withdrawal upon at-risk populations.
- Create voter guides for judicial elections and increase citizen access to court decisions by individual justices.
- Develop personal technology applications for local/global pricing algorithms that use GPS and real-time transactional data from locality to locality.
- Develop new theories for separation of powers within the justice system, including but not limited to the appellate and supreme court structures.
- Increase humane treatment, rehabilitation, and reentry procedures within local and global enforcement jurisdictions.
- Teach the fundamentals of the judicial system from primary through schools of higher learning.
- Teach the processes of the Golden Rule ethic in homes, communities, faith-based institutions and all areas of society.

The effects of a relational economy and judicial governance system on societal violence is being measured by the new technologies of the global consciousness. As we have seen, the Global Peace Index, compiled by the Institute for Economics & Peace, looks beyond the Gross Domestic Product in measuring national growth and progress. With the use of extensive data acquisition, the IEP is shifting the focus to peace as the positive and measurable means to well-being and progress.

In past decades, the Index has shown a decrease in militarization from the previous years. As indicated in the organization's statement, defense cuts driven by economic austerity were a major factor. "What comes across dramatically in this year's results and the six year trends is a shift in global priorities," notes Steve Killelea, founder and executive chairman of IEP. "Nations have become externally more peaceful as they compete through economic, rather than military means. The results for Sub Saharan Africa as a whole are particularly striking—regional wars have waned as the African Union strives to develop economic and political integration."[7]

Economics and governance are directly related to peace. If the world had been even more peaceful, says the group, the gain would have been an estimated $9 trillion per year. Yet on closer inspection of the Index, the multidimensional measurement of wars, killing, health, education, and other factors shows the decrease is due to more than simple economic activity. There will be temporary rises in wars and violence as society adapts to change.

Historical economic systems were, arguably, the most efficient for humanity during their specific time. Society's ability to produce and distribute what was needed to survive was based on the evolution of thought and ideas as well as the technology available. As humanity moved from tribalism to capitalism, we formed large political organizations and legislated laws to institutionalize the means of production.

Today, with technology and ideas evolving so quickly, laws need constant modification to keep up with changing circumstances. The decreasing importance of national boundaries has driven law to be increasingly global in scope. In fact, people have already begun to rely on the judiciary to keep local and national laws in line with international law. Currently, most laws can be changed only by passing new laws or through legislative processes of repeal. The historical process of codification allows laws to be set in stone. These statutes virtually freeze the law at all levels of government, from local to national, even international.

Still, contemporary history has shown, especially in light of the polarization of the legislatures and executive branches, the courts are by far the most efficient way of preventing laws from becoming static and inefficient. To reform the law is a normal act of democracy, and standard processes are in place to ensure stability during the transition. Law reform, or legal reform, is the action of examining and assessing existing laws, then advocating changes that will create a more just or efficient system.

Law commissions are set up by legislatures, executive offices, or the judiciary to reform the law. These commissions begin to research current laws and recommend minor to major changes in order to modernize, simplify, or make more efficient the law. Two types of reform bodies can be created. Statutory commissions are those set up by governments in certain jurisdictions and having specific missions. These bodies have a degree of independence in order to be relatively free of influence or control.

Other law reform organizations are created outside government through the action of independent citizen or organizations. Associations, lobbies, human rights groups, corporations, and many other organizations often present issues and demand reform or referendum. Think tanks write position papers that give the reasons for changes in law. Political action groups and individual citizens bring their cases for change to courts.

A route to changing from a legislative and executive governing structure to a judicial structure is shown by the many commissions set up to monitor, analyze, and make recommendations for changes in our system. These are both governmental and private organizations. As an example, the Colorado Commission on Judicial Performance was established by the state in 1988. This commission was charged with providing "fair, responsible, and constructive evaluation of trial and appellate judges and justices."

At the local level in many states, district commissions take a look at judges and other personnel within their jurisdiction. Through questionnaires and sampling, these commissions review cases, sentencing, and other issues. Citizen surveys and evaluations are utilized by judicial personnel to understand the need for additional training, equipment, and new skills on particular issues important to constituents. The information is also used by voters to make decisions on whether to retain or not to retain a particular judge.

Direct election by the citizenry of U.S. senators did not come until the Seventeenth Amendment in 1907. The Constitution's framers in the eighteenth century had decided against direct election for the senate due to their lack of trust in the technology and wisdom of direct democracy. Today, a new amendment to provide for direct election of the judiciary could be a major step in opening the door to justice and expanding democracy.

Withering of Power Blocks

Institutionalized blocks of power are created through legislated laws and executive orders. They are maintained and strengthened, in many cases, through judicial rulings. In the past, negotiations and deals could be made without much concern for citizen involvement in the back halls of power. Today, new technologies of transparency are shining light on the actions of politicians, board rooms, autocrats, diplomats, stockbrokers, and taxpayers everywhere whose decisions on economic and political transactions affect the lives of billions.

Things will change rapidly under that increasingly pervasive light. National industrial policies that encourage bureaucratic lobbying and competitive strategies will increasingly fade into local industrial output for the good of the community. Creating and maintaining the local infrastructure will become a more collaborative effort for the benefit of all residents. Keeping our elderly healthy and our children in schools will be part of the essential reciprocal missions for our industrial and political motives.

The withering away of the old systems is something humanity has been dealing with for thousands of years. The transitions in the current age are coming even more quickly. Our adaptation to new technologies is training us for a future that is upon us.

~

"In a near transaction-free economy, property still exists, but remains in the hands of the producer and is accessed by the consumer over a period of time. Why would anyone want to own anything in a world of continuous upgrades, where new product lines sweep in and out of the market in an instant?"[8]*—Jeremy Rifkin*

One particular facet of society will be difficult to envision in a relational society based on justice. The military-industrial complex, alluded to by former U.S. president Dwight D. Eisenhower, has never been inherently bad. It was, indeed, *of the people* and with their consent for lack of a better way to deal with dangers and prosperity in the era of the Golden Mean. As the legislative-executive roles in maintaining the competitive nation-states of the last few centuries begin to wane, the roles of the military as well as the industrial base change from supporting national goals to providing for local goals.

Even as the world grapples with the rise of terror, the military is already becoming a local-global police force. Targeted responses reduce the huge expenditures necessary to prepare for and carry out war. Humanitarian missions, which the military is well equipped and trained to handle, will be increasingly needed as natural disasters and human technological catastrophes become even more destructive.

In all aspects of society, the transition to a just economy will, of course, present new challenges. Yet the relational economic and judicial governance systems will create opportunities idealized but not realized under the current system.

- The defining value of society will shift from short-term competitive exploitation to the reciprocal responsibility and long-term benefits of the Golden Rule.
- The definition of a better society will move from monetary measures to health and wellness.

- Decision-making will shift from global to local.
- The spirit of ambition and greed will shift from win-loss competitive advantage to win-win personal excellence, cooperation, and collaborative advantage.
- Accumulation of individual fortunes will be replaced by the accumulation of community resources.
- Governance will shift from nation-state legislative and executive power to a local, judicial rule of law.
- The inherently adversarial, response-oriented and self-interested nature of current institutions and systems will shift to relational, intentional, collaborative, and integrative systems that will flourish under the Golden Rule reciprocal ethic.

These predictions may sound like an idealist's dream, yet current history is proving that practicality is the most powerful change agent. The shift toward relational economy and judicial governance systems is happening now. The cultural story of the transition from centralized wealth and power for the few to a society where local people and communities are controlling their own destinies is documented in newspapers and books and through online social networking memes.

The measures of a thriving economy will change from a focus on the Gross Domestic Product and stock markets of nation-states to local and global performance measures in health and well-being. The allocation of resources will be determined by the natural workings of an economy free of manipulation and control by power brokers. The arbiter of power, the currency and usury system, will be completely redefined in terms of basic delivery of value in goods and services. Money as a transaction method will become an inefficient mechanism, soon to be replaced by flexible, local-global transactional exchange.

Local economies are responding with more efficient resource allocation and distribution systems measured on whether or not they provide for the good of the community. Locally owned enterprises subject to the full value factors of distribution and innovation are becoming more human in scale. Local and regional economies are seen as ecosystems that live and breathe with the values of local people and the environment. The end result will be people enjoying a balanced life with self-sustaining systems that mimic the natural world and offer long-term sustainability.

The movement from legislative laws toward freely formed contractual relations is happening almost beneath the radar of the popular press. As we move toward the conditions that necessitate a relational economy, reliance on legislated laws is a hindrance to the free flow of goods and services. Contracts have become the standard for fast-changing relations between parties within the economy. When the tenets of a contract are in dispute, the judiciary is replacing the legislature as the most efficient way to respond to changing conditions.

From local courts to the World Trade Organization, the most important disputes are being resolved and new precedent is being created for use in future contracts. Rule of law has done wonders for our civilizations. Now the movement from the rule of legislative law to the rule of judicial law based on precedent will allow a rational, flexible means of developing our economic relations.

To reap the benefits of peace does not depend wholly on the mechanisms of our systems. Rather, peace is dependent on humanity instituting the Golden Rule as the central ethic of the new age. From there, the economic and governing systems that rule our lives will evolve to mirror our intentions. Changing our governing processes to allow for innovation will transform our civil society. When the judiciary begins to take its future place as the mediator and arbiter of justice, we will release ourselves from the chains of the powerful few. Only then can we achieve our purpose as creative beings within the larger peace of humankind.

Chapter 27

Our Future Is Golden

When we talk about peace, there is an elephant in the room that is not so easy to ignore. Is human nature good, evil, or a confusing mixture of both? Can any system, even one based on the Golden Rule, overcome the weaknesses and frailties inherited at birth? Is peace actually possible?

Aristotle spoke about the depths of human avarice and ambition two thousand years ago. Immanuel Kant wrote of a bad heart arising "from the frailty of human nature, which is not strong enough to follow its adopted principles." According to the Bible's Genesis 6:5, "The Lord saw that the wickedness of man was great in the earth, and that every intention of the thoughts of his heart was only evil continually."

What hope is there for human relations and justice if in our hearts we are continually evil? "I find, then, that man was constituted free by God," said Tertullian, known as the father of Latin Christianity. "He was master of his own will and power ... For a law would not be imposed upon one who did not have it in his power to render that obedience which is due to law. Nor again, would the penalty of death be threatened against sin, if a contempt of the law were impossible to man in the liberty of his will ... Man is free, with a will either for obedience or resistance."[1]

The debate on whether human nature is good or evil may be unending, yet the hope that humanity can rise to achieve greatness is little debated. "There is an electric fire in human nature tending to purify," wrote the poet John Keats, "so that among these human creatures there is continually some birth of new heroism. The pity is that we must wonder at it, as we should at finding a pearl in rubbish."[2]

Another persistent debate is whether human evolution increases our capacity to achieve peace. Are we better off than we were thousands of years ago? Margaret Mead noted, "Human nature is potentially aggressive and destructive and potentially orderly and constructive."[3] Does that potential

A new generation of global leaders, such as the Rotary Peace Fellows shown here at the Bangkok Rotary Peace Symposium, is helping the world move toward an active, unifying Golden Rule ethic (Rotary International).

exist solely in the promise of biological evolution, or can our systems provide a path for increased safety, prosperity, and quality of life? "The most beautiful as well as the most ugly inclinations of man," said psychologist Erich Fromm, "are not part of a fixed biologically given human nature, but result from the social process which creates man."[4]

The promise of peace is to make our economic and governing systems conform to the people's highest dreams and aspirations. Yet we temper our utopian enthusiasm with the raw understanding that there is no quick fix. "Only on paper," noted George Bernard Shaw, "has humanity yet achieved glory, beauty, truth, knowledge, virtue, and abiding love."[5]

The contention of this book is that we have reached a point in our history when our personal and collective empathy, our compassionate innovations and engagements, our unity in pursuit of transcendent love are moving the promise of peace from paper to implementation. The Golden Rule has been waiting since antiquity to facilitate the transition from amoral to moral systems of economy and governance. Our collective moral maxim provides tried-and-true processes to achieve the reciprocal relationships necessary for relational economic and judicial governance systems. The tensions of past and future have intersected at this particular present. Humanity has an extraordinary opportunity for transformation.

Why Is a Relational Economy Inevitable?

One by-product of the globalized world is that human relations have become central to economic activity. In the development of huge markets, the sales cycle is more dependent than ever on building one-to-one relationships between providers and customers. With real-time communications, our associations, innovations, distributions, and rewards are increasingly transparent. The mutual exchange of the Golden Rule ethic can now be measured more openly and precisely by its benefit to all parties concerned.

As a result, freedom can no longer be held at a distance from the earth's seven billion inhabitants. Justice cannot remain the richness of the powerful few. The hope in this reality does not come from fearing the change but rather through embracing the possibility that each and every child of the future has potential for achieving purpose within a climate of peace. The following are indicators of that hope:

- Business practices focus on reciprocal stakeholder benefits
- Faith-based initiatives focus on interfaith cooperation
- Recreations and sports focus on cooperative achievement
- Educational systems focus on achieving the global classroom
- Wellness alternatives focus on the interwoven matrix of life
- Environmentalism focuses on the unifying goal of sustainable practices
- Service groups focus on training those they help
- Arts and design focus on creativity as human purpose
- Safety initiatives focus on non-lethal security
- Civic organizations focus on transparent inclusion

Some contend there are over 50,000 peace organizations. When one considers the actions of people building community within the Golden Rule ethic, the profile of peace extends to every household around the globe. Peace is the spirit of the age, the new mode of thinking, the *zeitgeist* of our time. With new technologies and measurable strategies, each sector of our society is finding the reciprocating virtues of the Golden Rule can be applied for mutual benefit. Equality in association, purposeful innovation, collaborative distribution, and fair reward are all results of the give and take necessary for economic vitality entailed in the relational economy.

In addition, historic political transformation is under way as a result of failing legislative and executive governance, which are control mechanisms of the powerful. "Justice and power must be brought together," said Blaise Pascal, "so that whatever is just may be powerful, and whatever is powerful may be just."[6]

Reliance on the judiciary as the potential intersection of power and justice is increasing. Rule of law based on case law and precedent provides stability. Trial courts and alternative conflict resolution processes endeavor to produce justice. Democracy stands in waiting, and the science of fair enforcement seeks to stop the historical causes and cycles of violence.

To look with Golden Mean eyes at the human story and our present global realities, we might be less than hopeful that anything more than cautious balance can be achieved. "Pervading nationalism imposes its dominion on man today in many different forms and with an aggressiveness that spares no one," said Pope John Paul II. "The challenge that is already with us is the temptation to accept as true freedom what in reality is only a new form of slavery."[7]

A relational economic system based on the necessity of reciprocal associations can break the impositions of power. A judicial governance system based on constant attention to our social contracts can limit institutionalized power. Ever vigilant, humanity must move forward into the new age with several advances in mind.

- Emphasize contractual responsibility in our associations.
- Link our sense of individual purpose to innovation.
- Consider societal costs in our distributions.
- Localize fair exchange through algorithmic technologies.
- Move rule of law from legislated to adjudicated.
- Equalize access to justice for the current underclass.
- Democratize the judiciary.
- Use integrative methods to achieve just enforcement.

The most important of these actions, and perhaps the most difficult, is the democratization of the judiciary. Without a fair and competent judicial system, justice in our economic and governing systems is impossible. Wealth and power will continue to rule and benefit. The highest dreams of humanity for *freedom from* and *freedom to* will be restrained by the avarice and ambition of the few. New technologies and a global educational system have increased the potential for democratization of the judiciary, but an informed citizenry is key.

If we instill the Golden Rule in our children as the universal moral model, the result will be a society where the consensus value of mutually beneficial exchange is free to work. Individual purpose will be honored within the collective. The goal will evolve from survivalist greed to generosity of spirit, which opens the door to unity and purpose.

The Golden Rule is a genetic gift from antiquity, a memetic piece of cultural wisdom to modern humanity. Through thick and thin, through wars and plagues, we have carried the ethic forward. Children grasp its simplicity. Adults of all creeds advocate its use. We are in awe when we witness its application in everyday life. "Our special task is to iterate and reiterate to the people that society is organized love," said Henry Demarest Lloyd, "and the Golden Rule its law."[8]

This ancient maxim of human philosophy and faith releases humanity from the shackles of institutionalized amorality to let people embrace the freedom of moral consensus. To help the Golden Rule construct our future economic and governance systems is to personally apply the processes of empathy, compassion, engagement, and unity toward practical and transcendental love. We must allow it to work in society. We must encourage it. Protect it. Advocate it. Teach it. We must institutionalize it. And, most importantly, we must live the Golden Rule, so that others might reciprocate in kind.

Chapter Notes

Epigraph

1. Rudolph Steiner, A.O. Barfield and T. Gordon-Jones, trans., *World Economy: The Formation of a Science of World-Economics. Fourteen lectures given in Dornach, 24 July to 6 August 1922*, Version 2.5.3 (Sussex, England: Rudolph Steiner Press, 1972), Lecture 10.

Preface

1. Steiner, Lecture 11.
2. Kate Pickett and Richard Wilkinson, *The Spirit Level: Why Greater Equality Makes Societies Stronger* (New York: Bloomsbury Publishing, 2009), 144.
3. Jeffrey Wattles, *The Golden Rule* (Oxford: Oxford University Press, 1996), 156.
4. Philip J. Morledge, *"I Do Solemnly Swear": Presidential Inauguration Speeches from George Washington to George W. Bush* (Sheffield, England: PJM Publishing, 2008), 218.
5. Wattles, 157.
6. John Clinton Arment, Letter to Monna Ruth Arment on U.S. Army stationery, February 8, 1945, seven excerpts noted.
7. Walt Kelly, *Pogo: We Have Met the Enemy and He Is Us* (New York: Simon & Schuster, 1972), 11.

Section One

1. Abraham H. Maslow, *The Farther Reaches of Human Nature* (New York: Viking, 1971), 237.

Chapter 1

1. Andrew W. Cordier and Wilder Foote, ed., *Public Papers of the Secretaries-General of the United Nations, Vol. 3, 1956–1957* (New York: Columbia University Press, 1973), 141.
2. G.W.F. Hegel, *Reading Hegel: The Introductions,* Aakash Singh and Rimina Mohapatra, ed. (Melbourne: Re.Press, 2008), 122.
3. Eric J. Sundquist, *King's Dream* (New York: Yale University Press, 2009), 100.
4. Richard Vinen, *A History in Fragments: Europe in the Twentieth Century* (Cambridge: Da Capo Press, 2000), 15.
5. Lyndon B. Johnson, "An Excerpt from the Restatement of U.S. Aims by U.S. President Lyndon B. Johnson," *Time*, 4 March 1966, 30.
6. Peter McWilliams and Jane Sedilos, *Ain't Nobody's Business If You Do: The Absurdity of Consensual Crimes in Our Free Country* (Sidney: Prelude Press, 1996), 463.
7. Martin Luther King, Jr., Michael K. Honey, ed., "All Labor Has Dignity," Beacon Press, 2011, Local 1199, New York City, 10 March 1968.
8. Mikhail Aleksandrovich Bakunin, *The Selected Works of Mikhail Aleksandrovich Bakunin* (Library of Alexandria), Section on Revolutionary Catechism.
9. UNESCO, "Programme of Action on a Culture of Peace. U.N. Resolution A/RES/52/13, 15 January 1998," accessed 22 April 2014, http://www3.unesco.org/iycp/kits/TabPofAAng.PDF.
10. Doris Kerns Goodwin, *No Ordinary Time, Franklin & Eleanor Roosevelt: The Home Front in World War II* (New York: Simon & Schuster Paperbacks, 1994), 485.

11. Raymond Polin and Constance Polin, ed., *Foundations of American Political Thought: Readings and Commentary* (New York: Peter Lang Publishing, 2006), 506.

Chapter 2

1. United Nations, "Universal Declaration of Human Rights," accessed 17 April 2014, http://www.un.org/en/documents/udhr/.

2. Jennifer Crwys-Williams, ed., *In the Words of Nelson Mandela* (New York: Walker, 2010), 41.

3. Geert H. Hofstede, *Culture's Consequences: Comparing Values, Behaviors, Institutions, and Organizations Across Nations* (London: Sage Publications, 2001), 113.

4. Jeremy Rifkin, *The Third Industrial Revolution: How Lateral Power Is Transforming Energy, the Economy, and the World* (New York: Macmillan, 2011), 259.

5. Jeffery Wattles, *The Golden Rule* (New York: Oxford University Press, 1996), 79.

6. Wattles, 83.

7. Jean Piaget with the assistance of seven collaborators, Marjorie Gabain, trans., *The Moral Judgment of a Child* (New York: Free Press Paperbacks Edition, 1997), 323.

8. Piaget, 323.

9. Wattles, 144.

10. *International Journal of Ethics*, Vol. 22, 1911/12, First Reprinting (Philadelphia: International Journal of Ethics, 1912), 278.

11. Wattles, 4.

12. Wattles, 25.

Chapter 3

1. Annping Chin, *Confucius: A Life of Thought and Politics* (New Haven: Yale University Press, 2007), 168.

2. Wattles, 32.

3. Richard Dawkins, *The Selfish Gene: 30th Anniversary Edition* (Oxford: Oxford University Press, 2006), 192.

4. Immanuel Kant, James W. Ellington, trans., *Grounding for the Metaphysics of Morals: On a Supposed Right to Lie because of Philanthropic Concerns*, 3rd ed. (Cambridge: Hackett Publishing, 1993), 30.

5. Wattles, 157.

6. William S. Sahakian and Mabel Lewis Sahakian, *Ideas of the Great Philosophers* (New York: HarperCollins, 1966), 37.

7. Wattles, 4.

8. *The Presbyterian and Reformed Review*, Vol. 5, 1894 (Philadelphia: MacCalla, 1894) 569.

9. Craig A. Bubeck, ed., *The Bible Knowledge: Background Commentary* (Colorado Springs: Cook Communications Ministries, 2003), 140.

10. Arvind Sharma, ed., *The World's Religions: A Contemporary Reader* (Minneapolis: Fortress Press, 2011), 71.

11. Anthony J. Parel, *Gandhi, Freedom, and Self-Rule* (Lanham, Maryland: Lexington Books, 2000), 73.

12. Peter J. Frederick, *Knights of the Golden Rule: The Intellectual as Christian Social Reformer in the 1800s* (Lexington: University Press of Kentucky, 1976), 68.

Chapter 4

1. Adam Smith, *An Inquiry into the Nature and Causes of the Wealth of Nations,* J.C. Bullock, ed. (New York: P. F. Collier & Sons, 1909), 351.

2. Max J. Rosenthal, "Iraq War and Afghan Conflict Harmed the Economy, Study Says," *Huffington Post*, 1 March 2012.

3. David P. Barash and Charles P. Webel, *Peace and Conflict Studies*, 3rd ed. (Thousand Oaks, California: Sage Publications, 2014), 16.

4. Korten, David, "Path to a Peace Economy," *Yes!*, accessed 17 April 2014. http://www.yesmagazine.org/new-economy/path-to-a-peace-economy?b_start:int=0&-C=.

5. William James, John Roland, intro,. *The Moral Equivalent of War*, accessed 17 April 2014, http://www.constitution.org/wj/meow.htm.

Chapter 5

1. John F. Kennedy. "John F. Kennedy Address Before the Canadian Parliament in Ottawa, May 17, 1961," accessed 17 April 2014, http://www.presidency.ucsb.edu/ws/?pid=8136.

2. Robert Picciotto and Viesner Durán, ed., *Evaluation Ad Development: The Institutional Dimension* (Washington D.C.: The World Bank, 1998), 113.

Section Two

1. N.D. Arora, *Political Science for Civil Services Main Examination* (New Delhi: Tata McGraw Hill Education Private Limited, 2010), 11.25.

Chapter 6

1. Voltaire, *Candide*, (Minneapolis: Filiquarian Publishing, 2008), 8.
2. Aristotle and John Gillies, *Aristotle's Ethics and Politics: Politics* (London: A. Strahan and T. Cadell and W. Davies, 1797), 179.
3. Steiner, Lecture 5.
4. Steiner, Lecture 10.
5. Bartering, "Online Encyclopedia," *Inc.*, accessed 18 April 2014, http://www.inc.com/encyclopedia/bartering.html.
6. Rifdin, 37.
7. Cynthia C. Kelly, ed., *Oppenheimer and the Manhattan Project: Insights into J. Robert Oppenheimer, "Father of the Atomic Bomb"* (Singapore: World Scientific Publishing, 2006), 58.

Chapter 7

1. Rotary International, "Guiding Principles, Four-Way Test," accessed 18 April 2014, https://www.rotary.org/en/guiding-principles.
2. The Rotary Foundation of Rotary International, "Peace Is Possible," 4, accessed 18 April 2014, https://www.rotary.og/en/document/880.
3. District 6930 Rotary International, "Rotary Peace Fellows," accessed 23 April 2014, http://www.rotary6930.org/rotary-peace-fellows/.
4. Susan Smith Jones, *The Joy Factor: 10 Sacred Practices for Radiant Health* (San Francisco: Conari Press, 2011), 43.

Chapter 8

1. Salman Khan, *The One World Schoolhouse: Education Reimagined*, Kindle ed. (New York: Hachette Book Group, 2012), location 1883.
2. Harry J. Gensler, *Ethics and the Golden Rule* (New York: Routledge, 2013), 77.
3. Gudmundur Alfredsson and Asbjorn Eide, ed., *The Universal Declaration of Human Rights: A Common Standard for Achievement* (The Hague: Kluwer Law International, 1999), 417.
4. Werner Zollitsch, Christoph Winckler, Susanne Waiblinger and Alexander Haslberger, ed., *Sustainable Food Production and Ethics* (Wageningen, The Netherlands: Wageningen Academic Publishers, 2007), 154.
5. U.S. Department of State, "Fact Sheet: Non-Governmental Organizations (NGOs) in the United States, 2012–01–12," accessed 18 April 2014, http://www.humanrights.gov/2012/01/12/fact-sheet-non-governmental-organizations-ngos-in-the-united-states/.
6. Jessica Reeder, "2012: The Year of the Cooperative," *Yes!*, 1 February 2012.

Chapter 9

1. Michael Nojeim, *Gandhi and King: The Power of Nonviolent Resistance* (Westport, CT: Greenwood, 2004), 110–111.
2. PR Newswire, "Awearness: The Kenneth Cole Foundation, Announces Opening of the Kenneth Cole Haiti Health Center," accessed 23 April 2014, http://www.prnewswire.com/news-releases/awearness-the-kenneth-cole-foundation-announces-opening-of-the-kenneth-cole-haiti-health-center-168841416.html.
3. The Opus Prize, "Overview of the Prize," accessed 23 April 2014, http://www.opusprize.org/about/overview.cfm.
4. Catholic Relief Services, "Background of CRS Peacebuilding Program," accessed 23 April 2014, http://crs.org/peacebuilding/general_background.cfm.
5. Catholic Relief Services, "Technical Resources: Peacebuilding," accessed 23 April 2014, http://www.crsprogramquality.org/peacebuilding-description/.
6. Henry Wadsworth Longfellow, *Poems and Other Writings* (New York: Penguin, 2000), 746.

Chapter 10

1. Rifkin, 260.
2. Rifkin, 260.
3. Brychan Thomas, Christopher Miller and Lyndon Murphy, *Innovation and Small Business: Volume 1* (London: Ventus Publishing, 2011), 10.
4. Rifkin, 21.

5. John Fitzgerald Kennedy, "Address to the UN General Assembly, September 25, 1961," accessed 18 April 2014, http://miller center.org/president/speeches/detail/5741.

6. John Stossel, *The Daily Beast*, Interview on 6 December 2009 with Lloyd Grove, "Fitting in at Fox," accessed 25 July 2014, http://www.thedailybeast.com/articles/2009/12/06/fitting-in-at-fox.html.

Chapter 11

1. Walter Isaacson, *Steve Jobs* (New York: Simon & Schuster, 2011), 343.

2. Isaacson, 61.

3. Isaacson, 140.

4. Isaacson, 134.

5. Isaacson, 154.

6. Isaacson, 220.

7. Isaacson, 233.

8. Isaacson, 234.

9. Isaacson, 285.

10. Ben Klaiber, *Anatomy of an Apple: The Lessons Steve Taught Us*, Kindle ed. (Bookbaby, 2013), The Storm Before the Calm.

11. Isaacson, 370.

12. Walter Isaacson, *Great Innovators: Benjamin Franklin, Einstein, Steve Jobs* (New York: Simon & Schuster, 2011), The Whiteness of the Whale.

13. Walter Isaacson, *Steve Jobs* (New York: Simon & Schuster, 2011), 527.

14. Jay Green, *Design Is How It Works: How the Smartest Companies Turn Products into Icons* (New York: Penguin, 2010), Introduction.

15. Isaacson, vii.

Chapter 12

1. Rajesh Makwana, *Multinational Corporations (MNCs): Beyond the Profit Motive*. Share the World's Resources, 3 October 2006, accessed 18 July 2014, http://www.sharing.org/information-centre/reports/multinational-corporations-mncs-beyond-profit-motive#Part%202%20-%20The%20History%20Of%20The%20Corporation.

2. Rifkin, 116.

Chapter 13

1. Hindustan Unilever Limited, "Unilever Sustainability Living Plan: Progress Report, 2012" (Mumbai: Hindustan Unilever, 2012), 2.

2. Hindustan Unilever Limited, Annual Report, 2013 (Mumbai: Hindustan Unilever, 2013), 7.

3. Hindustan Unilever Limited, Annual Report, 2013 (Mumbai: Hindustan Unilever, 2013), 12–13.

4. Hindustan Unilever Limited, Unilever Sustainability Living Plan: Progress Report, 2012 (Mumbai: Hindustan Unilever, 2012), 9.

5. Charles F. Wilkinson, *Blood Struggle: The Rise of Modern Indian Nations* (New York: W. W. Norton, 2005), 159.

Chapter 14

1. Rifkin, 212.

2. "Newsletter of the Bahái International Community," April–June 2000, Vol. 12, Issue 1, accessed 19 April 2014, http://www.one country.org/story/un-civil-society-repre sentatives-gather-millennium-forum.

3. Orison Swett Marden, *Pushing to the Front* (Petersburg, NY: The Success Company, 1911). Chapter LXV: Why Some Succeed and Others Fail, accessed, 18 June 2014, http://www.gutenberg.org/files/21291/21291-h/21291-h.htm#chap65.

Chapter 15

1. "Widely quoted from Ben Cohen of Ben & Jerry's," accessed 19 April 2014, http://www.customerservicemanager.com/101-inspira tional-customer-service-quotes.htm.

2. Provided by Salesforce.com.

3. Ibid.

4. Ibid.

5. Ibid.

6. Bruno Ventelou, Gregory P. Nowell, trans. *Millennial Keynes: An Introduction to the Origin, Development, and Later Currents of Keynesian Thought* (Armonk, NY: M.E. Sharpe, 2005), 33.

Section Three

1. John W. Johnson, ed., *Historic U.S. Court Cases: An Encyclopedia*, Vol. 2, 2nd ed. (London: Routledge, 2001), 792.

Chapter 17

1. Barrie Houlihan and Mike Green, ed., *Routledge Handbook of Sports Development* (New York: Routledge, 2011), Chapter 24, Right to Play.
2. United Nations NOSDP, "Why Sport?" accessed 22 April 2014, http://www.un.org/wcm/content/site/sport/home/sport.
3. Kristine Toohey and A. J. Veal, *The Olympic Games: A Social Science Perspective*, 2nd ed. (Wallingford: CABI International, 2007), 42.
4. Bill Mallon and Jeroen Heijmans, *Historical Dictionary of the Olympic Movement*, 4th ed. (Lanham, MD: Scarecrow, 2011), xv.

Chapter 18

1. *Political Science*, Open Textbook (Boston: Boundless Learning, 2013), 1011.
2. Wattles, 78.
3. Edmund Burke, *Selected Letters of Edmund Burke,* Harvey C. Mansfield, Jr., ed. (Chicago: University of Chicago, 1984), 21.

Chapter 19

1. Christopher Pierson, *Just Property: A History in the Latin West. Volume One: Wealth, Virtue, and the Law* (Oxford: Oxford University Press, 2013), 28.
2. Andrew Zolli, "Learning to Bounce Back," *New York Times*, accessed 18 April 2014, http://www.nytimes.com/2012/11/03/opinion/forget-sustainability-its-about-resilience.html?pagewanted=all&_r=1&.
3. Ibid.

Chapter 20

1. Charles L. Zelden, *Thurgood Marshall: Race, Rights, and the Struggle for a More Perfect Union* (New York: Routledge, 2013), 117.

Chapter 21

1. Harold Greenwald, *Experimentation and Innovation in Psychotherapy* (New Brunswick, NJ: Transaction Publishers, 2010), 146.

2. Paul Simon and Arthur R. Simon, *The Politics of World Hunger: Grass-Roots Politics and World Poverty* (New York: Harper's Magazine Press, 1973), 146.
3. Carter Center, "Guinea Worm Eradication Program," accessed 20 April 2014, http://www.cartercenter.org/health/guinea_worm/index.html.
4. Leslie Stainton, *Lorca—A Dream of Life* (London: Bloomsbury Publishing, 2013). Citation from Lorca's interview in the Madrid daily La Voz.

Chapter 22

1. Philip G. Henderson, ed., *The Presidency Then and Now* (Lanham, MD: Rowman & Littlefield, 2000), 25.
2. Reinhold Niebuhr, *The Essential Reinhold Niebuhr: Selected Essays and Addresses,* Robert McAfee Brown, ed. (New Haven: Yale University Press, 1896), 160.
3. Charles Grove Haines, *The Role of the Supreme Court in American Government and Politics: 1789–1835,* Vol. 1 (Berkeley: University of California Press, 1944), 199.
4. Kenny Colston, "Former Justice O'Connor Says Direct Election of Judges Corrupts the System," WFPL News, accessed 20 April 2014, http://wfpl.org/post/former-justice-oconnor-says-direct-election-judges-corrupts-system.
5. Barbara Boxer, "Why I Must Object," Truthout, June 6, 2005. Accessed June 18, 2014, http://www.truth-out.org/archive/component/k2/item/51610:senator-boxer—why-i-must-object.

Chapter 23

1. Salman Khan, *The One World Schoolhouse: Education Reimagined*, Kindle ed. (New York: Hachette Book Group, 2012), Location 19.
2. Khan, Location 175.
3. Khan, Location 19.
4. Khan, Location 54.
5. James Temple, "Salman Khan, Math Master of the Internet," *SFGate online magazine,* 14 December 2009, accessed 23 April 2014, http://www.sfgate.com/business/article/Salman-Khan-math-master-of-the-Internet-3278578.php.
6. Khan, Location 141–142.

7. Bertrand Russell, *Uncertain Paths to Freedom: Russia and China, 1919–1922* (London: Routledge, 2000), 356.

8. Khan, Location 820.

9. Janet Benge and Geoff Benge, *George Washington Carver: From Slave to Scientist* (Bingley, England: Emerald Books, 2001), 91.

10. Khan, Location 141.

11. Kevin Devlin, "Khan Academy: Good, Bad, or Ugly?" *Huffington Post*, 20 March 2012, accessed 23 April 2014, http://www.huffingtonpost.com/dr-keith-devlin/khan-academy-good-bad-or-_b_1345925.html.

12. Khan, Location 234.

13. Khan, Location 2605.

14. Khan, Location 1066.

15. Khan, Location 1317.

16. "Guidelines, Richard P. Feynman Prize for Excellence in Teaching," Cal Tech, Office of the Provost, accessed 23 April 2014, http://provost.caltech.edu/FeynmanTeachingPrize/guidelines.

17. George Steiner, *Lessons of the Masters: Charles Eliot Norton Lectures, 2001–2002* (Cambridge: Harvard University Press, 2003), 183–184.

18. "Right to Education: International Covenant on Economics, Social and Cultural Rights, United Nations, 1966," UNESCO, Bangkok, accessed 23 April 2014, http://www.unescobkk.org/education/right-to-education/rights-based-approach-to-education/right-to-education-in-international-instruments/.

19. Khan, Location 54.

Chapter 24

1. Mahatma Gandhi, *The Gandhi Reader: A Sourcebook of His Life and Writings* (New York: Grove Press, 1956), 194.

2. Cutting Edge Law, *What if Lawyers Were Peacemakers, Problem Solvers, and Healers of Conflict?* accessed 28 April 2014, http://cuttingedgelaw.com/page/integrative-law-movement-introduction.

3. Mohandas Gandhi, edited by V. Geetha, *Soul Force: Gandhi's Writings on Peace* (India: Tara Publishing, 2004), 197.

4. Dwight Eisenhower, "General Eisenhower Speaks...," *Life Magazine*, 24 March 1947, 89.

Chapter 25

1. Isaac Asimov, *I, Robot* (New York: Bantam, 2004), 117.

Section Four

1. Khan, Location 399.

Chapter 26

1. Frederick, 68.

2. Frederick, 238.

3. Ibid.

4. Marnie Jones, *Holy Toledo: Religion and Politics in the Life of "Golden Rule" Jones.* (Lexington: University of Kentucky Press, 1998), 128.

5. Samuel Milton Jones. *The New Right; A Plea for Fair Play Through a More Just Social Order* (New York: Eastern Book Concern, 1899), 125.

6. Frederick, 239.

7. Reuters. "2012 Global Peace Index: World Slightly More Peaceful in 2012, Reversing Two-year Trend." Accessed April 20, 2014, http://www.reuters.com/article/2012/06/12/idUS42272+12-Jun-2012+PRN20120612.

8. Rifkin, 220.

Chapter 27

1. Tertullian, Peter Holmes, trans. *The Five Books against Marcion* (these documents, last modified 3 February 1998, were originally from the Christian Classics Electronic Library server, then at Wheaton College; accessed from the Ante-Nicene Fathers' website: http://www.ccel.org/fathers2), 542–3.

2. John Keats, *Bright Star: The Complete Poems and Selected Letters* (London: Vintage Books, 2010), 502–503.

3. Margaret Mead, ed., *The Study of Contemporary Western Cultures, Vol. 2.; And Keep Your Powder Dry: An Anthropologist Looks at America* (New York: Berghahn Books, 2000), 134.

4. Erich Fromm, *Escape from Freedom* (Open Road Media, 2013) Section 1.

5. Michael Holroyd, *Bernard Shaw: The One-Volume Definitive Edition* (New York: W.W. Norton, 2012) Section 3.

6. Michael C. Braswell, Belinda R. McCarthy and Bernard McCarthy, *Justice, Crime, and Ethics*, 6th ed. (Newark: Matthew Bender, 2008), 347.

7. Pope John Paul II and Tony Castle, *The Light of Christ: Meditations for Every Day of the Year* (Chicago: Crossroad Publications, 1987), 162.

8. Henry Demarest Lloyd, *Man, the Social Creator* (New York: Doubleday, Page, 1906), 24.

Select Bibliography

Abbink, Jon, and Gerti Hesseling, ed. *Election Observation and Democratization in Africa*. New York: St. Martin's Press, 2000.

Ackerman, Peter, and Jack DuVall. *A Force More Powerful: A Century of Nonviolent Conflict*. New York: St. Martin's Press, 2000.

Ackerman, Peter, and Christopher Kruegler. *Strategic Nonviolent Conflict: The Dynamics of People Power in the Twentieth Century*. Westport, CT: Praeger, 1994.

Amiram Raviv, Lou. *How Children Understand War and Peace: A Call for International Peace Education*. San Francisco: Jossey-Bass, 1999.

Anderlini, Sanam Naraghi. *Women Building Peace: What They Do, Why It Matters*. Boulder, CO: Lynne Rienner Publishers, 2007.

Arnson, Cynthia J., and I. William Zartman, ed. *Rethinking the Economic of War: The Intersection of Need, Creed, and Greed*. Washington, D.C.: Woodrow Wilson Center Press, 2005.

Barish, David P., and Charles P. Webel. *Peace and Conflict Studies*. Thousand Oaks, CA: Sage Publications, 2002.

Barrett, Scott. *Environment and Statecraft: The Strategy of Environmental Treaty-Making*. Oxford: Oxford University Press, 2005. Retrieved 10 March 2009, http://ebooks.ohiolink.edu/xtf-ebc/view?docId=tei/ox/0199286094/0199286094.xml&query=&brand=default.

Bekker, Peter H. F. *World Court Decisions at the Turn of the Millennium, 1997–2001*. The Hague and New York: M. Nijhoff, 2002.

Bennett, Steven C. *Arbitration: Essential Concepts*. New York: ALM Pub., 2002.

Benton, Barbara, ed. *Soldiers for Peace: Fifty Years of United Nations Peacekeeping*. New York: Facts on File, 1996.

Blackburn, William R. *The Sustainability Handbook: The Complete Management Guide to Achieving Social, Economic, and Environmental Responsibility*. Washington, D.C.: Environmental Law Institute, 2007.

Blakaby, Frank, and Joseph Rotblat, et al., ed. *A Nuclear-Weapon-Free World: Desirable?, Feasible?* Boulder, CO: Westview Press, 1993.

Bodine, Richard J., and Donna K. Crawford. *The Handbook of Conflict Resolution Education: A Guide to Building Quality Programs in School*. San Francisco: Jossey-Bass, 1998.

Booth, W. James. *Communities of Memory: On Witness, Identity, and Justice*. Ithaca: Cornell University Press, 2006.

Bosch, Olivia, and Peter van Ham, ed. *Global Non-Proliferation and Counter-Terrorism: The Impact of UNSCR 1540*. Washington, D.C.: Brookings Institution Press, 2007.

Braswell, Michael C., Belinda R. McCarthy, and Bernard McCarthy. *Justice, Crime, and Ethics*, Sixth Edition. Newark: Matthew Bender, 2008.

Brock, Peter. *The Quaker Peace Testimony:*

1660–1914. York, England: Sessions Book Trust, 1990.

Brown, Michael Barratt. *Fair Trade*. London: Zed Books, 1993.

Bush, Robert A. Baruch, and Joseph P. Folger. *The Promise of Mediation: Responding to Conflict through Empowerment and Recognition*. San Francisco: Jossey-Bass, 1994.

Carnegie Commission on Preventing Deadly Conflict. *Preventing Deadly Conflict: Final Report*. New York: Carnegie Corporation, 1997.

Chan, Steve, and A. Cooper Drury, ed. *Sanctions as Economic Statecraft: Theory and Practice*. New York: St. Martin's Press, 2000.

Chernus, Ira. *American Nonviolence: The History of an Idea*. Maryknoll, NY: Orbis Books, 2004.

Chin, Annping. *Confucius: A Life of Thought and Politics*. New Haven: Yale University Press, 2007.

Chinn, Peggy L. *Peace and Power: Creative Leadership for Building Community*. Boston: Jones and Bartlett, 2004.

Cloke, Kenneth, and Joan Goldsmith. *Resolving Personal and Organizational Conflict: Stories of Transformation and Forgiveness*. San Francisco: Jossey-Bass, 2000.

Coffin, William Sloane, and Morris I. Leibman. *Civil Disobedience: Aid or Hindrance to Justice?* Washington, D.C.: American Enterprise Institute for Public Policy Research, 1972.

Cohn, Ernist J., et al., ed. *Handbook of Institutional Arbitration in International Trade: Facts, Figures, and Rules*. Amsterdam: North Holland Publishers, 1977.

DeBenedetti, Charles. *Peace Heroes in Twentieth-Century America*. Bloomington: Indiana University Press, 1986.

DeChaine, D. Robert. *Global Humanitarianism: NGOs and the Crafting of Community*. Lanham, MD: Lexington Books, 2005.

Dill, Vicky Schreiber. *A Peaceable School: Cultivating a Culture of Nonviolence*. Bloomington, IN: Phi Delta Kappa Educational Foundation, 1998.

Dreher, Diane. *The Tao of Inner Peace: A Guide to Inner Peace*. New York: Plume, 2000.

Etzioni, Amitai. *The New Golden Rule: Community and Morality in a Democratic Society*. New York: Basic Books, 1996.

Evans, Alice Frazer, and Robert A. Evans. *Peace Skills: Leaders' Guide*. San Francisco: Jossey-Bass, 2001.

Falk, Richard A., Robert C. Johansen, and Samuel S. Kim, ed. *The Constitutional Foundations of World Peace*. Albany: State University of New York Press, 1993.

Fehr, Beverly, et al., ed. *The Science of Compassionate Love: Theory, Research, and Applications*. Malden, MA: Wiley-Blackwell, 2009.

Fisher, Ronald J. *Interactive Conflict Resolution*. New York: Syracuse University Press, 1997.

Forcey, Linda Rennie, and Ian Murray Harris. *Peacebuilding for Adolescents: Strategies for Educators and Community Leaders*. New York: Peter Lang Publishing, 1999.

Forsythe, David P. *Human Rights & World Peace*. 2nd ed. Lincoln: University of Nebraska Press, 1989.

Fort, Timothy L. *Business, Integrity, and Peace: Beyond Geopolitical and Disciplinary Boundaries*. Cambridge: Cambridge University Press, 2007.

Frederick, Peter J. *Knights of the Golden Rule: The Intellectual as Christian Social Reformer in the 1800s*. Lexington: University Press of Kentucky, 1976.

Freedman, Russell. *Confucius: The Golden Rule*. New York: Arthur A. Levine Books, 2002.

Gensler, Harry J. *Ethics and the Golden Rule*. New York: Routledge, 2013.

Girard, Kathryn, and Susan J. Koch. *Conflict Resolution in the Schools: A Manual for Educators*. San Francisco: Jossey-Bass, 1996.

Glickman, Lawrence B. *Buying Power: A History of Consumer Activism in America*. Chicago: University of Chicago Press, 2009.

Gosselin, Abigail. *Global Poverty and Individual Responsibility*. Lanham, MD: Lexington Books, 2009.

Graham, Thomas, Jr., and Damien J. LaVera. *Cornerstones of Security: Arms Control Treaties in the Nuclear Era*. Seattle: University of Washington Press, 2003.

Graybill, Lyn S. *Truth and Reconciliation in South Africa: Miracle or Model?* Boulder, CO: Lynne Rienner Publishers, 2002.

Guogi, Yu. *Olympic Dreams: China and Sports, 1895–2008.* Cambridge, MA: Harvard University Press, 2008.

Haines, Charles Grove. *The Role of the Supreme Court in American Government and Politics: 1789–1835,* Volume 1. Berkeley: University of California Press, 1944.

Harris, Ian M., and Mary Lee Morrison. *Peace Education.* Jefferson, NC: McFarland, 2003.

Hastings, Tom H. *The Lessons of Nonviolence: Theory and Practice in a World of Conflict.* Jefferson, NC: McFarland, 2006.

Hastings, Tom H. *Nonviolent Response to Terrorism.* Jefferson, NC: McFarland, 2004.

Helminiak, Lanham. *Spirituality for Our Global Community: Beyond Traditional Religion to a World at Peace.* Lanham, MD: Rowman & Littlefield, 2008.

Heydenberk, Warren, and Roberta Heydenberk. *A Powerful Peace: The Integrative Thinking Classroom.* Boston: Allyn and Bacon, 2000.

Holbrooke, Richard. *To End a War.* New York: Modern Library, 1999.

Hope, Ronald H. *Poverty, Livelihoods, and Governance in Africa: Fulfilling the Development Promise.* New York: Palgrave Macmillan, 2008.

Howard, Lisa Morjé. *U.N. Peacekeeping in Civil Wars.* Cambridge: Cambridge University Press, 2008.

The International Bill of Human Rights. Foreword by Jimmy Carter. Introduction by Tom J. Farer. Glen Ellen, CA: Entwhistle Books, 1981.

International Development Research Center. *Cultivating Peace: Conflict and Collaboration in Natural Resource Management.* Ottawa: International Development Research Center, 1999. Retrieved 10 March 2009, http://www.netlibrary.com/Search/BasicSearch.aspx.

Isaacson, Walter. *Steve Jobs.* New York: Simon & Schuster, 2011.

Isard, Walter. *Understanding Conflict & the Science of Peace.* Cambridge: Blackwell, 1992.

Iyer, Raghavan, *The Moral and Political Writings of Mahatma Gandhi, Vol. III Non-Violent Resistance and Social Transformation.* Oxford: Clarendon Press, 1987.

Jamner, Margaret Schneider, and Daniel Stokols, ed. *Promoting Human Wellness: New Frontiers for Research, Practice, and Policy.* Berkeley: University of California Press, 2000.

Johnson, John W., ed. *Historic U.S. Court Cases: An Encyclopedia,* Vol. 2, Second Ed. London: Routledge, 2001.

Jones, Marnie. *Holy Toledo: Religion and Politics in the Life of "Golden Rule."* Lexington: University Press of Kentucky, 1998.

Jones, Samuel Milton. *The New Right: A Plea for Fair Play Through a More Just Social Order.* New York: Eastern Book Concern, 1899.

Khan, Salman. *The One World School House: Education Reimagined.* New York: Twelve, Hatchette Book Group, 2012.

King, Robert Harlen. *Thomas Merton and Thich Nhat Hanh: Engaged Spirituality in an Age of Globalization.* New York: Continuum International Publishing Group, 2001.

Kool, V.L. *The Psychology of Nonviolence and Aggression.* New York: Palgrave Macmillan, 2008.

Korey, William. *NGOs and the Universal Declaration of Human Rights.* New York: St. Martin's, 1998.

Kriegel, Blandine, Marc A. LePain and Jeffrey C. Cohen, trans. *The State and the Rule of Law.* Princeton, NJ: Princeton University Press, 1995.

Kurlansky, Mark. *Nonviolence: Twenty-five Lessons from the History of a Dangerous Idea.* New York: Random House, Modern Library, 2006.

LaBotz, Dan. *César Chávez and la Causa.* New York: Pearson/Longman, 2006.

Lauren, Gordon. *The Evolution of International Human Rights: Visions Seen.* 2nd ed. Philadelphia: University of Pennsylvania Press, 2003.

Leys, Simon, trans. *The Analects of Confucius.* New York: W.W. Norton, 1997.

Lederach, John Paul. *The Moral Imagination: The Art and Soul of Building Peace.* New York: Oxford University Press, 2005.

Marden, Orison Swett. *Pushing to the Front.* Petersburg, NY: Success Company, 1911. Chapter LXV: Why Some Succeed and Others Fail. http://www.gutenberg.org/files/21291/21291-h/21291-h.htm#chap65.

Maslow, Abraham H. *Motivation and Personality.* 2nd ed. New York: Harper & Row, 1970.

McFaul, Thomas R. *The Future of Peace and Justice in the Global Village: The Role of World Religions in the Twenty-first Century.* Westport, CT: Praeger, 2006.

Meyer, Aleta Lynn. *Promoting Nonviolence in Early Adolescence: Responding in Peaceful and Positive Ways.* New York: Kluwer Academic/Plenum Publishers, 2000.

Meyer, Howard N. *The World Court in Action.* Lanham, MD: Rowman & Littlefield, 2002.

Milko, Matthew. *Peaceful Societies.* Oakville, Ontario: CPRI Press, 1973.

Mills, Nicolaus. *Winning the Peace.* Hoboken, NJ: John Wiley & Sons, 2008.

Mitchell, George J. *Making Peace.* New York: Knopf, 1999.

Mollin, Marian. *Radical Pacifism in Modern America: Egalitarianism and Protest.* Philadelphia: University of Pennsylvania Press, 2006.

Moore, Christopher W. *The Mediation Process: Practical Strategies for Resolving Conflict.* San Francisco: Jossey-Bass, 2003.

Moore, John Allphin, Jr., and Jerry Pubantz. *The New United Nations: International Organization in the Twenty-first Century.* Upper Saddle River, NJ: Pearson Prentice Hall, 2006.

Mortenson, Greg, and David Oliver Relin. *Three Cups of Tea: One Man's Mission to Promote Peace... One School at a Time.* New York: Penguin Books, 2006.

Muscat, Robert J. *Investing in Peace: How Development Aid Can Prevent or Promote Conflict.* Armonk, NY: M.E. Sharpe, 2002.

Myers, N., and J. Kent. *Environmental Refugees: A Growing Phenomenon in the 21st Century.* Washington, D.C.: The Climate Institute, 2001.

Nafziger, E. Wayne, and Juha Auvinen. *Economic Development, Inequality, and War: Humanitarian Emergencies in Developing Countries.* New York: Palgrave Macmillan, 2003.

Nagel, Stuart S., ed. *Handbook of Global Economic Policy.* New York: Marcel Dekker, 2000.

Narlikar, Amrita. *The World Trade Organization: A Very Short Introduction.* Oxford: Oxford University Press, 2005.

Newton, David E. *Environmental Justice: A Reference Handbook.* Santa Barbara, CA: ABC-CLIO, 1996.

Oliner, Samuel P. *Do Unto Others.* Cambridge, MA: Westview Press, 2003.

Osa, Maryjane. *Solidarity and Contention: Networks of Polish Opposition.* Minneapolis: University of Minnesota Press, 2003.

Otto, Nathan, and Heinz Norden, ed. *Einstein on Peace.* New York: Simon & Schuster, 1960.

Pickett, Kate, and Richard Wilkinson. *The Spirit Level: Why Greater Equality Makes Societies Stronger.* New York: Bloomsbury Publishing, 2009.

Pierson, Christopher. *Just Property: A History in the Latin West. Volume One: Wealth, Virtue, and the Law.* Oxford: Oxford University Press, 2013.

Pikas, Anatol. *Rational Conflict Resolution.* Uppsala, Sweden: Stencile Edition, 1973.

Pinker, Steven. *The Better Angels of Our Nature.* London: Penguin, 2011.

Plante, Thomas G., and Carl E. Thoresen, ed. *Spirit, Science, and Health: How the Spiritual Mind Fuels Physical Wellness.* Westport, CT: Praeger, 2007.

Pogue, Alan, and Roy Flukinger. *Witness for Justice: The Documentary Photographs of Alan Pogue.* Austin: University of Texas Press, 2007.

Ransom, David. *The No-nonsense Guide to Fair Trade.* Oxford: New Internationalist Publications, 2001.

Rao, K. Ramakrishna, ed. *Cultivating Consciousness: Enhancing Human Potential, Wellness, and Healing.* Westport, CT: Praeger, 1993.

Rawls, John. *A Theory of Justice.* Cambridge, MA: Belknap Press of Harvard University Press, 1999.

Reiss, Albert J., Jr., and Jeffrey A. Roth, ed. *Violence: Understanding and Preventing.* Washington, D.C.: National Academy Press, 1993.

Requejo, William Hernandez, and John L. Graham. *Global Negotiation: The New Rules.* New York: Palgrave Macmillan, 2008.

Reychler, Luc, and Thania Paffenholz, ed. *Peacebuilding: A Field Guide.* Boulder, CO: Lynne Rienner Publishers, 2001.

Rifkin, Jeremy. *The Third Industrial Revolution: How Lateral Power Is Transforming Energy, the Economy, and the World.* New York: Macmillan, 2011.

Rigby, Andrew. *Justice and Reconciliation: After the Violence.* Boulder, CO: Lynne Rienner Publishers, 2001.

Ross, Fiona C. *Bearing Witness: Women and the Truth and Reconciliation Commission in South Africa.* Sterling, VA: Pluto Press, 2003.

Schrumpf, Fred, Donna K. Crawford, and Richard J. Bodine. *Peer Mediation: Conflict Resolution in Schools: Program Guide.* Champaign, IL: Research Press, 1997.

Shermer, Michael. *The Science of Good and Evil: Why People Cheat, Gossip, Care, Share and Follow the Golden Rule.* New York: Times Books, 2004.

Smoker, Paul, et al., ed. *A Reader in Peace Studies.* Oxford: Pergamon Press, 1990.

Solimano, Andrés, Eduardo Aninat, and Nancy Birdstall, ed. *Distributive Justice and Economic Development: The Case of Chile and Developing Countries.* Ann Arbor: University of Michigan Press, 2000.

Stainton, Leslie. *Lorca—A Dream of Life.* London: Bloomsbury Publishing, 2013.

Starke, J. G. *An Introduction to the Science of Peace (Irenology).* Leyden: A.W. Sijthoff, 1968.

Stegar, Manfred B. *Gandhi's Dilemma: Nonviolent Principles and Nationalist Power.* New York: St. Martin's, 2000.

Steiner, Rudolph, A.O. Barfield, and T. Gordon-Jones, trans. *World Economy: The Formation of a Science of World-Economics. Fourteen Lectures Given in Dornach, 24th July to 6th August, 1922.* Version 2.5.3. Sussex, England: Rudolph Steiner Press, 1972.

Stiglitz, Joseph E., and Andrew Charlton. *Fair Trade for All: How Trade Can Promote Development.* Oxford: Oxford University Press, 2005.

Tal, Alon, ed. *Speaking of Earth: Environmental Speeches that Moved the World.* New Brunswick, NJ: Rutgers University Press, 2006.

Tov, Yaacov Bar-Siman, ed. *From Conflict Resolution to Reconciliation.* New York: Oxford University Press, 2004.

Truth and Reconciliation Commission of South Africa Report. Foreword by Desmond Tutu. London: Macmillan Reference, 1999. 10 March 2009, http://www.netlibrary.com/Details.aspx.

United States Institute of Peace. *Dialogues on Conflict Resolution: Bridging Theory and Practice.* Washington, D.C.: United States Institute of Peace, 1993.

The University of California. *The New Wellness Encyclopedia.* Boston: Houghton Mifflin, 1995.

Ventelou, Bruno, Gregory P. Nowell, trans. *Millennial Keynes: An Introduction to the Origin, Development, and Later Currents of Keynesian Thought.* Armonk, NY: M.E. Sharpe, 2005.

Walker, Goeffrey de Q. *The Rule of Law: Foundation of Constitutional Democracy.* Carlton, Victoria: Melbourne University Press, 1988.

Wattles, Jeffrey. *The Golden Rule.* New York: Oxford University Press, 1996.

Weddle, Meredith Baldwin. *Walking in the Way of Peace: Quaker Pacifism in the Seventeenth Century.* Oxford: Oxford University Press, 2001.

Williams, Oliver F. *Peace through Commerce: Responsible Corporate Citizenship and the Ideals of the United Nations Global Compact.* Notre Dame, IN: University of Notre Dame Press, 2008.

Wilson, Mike, ed. *World Religion.* Detroit: Greenhaven Press, 2006.

Wilson, Richard Ashby. *Humanitarianism and Suffering: The Mobilization of Empathy.* Cambridge: Cambridge University Press, 2009.

Worthington, Everett L., Jr., ed. *Handbook*

of Forgiveness. New York: Routledge, 2005.

Young-Eisendrath, Polly, and Melvin E. Miller, ed. *The Psychology of Mature Spirituality: Integrity, Wisdom, Transcendence*. London: Routledge, 2000.

Zifcak, Spencer, ed. *Globalisation and the Rule of Law*. New York: Routledge, 2005.

Zucker, Ross. *Democratic Distributive Justice*. Cambridge: Cambridge University Press, 2001.

Index